The Divided City

Translated by Corinne Pache with Jeff Fort

The Divided City

On Memory and Forgetting in Ancient Athens

Nicole Loraux

ZONE BOOKS · NEW YORK

2002

The publisher would like to thank the French Ministry of
Culture for its assistance with this translation.

Originally published in France as *La Cité divisée* © 1997 Editions
Payot & Rivages.

Printed in the United States of America.

Distributed by The MIT Press,
Cambridge, Massachusetts, and London, England

Library of Congress Cataloging-in-Publication Data

Loraux, Nicole
    [Cité divisée. English]
    The divided city : on memory and forgetting in Ancient
Athens / Nicole Loraux.
        p.   cm.
    Includes bibliographical references and index.
    ISBN 1-890951-08-0 (cloth) — ISBN 1-890951-09-9 (pbk. :
alk. paper).
    1. Athens (Greece) — Politics and government — Philosophy.
2. Athens (Greece) — History— Thirty Tyrants, 404–403 B.C.
3. Amnesty — Greece — Athens. 4. Democracy — Greece —
Athens. I. Title.
DF231.L6713   2001
938′.506—dc21   2001017970
                                                              CIP

Contents

Acknowledgments 7

Preface 9

PART ONE: THE DIVIDED CITY: MAPPINGS

  I *To Forget in the City* 15
 II *To Repoliticize the City* 45
III *The Soul of the City* 63

PART TWO: UNDER THE SIGN OF ERIS AND
           SOME OF HER CHILDREN

 IV *The Bond of Division* 93
  V *Oath, Son of Discord* 123
 VI *Of Amnesty and Its Opposite* 145
VII *On a Day Banned from
      the Athenian Calendar* 171

PART THREE: POLITICS OF RECONCILIATION

VIII *Politics of Brothers* 197
  IX *A Reconciliation in Sicily* 215
   X *Of Justice as Division* 229
  XI *And Athenian Democracy Forgot* Kratos 245

Notes 265
Bibliography 343
Index 355

Acknowledgments

My greatest thanks go to Miguel Abensour, who was eager to have this book — the product of fifteen years of study — appear in his series.

I would also like to thank Philippe Lacoue-Labarthe, who acted as respondent for a talk on *stasis* in 1987 at the Collège international de philosophie, Yan Thomas, and Hélène Monsacré.

And, for the third time, I dedicate *The Divided City* to Patrice, who knows that this is my book par excellence.

Preface

It all began with Cleocritus's speech in Xenophon's *Hellenica*. The Athenian democrats had just overcome the army of the Thirty. Some of the most important oligarchs — including Critias and Charmides, Socrates's erstwhile listeners whose names would later appear in Plato's dialogues — were among the dead. Most of the "city" troops were no doubt demoralized, a large number of hoplites having been vanquished by a motley crew equipped with whatever weapons they could find. . . . In the exultation of victory, the time was ripe for revenge, especially for those democrats who just before battle had been reminded by Thrasybulus of the "war" that the Thirty had waged against them and of the abuses suffered at their hands. Yet at that moment, an Athenian citizen, bearing the mystical seal of Eleusis, stepped before the democrats' lines to ask his hostile countrymen: "You who share the city with us, why do you kill us?" The question itself was incongruous (or, on the contrary, anachronistically familiar); it was a democrat's question, to be sure, because an oligarch would already know the answer: one's opponent is the *enemy*. But it was no more incongruous than the amnesty it announced, through which the victors would bind themselves to their former opponents, swearing the most solemn oath "not to recall misfortunes of the past."

The problem was to understand why, on that day in 403 B.C., the pacifist Cleocritus became the spokesman for the victorious army of the "Piraeus democrats."

This was the point of departure for a long-term inquiry into what the city experiences as *stasis*, to use the Greek term for what is simultaneously partisanship, faction, sedition, and — as we say in an expression with very Roman connotations — civil war. The initial project, occasionally shelved over the years but never forgotten, was to interrogate in a Greek context the specifically *democratic* — and therefore, in this case, Athenian — thinking on conflict, insofar as conflict is bound together, whether in opposition or affinity, with the definition of the political.[1] Along the way, I saw that it was necessary to establish and locate conflict in the city, because, under the name of politics, conflict is always already constitutive of the city. It is perhaps this primal link, rather than more recent "misfortunes," that the Greeks — and not only the Greeks — would like to forget in their proclamation of amnesty.

But did I ever expect to find anything else?

I had to find a way to begin. I started my investigation — caught up in the enthusiasm that comes with beginnings — by laying out a sort of program, one that I have never ceased to develop since. After that, things became complicated, as I knew they would. It is no doubt impossible to work on conflict without repercussions, and it is futile to hope that one can approach the forgetting that founds the political without triggering a return of the repressed. . . . Linking the divided city with the peaceful *polis* — a project caught between history and anthropology — turned out to be a less serene task than one might at first have hoped (however unadvisedly), especially when it became apparent that it would be impossible to avoid questioning what the *polis*, as a thinking and willing authority, was for the Greeks. Hence my conviction that it was necessary to risk a confrontation with the interdiction of the "subject," that lowest common denominator, around which, in something resembling unanimity, gather the researchers who, in every other respect, remain separated.

The following texts, composed for journals or research institutions over eight years, bear witness to these earlier mappings of the divided city, to the permanent features found there, and to the deviations and divergent movements in the questioning itself.

PART ONE

The Divided City: Mappings

CHAPTER ONE

To Forget in the City

[In the Erechtheion], there is moreover an altar dedicated to
Oblivion [Lêthê].

— Plutarch, *Table Talk*[1]

I begin with a project: to understand what motivated the Athenians in 403 B.C. to swear "not to recall misfortunes of the past." In
other words, I begin with a political event. I will end, very provi-
sionally, to be sure, with a passage from the *Oresteia*: a few lines
from Aeschylus, an entirely different order of reality, a mode of
thought from fifty years earlier (and half a century is a long time in
the very short history of classical Athens). Along the way arise the
questions and concerns of an investigation still in its first stages.

I begin with the project of understanding a crucial moment in
Athenian political history: after the final defeat in the Peloponnesian War, after the oligarchic coup of the Thirty Tyrants and the
abuses they inflicted, there is the victorious return of the democratic resistance, whose members reunited with their fellow citizens — their recent opponents — and swore an oath with them to
forget the past in a harmonious consensus. Modern historians of
Greece often identify this as the first example, at once surprising
and familiar, of amnesty. In textbooks — and even in ancient writings and speeches after 400 B.C.[2] — this is the point at which the
century of Pericles ends and what is called "the crisis of the fourth
century" begins. Why situate this investigation in relation to one
event, and why this event in particular? Perhaps to escape the

15

atemporal schemes of universal history. But also for the pleasure and, I hope, the benefit of attempting to wrench an event away from narrative history, as well as from commemorative historiography, so as to open it up to some very ancient Greek questions. The year 403 B.C. weighs heavily in the history of the model city, for this is when it "invents" amnesty.[3] Yet it does so with the conceptual tools of a long tradition, one in which politics and religion are inseparable. The city — the one that interests historians — makes decisions, but the *polis* — a figure dear to anthropologists of ancient Greece — is also confronted with its own division, in the time of men and in the time of gods. In short, I will attempt to understand the city through the *polis*.

Such an approach might seem self-evident, but things are not quite so simple.[4] Imagine a historian who is preoccupied with politics and looks for it in Greece, but in a Greece that is not exemplary, which he believes can be found among the anthropologists. This is where the difficulties begin, because the *polis*, as the site of the political, is for both historians and anthropologists the very object in question in a new version of the parable of the two cities. I will first examine the central perplexities that such a political historian would encounter.

The Two Cities

In book 18 of the *Iliad*, Hephaestus fashions two human cities on Achilles's shield, both of which the poet calls beautiful: one is engaged in the peacetime activities of marriage and justice, whereas the other confronts the war that rages at its gates. How shall we figure these two cities, which modern researchers, historians, and anthropologists of Greece have taken pleasure in depicting again and again as they wish and as if they had turned their backs on each other?

On one side, there is the classical city, the city of classical historians. Clearly separated from those on the margins of society and cut off in large part from its social roots — even in religious matters — the city is a group of men (that is, males — *andres*) connected by a constitution (*politeia*) that can be either democratic or oligarchic. (At this level of generalization, the tyrant would have no place, because, as the Greeks themselves say, he is outside the city; at most, he is seen as a moment, always outmoded, in the irresistible evolution of the constitutional history of Greek cities.)[5] The life of the city is military and political, because the *andres* wage war and, gathering in the assembly, make decisions based on a majority vote. The city has a history that Greek historians, much to the benefit of their modern "colleagues," have already written.[6] This history deals with constitutions and wars but has no place for the silent lives of women, foreigners, and slaves. The city recounts its own *erga* (its deeds — in this case, great military exploits). The city recounts itself.

The city of anthropologists operates not in the time of punctuated events but in the repetitive time of social practices — marriage, sacrifice — in which doing is still a form of thinking. It is a form of thinking of oneself by assigning, or attempting to assign, a place to the other, to every kind of other, and consequently to the same: by fastening the margins to the center, to the *andres* who make up the city but who still need women, for example, to constitute it. Thus marriage founds the city by ensuring its reproduction. Subsequently, once the *polis* is constituted as a human society, it is possible to situate it in relation to an elsewhere. More precisely, the city proclaims the distance of this elsewhere, be it the time of gods or the untamed world of animals, in order to integrate it more fully. The city has absorbed the outside, and sacrifice founds the *polis*: far from the gods but endowed with civilization, men sacrifice animals to the gods, and this gesture carries the system of exclusion and assimilation around the nucleus of the *andres*.

17

With each ceremony, the political is born from this sacrificial cutting and dividing and from its interpretation in the act itself: as egalitarian as the sharing out that results, isomorphic....[7] Should we say neutralized? The political can be understood as immobile circulation, as the city at rest.

City of historians, city of anthropologists. Because there is nothing about ancient Greece that the Greeks have not already thought before us, these two cities are first and foremost Greek. The city that makes decisions, fights, makes and breaks the peace is the object of the so-called Hellenic writings: precisely what we call History. The other city, the one that renews its identity in the atemporal return of ritual gestures, constitutes a common model of intelligibility, beyond all differences of literary genre: it is a discourse on the human whose essential propositions, taken up again and again, are used to separate the normal from the strange or else lend themselves to the mixed signals and distortions that provoke thought.

In the lived experience of a Greek man — an experience that is forever lost — it was no doubt unnecessary to choose between these two notions of the city. But the necessity of this choice pervades Greek discourse. This is true of Herodotus, for example, whose work is dominated by the anthropological model of the *polis* whenever he ventures into barbarian lands and by the city of the *andres* when, with the arrival of the Persian troops, the backdrop changes to Greece. In the end, Herodotus made a choice between the two definitions of the city, and the moderns, too, make their choices between these definitions and what they historically became for us.[8] This choice is inscribed within the perennial dispute at the heart of Hellenist studies between conformism and heterodoxy (or what would like to be heterodoxy) in the Academy. Either one is faithful to Thucydides and adopts narrative history, or, rejecting tradition, one seeks in Greek discourse itself arguments to "cool off" the object defined as the Greek city.[9]

By choosing, of course, we exclude. "History" excludes from the political everything in the life of the city that is not an event, as well as any event that cannot be explained, however vaguely, by invoking Greek "reason." The time of religion and the long work of myth are easily disposed of in a single chapter, with a few pages or even sentences recalling that this was an important aspect of civic life.[10] And so the entire question is overlooked, just as, in studies of the events of 404–403 b.c., little notice is taken of a speech by the leader of the democrats in which he claims that the gods are visibly fighting alongside their troops, for whom they bring both storms and fair weather.[11] What are we to do with this information? Typically, nothing is done except to assume that it has slipped through the imperfect filter of an indiscriminate narrative written by a historian we cannot completely trust. The modern historian of Antiquity prefers to ignore the links between the gods and the democrats, because he wants to keep religion and democracy separate.

For anthropologists, on the other hand, it is no longer necessary to argue for the "politico-religious," which is an undeniable benefit for anyone who, like our political enthusiast, is not content to secularize the city on principle.[12] Yet because it arises in the suspended time of sacrifice, and because it is ceaselessly born and reborn in the slow and idle gestures of ritual, the political thus constructed looks very much like the *myth* of the political. A homogeneous environment, an egalitarian operation — such would be the city. Or, more precisely: such is the idea of *the* city. In the daily life of the city, there is no doubt that the most widespread practices reinforced the inequality among citizens; nor is there any doubt that the question of how much equality each citizen deserved regularly produced a rupture. There is no need to

19

rely on the narratives of Thucydides and Xenophon to corroborate this: it is enough to read Aristotle, that "anthropologist."[13] The proponents of isomorphic politics have read Thucydides, Xenophon, Aristotle, and many others: they know the city is affected by activities that cannot be reduced to the regular and repetitive rotation of duties, that annual redistribution of the political in which the equal sharing out of power is incarnated. But the difficulty remains: how can one plausibly claim that violence arises from homogeneity except by invoking the regression of men who "return to savagery" somewhere on this side of the human,[14] or by raising the figure of the tyrant, the wolf man, beast, or god, who is excluded from the city because he weighs too heavily on it?[15]

Consider, for example, the murder of Ephialtes, the democratic leader and adviser to Pericles. Ephialtes was assassinated in 461 B.C. for daring to reduce the vast powers of the Areopagus, the aristocratic council that had an aura of sacred terror. This was without question a political assassination, and it is mentioned as such in narrative history, where it is seen as a very important event but receives little commentary. Theorists of the politico-religious would no doubt like to know more about the reversal that transformed the reformer into the victim of a "treacherous murder" (*dolophonetheis*) after he limited the ancient council to sentencing murder cases (*phonou dikai*).[16] But at the general level of the political, little is said about this death — just as little, it seems, as in the discourse of the Athenians, who were remarkably discreet on this point in the history of Athens. . . .

So one must choose: either decisions lacking in ulterior motives or a thought that lags far behind all acts. In order to take an interest in Greek politics, must we first decide what shall be purged from it?

The political enthusiast — who will serve here as a true fiction

20

— is intent on refusing such an alternative, and rightly so. Thus, returning to the modern idea of the Greek *polis* as the source of the political, he goes back to the city in order to seek that "inaugural gesture" of the political — the "acknowledgment of conflict in society."[17] He does this above all in order to determine the function of speech, so easy to lose sight of when all attention is focused on the before or the after of the political. He is content neither to end, like the anthropologists, with the sacrifice that opens any assembly of the people nor to begin with the decree that closes every session of the *ekklēsia* and introduces the speeches. For, in the interval between the beginning and the end is that distinctive Greek invention: open debate, followed by a vote.[18]

A vote: that is, the victory of one *logos* over another. The Greeks actually say *nikē* (victory), borrowing a word from the vocabulary of war and competition. Because the political historian stubbornly refuses to take a side in the rivalry between the two cities, he focuses instead on rivalry in the city — which helps us not to forget that the events at the end of the fifth century in Athens have provided our starting point.

One Divided into Two

It is pointless to entertain the illusion that we have immediate access to the reality of this open debate or to the modalities of conflict. The historian of classical Greece knows that there are no documents that would allow him to imagine attending a session of the assembly or that would provide sufficient details on the exact course of a political struggle. Without archives, without any plausible representation of a vote, whether textual or visual, he must rely on discourse. Discourse is the historiographical narrative that makes a permanent selection from reality. For instance, without the discovery, during the excavation of the *agora*, of countless tokens of ostracism bearing the name of one Callixenos, this character, who was important enough for numerous Athenians to fear him, would have remained unknown in Athenian political history; and, in the absence of a historical narrative about him, he has indeed remained unknown.[19] Discourse, and discourse after the fact: these are the decrees that, far from giving an accurate account of a session of the assembly, construct and limit our knowledge of it.

Discourse for discourse: it is better to step back and try to delimit what the Greeks say about a victory in the assembly, because it is also true that they invented the political in the mode of victory.

What they say about it, from the *Odyssey* to the *Peloponnesian War,* is this: that the worst argument wins, would have won if..., threatens to win, has already won. Every once in a while, of course, a good decision is made, one that makes it possible to forget the threat, or even cancels the harmful effects, of an earlier vote. It is curious, however, that in relating this good news, the texts often decline to use the vocabulary of victory. It is as if the very existence of victory were a fundamental evil. There do exist more reassuring ideas, such as the law of the majority which governs all votes and should be a guarantee. But whenever the majority wins "for the good," such a victory is usually gained by a narrow margin; and the ideal remains that of unanimous decision, as if, in loudly proclaiming the unity of that totality called the *polis*, it were a matter of forgetting that for the space of a moment — the moment of debate, that is, of the assembly — the city is necessarily divided.[20] To forget division, to forget debate.... Some have said that the Greek *polis* "is known only behind a mask."[21] I will add a hypothesis to this observation: this is the case because the *polis*, with great consistency, masks itself from the reality of its own processes.

An interest in the legitimacy of conflict requires that one try to understand what the Greeks said about its illegitimacy. It means reflecting on the effort — constitutive, so to speak, of the unity of Greek political thought — to neutralize the existence of the political as *nikē* and *kratos*: as the victory and domination of one party over another. Book 18 of the *Iliad* opposes the peaceful city of the wedding and of justice to the city at war. In the midst of peace, however, justice is actually conflict (*neikos*), which is not very surprising in Greece, where every trial was a fight and in this case a serious fight in which a man's life is at stake.[22] We see that in this beautiful city, "the people were crying out in favor of one or the other, and formed two sides in support of them."[23] Is this a serene acknowledgment of the legitimacy of conflict? It might be objected that the decision belongs not to either of the two groups but to a complex procedure involving a *histor* and the council of elders. Could it be that in this city that is not yet *the* city, we can conceive of a temporary division that does not involve the fate of the community because there is nothing to sanction it? It is still the case that the matter ends with the contest of the "straightest judgment,"[24] the effective speech that can defuse a situation "with sweetness," like the words of the good Hesiodic king. Nothing indeed seems to threaten the beautiful Homeric city from within. By contrast, the poet of the *Iliad* clearly gives a name and a place to absolute evil on the other side: Eris (Strife) or Kēr oloē (Death the destruction), whose place is not within the walls but at the gates of the city besieged by the enemy army. A few centuries later, a reshuffling of these particulars occurred, and at the end of the *Eumenides*, Aeschylus opposes war against a foreign enemy, in which one may win fame — the only good war, because it is the only war that brings glory to the *polis* — to the scourge of internal war. Thus only the city that enjoys internal peace can wage war outside, and that is both its duty and its fate; it is not death the destructive that presides over this kind of war but the "beautiful death" of the citizens for the sake of the fatherland. The two

23

Homeric cities, the city that performs marriages and the city that goes to war, become one, the very figure of the good city, while division, now the absolute threat, settles into the sick city torn apart by citizens confronting each other.[25]

To be sure, there is a great distance between a division of opinions and bloody confrontation. And yet in taking this step — such at least is my hypothesis — we imitate the Greeks, who themselves never ceased to do so.

Civil war: for the Greeks it was the abomination of desolation. Rather than linger over reflections on what is "natural" in such a condemnation (what is the status of nature for a historian?), I will focus on the name that the Greeks give to this confrontation: *stasis*. As Moses I. Finley notes simply and forcefully, *stasis* refers etymologically only to a position; that the position should become a party, that a party should be constituted for the purpose of sedition, that one faction should always call forth another, and that civil war should then rage is a semantic evolution whose interpretation should be sought not "in philology but in Greek society itself."[26] I would add that it should also be sought in Greek thought about the city, where the same condemnation is manifest: from Hesiod's establishing an equivalence between *agora* and *neikos* — between the place where words are exchanged and the conflicts that are an unfortunate incarnation of Bad Strife — to Athens in 403 B.C., when the city does not know what to do with the men "rising up for the cause of democracy [*stasiasantes huper tēs dēmokratias*]," and passing through Aeschylus's *Eumenides*, where Athena wishes for "something that has no traffic with evil success [*nikē mē kakē*]," that is, with a victory of one part of the city over the other.[27] *Stasis* as the division that tears apart and tears open: from Solon to Aeschylus, *stasis* is a deep wound in the body of the city.

In the city of *andres* dear to Greek historians, *stasis* introduces disorder, and suddenly, in Thucydides's account of the events of

427 B.C. at Corcyra, women and slaves, usually forgotten in such narratives, slip through the crack thus opened and are fighting alongside the popular party.[28] Thus battle rages in the midst of the *polis*: a battle without great deeds, without trophies, but not without victory; one that mimics and degrades the more legitimate battle waged against external enemies. Here, in a monstrous displacement of sacrifice, slaughter (*sphagē*) takes citizens for its victims. Here we see women, usually confined to the house, climbing up on roofs and slaves serving as comrades in arms.

Clearly, *stasis* unsettles established models, as well as their reassuring certitudes. Modern historians of Antiquity have not failed to place some emphasis on it. Translated as "civil war," it appears in the work of Gustave Glotz — or, earlier still, in that of Numa Fustel de Coulanges — as the event whose recurrence constitutes the framework of "the history of Greece."[29] (Although, according to Glotz's own categories, civil war is precisely what the invention of the political is supposed to avert, since the city would have introduced voting as a "preventive remedy" for bloody division. Is civil war, then — in the beginning, but also in the middle and at the end — the unavoidable recurrence of an evil on which the city is founded?)[30] When historians designate civil war with its Greek name, they often locate its origin in competition, in the agonistic mentality that, ever since Jakob Burckhardt, has constituted the Greek spirit of life in the city.[31] We should observe — as we often forget to do — that if this is indeed the case, whenever Greek civic thought condemns *stasis*, it must erase its *political* origin — for example, by assimilating it to an illness (*nosos*) malevolently fallen from the sky — in order to preserve the consensual form of the political, which is supposedly the political itself. What becomes of Greek consciousness of the political during this rescue operation that looks so much like denial?

We must reconsider this operation of thought for several

reasons: to understand *stasis*; to return better equipped to the Athens of 403 B.C., a convalescent city that refuses even the memory of division; and perhaps also to assign a status to the egalitarian consensus of the *polis* by confronting it with the effective tearing apart of the *polis*.

Such, then, is the project, which for now has merely been described. Such is the goal of my inquiry, which will no doubt engage me for a long time to come. Let us henceforth do away with the fiction of the historian-enthusiast of politics: the encounter with the object *stasis* is not the end point of a theoretical path traveled in a single go, like the one I have attempted to describe up to now. Neither sudden nor controlled, the encounter with an object results from the unexpected twists and turns of research, and often it has taken place long before one is aware of it, in the course of meanderings — a large part of which remains unconscious — through various theoretical investments that coexist for a long time before ever crossing paths.

At the Intersection: Stasis

Afterward, once the encounter has taken place, things seem clear. It is then possible to reconstruct a process and to say, for example, that an inquiry about *stasis* is located at the intersection of two research projects originally carried out independently but now pursued together. That is easily said. But it is better to avoid the illusion of total clarity. We move forward only by groping along, and sometimes we find our way. In this case, a journey through the Athenian imaginary as it touches on autochthony was followed by a study on the idea of the city, until, by one of those swings of the pendulum that in research seems to cancel divergences after the fact, I suddenly realized that I had been thrown back toward the idea of the city; but this time it was the city in its relationship to its own division.

26

In the long tradition of Greek history, the city is Athens, and everyone points this out, whether with satisfaction or irritation. But no one could be so confident of this identification if the Athenians had not already, and insistently, elaborated this idea themselves, if Athens had not thought itself and successfully imposed itself as the city. I thought it possible to identify one site of this elaboration by studying the Athenian funeral oration. Central to funeral orations in honor of Athenian citizens who died in action is the model of the "beautiful death," the death of the worthy warrior who finds immortality in glory. Men pass on, the city remains, all-powerful, as indivisible as the idea of unity itself. When the orator arrives at the point in his speech where he exalts Athens through the Athenians, the citizens are already dead, and the city builds its ideality over these abstract dead. Through this transference of glory, Athens enters into the timelessness of nobility; and democracy, which is praised constantly by the orators, finds its principle in *aretē*, the conspicuously aristocratic quality of excellence. At the time, the essential point was to be found in the impossibility proper to Greek democracy — that model system — of inventing a democratic language to speak itself.[32] This invention begins, in fact, with the very word *dēmokratia*, which speaks of the victory or the superiority (*kratos*) of the people and is not uttered without countless rhetorical safeguards.[33] Is democracy a victory so dangerous that it can come to terms with itself only in the register of *aretē*, at once noble and warlike? The fear of *stasis* is never far, and in fact while working on the funeral oration, I did encounter this problem. But the time had not yet come to interrogate civic thought on division: in the field of value, everything is absorbed into the unity of the city, which as the locus of equals must be One. What caught my attention in democracy's discourse on its own value was precisely this process whereby the funeral oration can function for us as an ideology, whereas for the

27

Athenians it functioned as one of the privileged voices of the city's imaginary.

My concern at that time was to delimit the place and the role of myth in the shifting play of this imaginary. The example of the Athenian myth of autochthony came from the funeral oration as well, but I wanted to move away from the oration, in an attempt to ground the myth *in* the city, in the complex density of its different "levels," in the cartography of its sites, and in its multiple discourses. In the funeral oration, as in the rituals of the Acropolis and on the tragic stage, all Athenians are autochthonous insofar as they are heirs of the child Erichthonius, the primordial autochthon born from the civic earth. In Athenian reflections on citizenship, a citizenship mythically founded by the birth of Erichthonius, two basic issues emerge barely concealed within discourse and imagery: the place of women — and the division of the sexes — and the forms of kinship at the heart of the city. The *andres* are autochthonous in contrast with women, who are grafted onto the city from elsewhere, or so the *andres* liked to think. Thus the autochthonous *andres* assemble themselves in a place far from women, a place where they can think themselves, where the city is a single whole because all its members are the same: the originary kinship bond of those who individually have their own father, while collectively they share the same mother. I then attempted to understand how the name of this mother was thought in the Athenian idiom — Ge, Earth? or the virgin Athena? — and consequently to determine what place women occupy in Athenian thought on citizenship.[34] The question of kinship would come later, in the city given over to *stasis*. ... But let us not anticipate, and more important, let us not yield to the temptation to reconstruct a simple linear development: it was after the fact, and only after the fact, that I realized how a reflection on the division of the sexes followed from a study of the unitary city and that the

28

division of the sexes surreptitiously led the way into the city conceived as a divided family.

To understand what happened and what was said in Athens in 403 B.C., I intended to return to the event itself after a detour through the atemporal figures of the Athenian imaginary. This apparently meant a return to a form of the political that does not exhaust itself in rethinking the difference between the sexes and that abandons its dream of origins for more immediate concerns. The year 405 B.C.: the Peloponnesian War ends with the defeat of Athenian imperialism as the Long Walls of Athens are destroyed to the music of Spartan flutes. The year 404 B.C.: civil war settles in the city, with the proscriptions and oligarchic violence of those who are called the Thirty Tyrants, the better to place them outside the *polis*. The year 403, then 401 B.C.: at last, the restoration of democracy and the oath solemnly sworn again by all the citizens *not to recall the misfortunes*, now past and thrown back into the nonbeing of oblivion. *Mē mnēsikakein*: this model amnesty (already considered such in the decades following 403 B.C.) fixes in chronological time the very Greek decision to forget the division of the city. Thus I quickly realized that to understand what was played out in 403 B.C., I would need to knot together two temporalities by situating this political gesture from the end of the fifth century B.C. within the long Greek history of *stasis*, which is constantly in effect in one or several cities but always rejected in Greek thinking on the political.

In Xenophon's account of the years 405–403 B.C., everything has been decided well before the day when the victory procession of the armed democrats goes up to the Acropolis to offer a sacrifice to Athena. Everything is played out in the battle in which the democrats prevail and Critias, the most tyrannical of the Thirty, dies. It is then that the herald of the Eleusinian mysteries, who fought on the democrats' side, stands between the two armies to

29

give them a political lesson: "Fellow citizens, why do you drive us out of the city? Why do you wish to kill us? We are not the ones who have done wrong." In a word, *stasis* is meaningless. What is meaningful is the shared community of social activities, military dangers, and above all kinship, which weaves enough ties between the citizens so that what unites can allow them to avoid the thought of what separates. This is because, in this lesson about the *polis*, it will only later be a question of the political, in a verb that gives it its most neutral designation: *politeuesthai*, to live in the city.[35] Studying this text led to a hypothesis and a surprise. The hypothesis can be formulated as follows: the egalitarian *polis* of consensus (the model dear to anthropologists), whose essential propositions are disseminated throughout Greek discourse, exists because actual cities are divided (because, in large and small cities alike, decision and combat, these two subjects of historians, suddenly interfere with each other). This *polis* becomes ideology for the divided city because it denies the very possibility of thinking about real divisions. As for the surprise, it came later, when I compared this text with a passage of the *Menexenus*, which led me once again to the funeral orations. Evoking the reconciliation of 403 B.C. in his *Menexenus*, Plato praises the Athenians for "mingling" together with a truly familial joy, due to the real kinship created by their common race (*to homophulon*). Now, officially, the *homophuloi* are the Athenians as autochthons; and a few pages earlier, Plato had derived democratic *isonomia*, the Greek term for equality in the political realm, from this kinship, which he turns into fraternity.[36] It is thus that in the inquiry into *stasis*, autochthony returned in the form of an originary kinship of Athenian citizens, invoked as an aid in effectively repressing the memory of *stasis*:[37] it became necessary to reorient the inquiry toward an examination of the many texts in which *stasis* is accused of affecting the family as the city's basic unit, indeed as the very metaphor of the *polis*.[38]

This led me to reread the lines from the *Eumenides* alluded to above, which make of *stasis* — a word absent from this passage but appearing some hundred lines later — the *ares emphulios*: war within the family.

Ares *in the Family*

Athena addresses the chorus of Erinyes, who are slow to be persuaded by her:

> Only in this place that I haunt do not inflict
> your bloody stimulus to twist the inward hearts
> of young men, raging in a fury not of wine,
> nor, as if plucking the heart from fighting roosters,
> engraft among my citizens that spirit of war
> that turns their battle fury inward on themselves.
> No, let our wars range outward hard against the man
> who has fallen horribly in love with high renown.
> No true fighter I call the bird that fights at home.[39]

In the Athens of myth, a court of citizens, with Athena joining in their vote, has just absolved Orestes of his mother's murder. A decisive ruling, yet ambiguous, as is any ruling that ends in a tie vote — and even more so than any other *isopsephos* ruling, because of the disparity between the voters: men and a goddess. (Without the divine vote, the son of Agamemnon would have been judged guilty.)[40] The winner of this trial is nevertheless Orestes. Exit the winner. The Erinyes, whose dreadful wrath threatens Athens, remain on stage. Athena must convince them to relinquish their anger by explaining to them that they were not truly defeated. Settled within the city, they will be honored as long as they hold off *stasis*. Here is where the text I just quoted comes in.

A text. Yet another. One that does not belong to the textual

31

territory of historians. One that has nothing to do with the events of 403 B.C. and the ban on remembering misfortunes of the past.

Perhaps. But this text, already encountered because of its extremely clear formulation of the opposition between *stasis* and *polemos*, makes an ideal distinction between what is a vocation for the city and what is an absolute threat. The ideal figure of the *polis* can be distinguished in outline: warlike outside its gates, civil and peaceful within. The outside belongs to Athena; the inside belongs to the Erinyes, who can unleash discord or, once they become Eumenides, preside over the reproduction of the city in the repetitive time of succeeding generations. There is no sign of the political functioning of the city at peace with itself until the very end of the play: Athena has created the Areopagus to keep watch over the sleeping city; the Erinyes must ensure the fecundity of Athens; and the "people," finally, are repeatedly designated as *stratos* (army), as if they had no other task than to wage wars outside the city. An instructive moment: on the proper usage of the city, or how, between the ban on *stasis* and glorification of foreign wars, to lose the political.

This is clearly an essential text, which any inquiry into *stasis* must confront.

But it is also a tragic text, and historians are supposed to distrust tragedy. At any rate, they distrust tragedy as *text* and limit themselves to those works that, they think, can be used as documents. At most, they refer each play to the year of its production, assuming it is a reflection of its historical context. I will not indulge in this exercise, even if it would establish a connection between the date of the production of the *Oresteia* (458 B.C.) and the date of Ephialtes's reform of the Areopagus (461 B.C.). My intention is to reject border disputes once and for all in order to read these lines differently from how historians or "literary critics" would read them. Because we must not leave tragedy to literary specialists alone, I also reject the premises of a reading that academics portray as literary. Though implicit, these premises have the force of law. They can be summarized thus: (1) in tragedy, words do not have their usual meanings — including their political or social meanings — because it is poetic language (the word *turannos*, for example, would simply designate a king, which makes it unnecessary to pose the question of Oedipus as a tyrant; and in the lines quoted above, *splankhna,* entrails, is translated as "inward hearts");[41] (2) a text has one meaning, and one only (nothing is said of the obvious contradiction in requiring words that have only approximate meanings to have a single meaning). Overturning these postulates, I shall apply, as others have before me, the following rules for reading: (1) No word can be simply substituted for another, and nowhere is this more the case than in a tragic text;[42] if Aeschylus names the entrails and not the heart, that is precisely what must be interpreted; (2) A tragic text, more than any other, is ruled by polysemy; a single word, *splankhna,* entrails, is enough to express several subversions of sacrifice, because it evokes at once the fantasy of corrupted sacrifice in a civil war that kills young men and the foul feast at which Thyestes devoured the roasted viscera of his children.[43]

In reading lines 858–66 of the *Eumenides,* I will not extract "historical" information about the year 458 B.C. or a meaning that is somehow both unique and poetically ambiguous. Instead, I will seek a properly tragic thought concerning *stasis.* Athena's speech attempts to avert the threat of *stasis* for two reasons: because all Greek thought strives to do this, and especially because the distinctive property of tragedy is to keep at a distance the crucial problems and "inner ills" of the city.[44] *Stasis* is denounced at the end of a trilogy that shows how, from ancient murders to more recent ones, crime is engendered within a single family. I have isolated these few lines in part, of course, to use them as the basis for

33

a close reading; but I would like above all to do justice to a text that has revealed, on the horizon of this inquiry, perspectives I had not at first suspected.

Because the tragic signifier resonates with ambiguous echoes, a first attempt to decipher it must open the selected passage onto the text as a whole, in this case a trilogy. Thus the "bloody stimulus" of civil war joins together the blood that has been shed — the constant obsession of tragedy — and the sting of a fate who, in lines 1535–36 of the *Agamemnon*, sharpens the blade of disasters to come after Clytemnestra murders the king. The meaning of the phrase is made clear by two appositions that weave together a complex network of images borrowed from other associative sequences and that, in relation both to each other and to *haimateras thēganas*, form something of an equivalence. I have already discussed *splankhnon blabas neon*: by destroying young entrails, the stings of *stasis* become monstrous sacrificial instruments that carry out in the body of the citizens an impious division and redistribution. *Aoinois emmaneis thumomasin* describes the mad, wineless intoxication of wrath. The madness of mutual murders (*mania allēlophonos*), which Clytemnestra evokes at the end of the *Agamemnon* — this familial wrath that destroys the family — is the prerogative of the Erinyes. Madness meets wrath in these Furies but also in each of their victims, so strong is the bond uniting these "bitches" to their prey, and indeed the Furies threaten Athens with the consequences of unleashing their wrath in the city.[45] Political intoxication is unleashed without wine, as are the libations offered to the Erinyes, but in the divided city as well as in the offerings to the forces of revenge, spilled human blood will do just as well.[46] Thus in the space of two verses, semantic fields that have coexisted throughout the *Oresteia* are suddenly in conflict. As if such a conflict were enough to express the disruption of order caused by civil war, Athena can now oppose *stasis* to the good war that does not cross the city gates. On one side is Ares, god of murder, Murder itself, Ares installed in the family hearth and in the city, as well as among the Atreids, unleashing mutual effrontery among relatives. On the other side is the desire for glory, which the funeral oration attributes to the citizens killed by the enemy.

Yet before *Ares emphulios* and after the desire for glory, there are roosters in the text. Encompassing the opposition between the two wars, the strange birds come to signify that *stasis* is family war ensconced in the city. Because *ornis* (bird) commonly means rooster, especially when the bird is described as domesticated (*enoikios*), it is not hard to understand the metaphor in line 866 ("no true fighter I call the bird that fights at home") as an echo of line 861 ("as if plucking the heart from fighting roosters" or, more literally, "rousing the heart of fighting roosters in my fellow citizens"). The roosters lead to the familial Ares; the glory of warfare, once named, forbids the use of the vocabulary of combat within the city. That may be. But what are we to make of the roosters? No doubt, they force us to go outside the text, and also outside the reading that tries to shed light on the strangeness of certain figures by referring to the vast Greek imaginary. Behind these symbolic birds, then, appears *nikē*, together with subversion in the family.

Consider the theater of Dionysos, where tragedians compete for peaceful victory before an audience of citizens. Every year, the Athenians also organized rooster fights there at public expense, an animal counterpoint to the tragic competition (but a bloody and therefore disturbing one). Many texts and images allude to this practice, which makes it easy for us to believe that for the Athenians — indeed for the Greeks — rooster fights symbol-ized the desire for victory in its purest form, which in any fight

35

outstrips all other motivations, even the most noble.[47] It will suffice to mention a text by Aelian, a late text to be sure (its author is among those distrusted by historians of the fifth century B.C.) but one that vividly expresses this idea. A speech by Themistocles serves to account for the origins of the Athenian practice. Leading the army of citizens against the barbarians during the Persian Wars, Themistocles, it is said, saw two roosters, placed as if by chance in his path and engaged in a relentless fight. "These birds," he exclaimed, "are not fighting for their country or their fathers' gods; they are not enduring pain to defend the tombs of their ancestors, their reputation, freedom, and children; each of the pair aims to avoid defeat and not to yield to the other."[48] To defeat in order not to be defeated: victory for victory's sake. According to Aelian, this example gave new life to the Athenian troops. On closer examination, it is clear that the words attributed to Themistocles deny, in a troubling way, all the reasons the Greeks gave for waging war: glory, of course, but also, very specifically, the values listed in Aeschylus's *Persians* that lead the Greeks to victory at Salamis.[49] There is only one reason left, which is a *desire*: the desire to defeat for the sake of defeating, which the discourse of war usually tries to hide (at the end of the *Eumenides*, the only *erōs* is for beautiful glory) but which the Greeks detect and condemn in *stasis*.[50] Should we go further and claim that they confine it within *stasis* only to ward off its threat? The anecdote about Themistocles suggests that the Greeks clearly recognized the troubling boundary zone where war too closely resembles civil war. To pursue this line of inquiry would lead beyond the scope of my present concerns.[51] I will only note that it is perfectly appropriate to find the fighting roosters in these lines of the *Eumenides* devoted to civil war.

But this is not all. The roosters lead us in yet another direction, toward a Greek understanding of animal virtues in which the rooster is anything but respectable. The rooster is a tyrant, sometimes even a Persian. It beats its father, when it doesn't kill him. In fact, one is equivalent to the other, because the Greek noun for parricide speaks of beating, not of killing.[52] Here we see already, insinuating itself among birds of the same flock, the parricide and familial murder that transformed Aigisthos, the killer of Agamemnon, into a rooster strutting to please his female mate. Even without leaving Aeschylus, we can extend the list of the rooster's crimes by evoking the line from the *Suppliant Maidens* about the bird that "preys on bird," fearsome figure of incest.[53]

And *stasis*? No need to worry, it has not been lost along the way. Like incest, *stasis* is no doubt "domestic fodder" (*oikea bora*), and the supposedly civilized birds of Aristophanes eat the oligarch birds that rebelled against their *dēmos* and were defeated,[54] echoing the dreadful vow made by Theognis ("Whose [my enemies'] red blood be it mine to drink").[55] This invites us to go very far back, to Hesiod's definition of the status of man in terms of his well-regulated diet, in contrast with animals and especially the "winged birds," for whom devouring each other is the rule.[56] I will end here this digression that began with the rooster fights and drew the "bad victory" toward familial war in order finally to take *stasis* in the direction of a cosmic thought in which it is a scourge for the city of men, an irruption into the civilized world of a savagery often described as animal yet that threatens the human family from the inside, as is shown in tragedy in the story of the Atreids.[57]

Is all of *stasis* contained in nine lines of Aeschylus? The risk of a microscopic reading — and there would be no point in denying that this has been one — is, in opening the small onto the large at every step, to lose the text by wandering into the generality of the Greek imaginary. Now it is time to return to the text to compare it again with the whole of the *Oresteia*. But we return to it with new hypotheses suggesting that the rejection of *stasis* should be understood in relation to Greek anthropological thought, which tirelessly enumerates all the behaviors that make a man cease to be a man. A purely "historical" approach, however, would probably have overlooked this cosmic dimension of civil war.

It remains, then — or rather would remain, because an explanation would require much more than one paragraph — to explain why the end of the *Eumenides* is about civil war. This would entail explaining how the *Oresteia* stages the begetting of crime by crime within the family, inhabited by *neikos* (conflict), *Eris* (Strife), *stasis* (already alluded to in lines 1117–19 of the *Agamemnon* — a network of correspondences leads to it even before the fatal name is pronounced), and the Erinys (divine figure of Wrath); how the revenge of Orestes sets Ares against Ares; how everything comes to an end in the *Eumenides*, where it is the responsibility of the city of Athena to put a stop to this murderous begetting — dramatically through the recourse to an institution, a vote ending in a tie, but also, at the deepest level of tragic thought, by making a collectivity of all the families that the *polis* encompasses and supersedes. Then we understand why Athena assigns the protection of her city to the Erinyes ("it is your task to watch over fecundity," she says, "and I will take care of war and its true victories"), why they must at all costs renounce the scourge of their anger or, what comes to the same thing, renounce surrendering the city to *Ares emphulios*: it is necessary to protect the city from familial evil and to transform murderous begetting into blessed fecundity. The Erinys, as the spirit of Wrath, unleashes the scourge — on the family, the genealogy of murders; on the city, the triple "plague" (sterility of the earth, of flocks, of women), which all the Greeks attempt to avert by swearing an oath;[58] and among the *andres*, the "fury of mutual homicides" — but the Erinyes can also hold the scourge back, turning the curse into its opposite.[59] Transformed into Eumenides, they will protect the city: from their own fury, and from its internal fits of fury. Moreover, because they "hold memory of evil [*mnēmones kakōn*]," as Aeschylus has them say at line 382, the Erinyes are marked to become the custodians of memory within the city, a timeless memory, airtight and as if curled up inside itself, a Memory that will preventively exempt the citizens from having to "recall the misfortunes" they inflicted on each other in *stasis*.

Toward a History of Memorable Forgetting

The aim of my detour through the *Eumenides* was not simply to have the pleasure of a close reading. It was instead a matter of reconstructing in all its complexity the essential moment that opens a research project to new and often unexpected horizons.

I was seeking in the nine lines of Aeschylus a confirmation that *stasis* deeply affects the family within the city. But the familial Ares of the *Eumenides* is only Aeschylus's way of renaming what the lyric poets call *makhē emphulos, phonoi emphuloi*, or, more simply, *stasis emphulos* (fight, murders, civil war within the lineage); and this is an invitation to go back through archaic poetry to the most ancient history of the idea of civil war, from Aeschylus to Solon and from Solon to Alcaeus by way of Theognis. All this before coming back to the fifth century and Thucydides, who, before proceeding to a long development on *stasis*, would have liked to condense all its horror in the murder of a son by his father. And from here to the fourth century, which, as expected, interrogates the difference between the city and the *oikia*, the family house, and glosses *stasis* as *oikeios polemos*, internal war.[60] Along the way, we will also come upon Cleocritus, orator of the democratic party who in Xenophon flaunts the existence of familial relations against the reality of division.

Aeschylus leads us back to Solon, the thinker of the divided

39

city, and invites us to enter the ongoing debate among lyric poets about the origin of *stasis*.[61] Purely human, *stasis* sleeps within the *polis* and is always ready to stir, according to Solon, who refuses to ascribe responsibility to the gods, whereas Alcaeus sees *stasis* as a "plague that gnaws at the heart" (*thumoboros*) sent by one of the Olympians; this idea easily leads us to the Hesiodic picture of the bad king's city, abandoned by the gods and prey to the scourge that dries up the source of all life within it. This is an opportunity to reflect on the surprising fate of Hesiod, whose poetry is supposedly ignorant of the city as a political world yet ceaselessly provides models to think the *polis*, from Solon to Plato and beyond, including — surprise of surprises — the rationalist Thucydides.[62] It is also an opportunity to include *stasis* among the transgressions that, like so many threats, form the terrifying figure of an inhuman humanity around the city. It is an opportunity, above all, to understand how, for the Greeks of the archaic and classical period, condemnation of *stasis* is a way of denying the reality of the political as it verges toward terrifying horizons: how could anyone who has been absorbed in the horrible spectacle of parricide go back to the idea of a regulated operation of "victory" in the city or of a legitimately carried-out division of the civic body? The inverse of the egalitarian city without history — the city of the anthropologists — the specter of *stasis* takes the terrifying form of a curse. The historian can now go back to the facts, if he so desires, enriched by the anthropological detour: for example, to the denial of victory among the Athenian democrats who in 403 B.C. swore an oath that threatened to weigh more heavily on themselves than on their political adversaries, forgotten as such under the name of fellow citizens and brothers. Then, perhaps, the historian of the city seeking to understand this event will realize that he cannot do without the anthropologists' atemporal model, even if he must ascribe to it a mode of existence that belongs to ideology: the dream of equality, like the condemnation of the scourge, is indeed an *ideology* of the political — for we need not abandon the question raised by this word under the pretext that the word itself has lost currency. To speak of ideology is to believe that we have a chance of attaining something other than the eternal *logos*, or at any rate that all discourse does not function on the same level.

I have not yet finished enumerating the perspectives opened by Aeschylus's evocation of *stasis*. The establishment of the Erinyes at the foot of the Areopagus indeed symbolizes the domesticated yet always threatening presence of terror and wrath in the city. Terror and wrath: the terror attached to the oath — a terror that guards against perjury — and the wrath that from the *Eumenides* to Thucydides is one name for civil war.[63] How can we disentangle the two? We might as well try to disentangle politics from religion, and Aeschylus's text supports the idea that this is indeed impossible. What about the Athenians' oath in 403 B.C.? Within it is something like an oath not to recall that the recollection itself is a wound — a bloody stimulus — the solemnly sworn promise to erase what the evocation has already realized, since in the discourse about violence there is the latent and sinister effectiveness of the Erinyes' word "whose fruit would be a catastrophe for all."[64] Historians of religion are indeed mistaken to consider the Erinyes only in connection with myth and cult, and historians of the city would do well to note that the Erinyes dwell in Athens, fixed at the foot of the Areopagus under the name Semnai (the Awful Ones), a protection that also constitutes a threat, in 403 B.C. as well as in Ephialtes's time. The "democratic reconciliation"? At the end of the century of Pericles, this is perhaps the politico-religious at work, *hic et nunc*.

This leads us back to Aeschylus one last time before returning to the event of 403 B.C. The Erinyes "hold memory of evil," and the citizens commit themselves to forgetting their misfortunes. An entire trilogy is necessary to domesticate the memory of murder and to assign it a place from which it will not overflow, but in 403 B.C., after two dramatic years, it is hoped that the city will have done with division. Once the tyrants, the same men who had provoked what Cleocritus described as "the most awful war, the hardest, the most sacrilegious, the most odious to gods and men," are expelled, once they are charged with all the crimes from which Athens must be exonerated, after all this, well, let's forget it! Officially and institutionally. Forget that there were two parties; and the winners themselves solicit the forgetting, those same men who had knowingly chosen their side. Fourth-century democracy, whose name it is no longer dangerous to evoke, perhaps because the thing itself is no longer dangerous, will feel the effects of this.

As if the memory of the city were founded on the *forgetting of the political as such.* It is with this hypothesis — the one most important to me and that I have attempted to formulate in these pages — that I will break off this enumeration of the paths leading to the memorable forgetting of 403 B.C.

The itinerary whose future directions I have just outlined is not very economical. Yet to assess what is conventionally called a work in progress, I have anchored myself more firmly in the conviction that if the anthropologist suffers from avoiding the event, the historian can examine no event without opening it up to the slow temporality of the networks of signification that give it meaning. These problems are already solved, perhaps, for historians of other periods, who, because they do not have Greece as their object, are not called on to fight day in and day out against the weightiness of classicism. Yet the historian of Greece knows that in order to give a meaning to the word "city," he must hound out of the *polis* the forgetting — a founding forgetting — of the division that its unity implies, even if only temporarily.

A founding forgetting... To conclude, I will say a few words about a text that tells of forgetting. An almost too beautiful text that in mythical time places at the origin of the Athenian city a loss of memory on the Acropolis.

I became aware of Plutarch's reference to the altar to Lēthē (Oblivion) through a mention of it in a scholarly note. Because it seemed important to me from the start that oblivion was worshiped within the Erechtheion, the most symbolic of all the Acropolis's sanctuaries, I decided to begin this chapter by quoting Plutarch. But when I read Plutarch, what was my surprise, not to mention my joy! My hypothesis was borne out beyond all my hopes: in *Table Talk*, the altar to Lēthē sanctions a reconciliation after a quarrel. True, forgetting is often associated with a quarrel in Greek mythological thought: thus Hesiod's *Theogony* makes Lēthē the child of Eris;[65] but the Athenian version of the story is even more telling, because the reconciliation there puts an end to the quarrel between Athena and Poseidon over possession of the new city. Divine Eris: a mythical model of human *stasis*?[66] To anyone who still has doubts I would only quote the rest of Plutarch's text: "How much more political [*politikoteros*] than Thrasybulus did Poseidon show himself to be when he was not the winner [*kraton*] like the former but the conquered one."

We shall not know more: as if to arouse speculation, the end of the text is lost. But I would venture to say we know enough: *politikos* is the name of one who knows how to agree to oblivion; and if myth locates at the origin of Athens a *stasis* that is quickly erased, it is not by chance that the only counterexample of Poseidon's moderation Plutarch's drinkers can find is that of Thrasybulus, the democrats' leader in 403 B.C. Of course, we must also read things

43

in the other direction: the history of Athens turns back to the myth, and 403 B.C. itself serves as a model for an entire rhetorico-political tradition inherited from Isocrates, among others. As if, by swearing not to recall the past, the Athenian city had once again founded its political existence on a loss of memory.

CHAPTER TWO

To Repoliticize the City

The connection between history and anthropology is supposedly an established fact. Claude Lévi-Strauss recalled that this is "one of the most original aspects of the evolution of the social sciences in France," but he went on to suggest that this connection is also something that remains to be accomplished.[1] Is it too pessimistic to point out that there are fields in which this connection cannot be made without serious difficulties? Studies of ancient Greece provide an example, one that may indeed be considered exemplary, of the difficulties encountered in making this connection. In fact, the quarrel about boundaries, or rather — because to speak of a quarrel might imply that the practice of encroachment is common to both sides — the strict delimitation of boundaries, is far from recent: this distinction goes back to the Greeks themselves, among whom, from Homeric epic to classical thought, two ways of thinking the city clash with each other.[2]

In the social sciences of the early twentieth century, history and ethnology were distinguished by their subjects: "History treated ... the upper classes, the deeds of war, the reigns, treaties, conflicts, and alliances; ethnology treated popular life, customs, beliefs, and the elementary relations men have with their environment."[3] Likewise, in the Greek way of thinking the city we can

45

distinguish a historical and an anthropological mode. To be sure, the two ways (or the two cities) easily coexist within a single work, either side by side or in succession: this is the case in Herodotus, where the city that performs sacrifices, weddings, and funerals is a criterion of intelligibility for the investigator passing through barbarian lands, but during times of conflict in Greece, this city is effaced in favor of the city of political decisions and armed combat;[4] the shield of Achilles already revealed this by showing the peaceful city resounding with wedding songs along-side the city at war with armies camped at its gates. This division is easily discovered and demands to be thought, and in fact, modern anthropologists and historians of Greece have faithfully brought it to our attention. Too faithfully, perhaps, since they stress the boundary between the two, as if one approach had to exclude the other and as if it were necessary to choose one city over the other.

Anthropologists of Greece, then, have chosen their side. Against the Greece of the humanities, which in its own history is associated with the city of the historians, and against the prestige of the same, which is deeply implicated in Greek politics and reason, the anthropologists have tried to de-center the object "city." They have sought in the cities of archaic and classical Greece the other: the suspended time of ritual, the other of political time, but especially those who represent the other of the citizens — that is, the young, women, slaves, even craftsmen, until bowmen and peltasts, the other of the hoplites, came to swell the ranks of the battalion of alterity. In other words, as François Hartog puts it: "Behind the same, to find the other, behind Apollo, Dionysos, . . . but at the risk of moving, for the general public, from the traditional 'Greek miracle' to the exotic Greeks."[5]

Respecting this demarcation, anthropologists of Greece have made a distinction among the texts that they consider documents.

46

Thus they gladly read Herodotus, but very little Thucydides, the paradigmatic historian whom they typically leave to historians. Because Thucydides says that he expelled the *muthōdēs* and because myth is essential to anthropological reflection on Greece, they take Thucydides at his word, too quickly forgetting that in 1907, at the very core of the Cambridge School, a disciple of Jane Harrison's was bold enough to write a study titled *Thucydides Mythistoricus.*[6] Because interest in anthropological criteria is explicitly limited in Thucydides's work to the "archaeology" at the beginning of book 1, which attempts to reconstruct the most distant past of Greece — anthropology for the Greeks being an instrument for the time before history or, as in Herodotus, for non-Greek space[7] — modern anthropologists have not sought the elements for a different framework for reading, elements that may be disseminated throughout the *logos* of historical reason.[8]

But, anticipating my argument, I had already begun to wonder about the options involved in choosing one city over the other. It is worth trying to elucidate the principle of this choice and its consequences.

The inaugural act of the anthropology of Greece seems to have been to arrest civic time, to present it as immobilized around certain practices, rites, or gestures labeled fundamental, which, in the *aiōn* (the always renewed eternity) of social life, actually are fundamental.[9] These rites and gestures are grasped in their repetitive periodicity and have no other duration than that of the strictly limited unfolding of their sequences, which is always the same.

This immobilization makes it possible to generalize, that is, to have recourse to types, isolated in their particularity (the child, the ephebe, the woman, the warrior, the old man) or linked in pairs of opposites (master and slave, man and woman, citizen and foreigner, adult and child, warrior and artisan).[10] And by assigning these generic characters their places, social practices become types as well: there is sacrifice, war, or marriage, and there is the all-encompassing ideality of the city, the most important of all these types.[11] Greek reflection, whenever it generalizes, often takes the form of a typology, as it does in Aristotle when the city becomes the object of his thinking. Still, it is necessary to question the anthropologist's willingness to seize on everything in a society that "speaks in the singular."[12]

When it comes to the anthropology of Greece, the answer to this question might be found by analyzing its very last option: the domination of iconography or, as its practitioners put it, of the reading of images. Images painted on vases, motionless scenes whose characters — types, precisely — "represent the city." *The* city would be found entirely in images. One more step and we will hear — we do hear — about the *city of images*.[13] "The city" has passed over to the figuration that the Greeks call *zōographia* (drawing from life), which Plato accused of saying "the same thing forever."[14] The same thing forever: hunting, war, marriage, sacrifice, banquet; funerals, erotic life, religious festivals, the Dionysian universe. Through rites and practices, the city appears as it is in itself.

In a word, the "city as a whole" is everything except the political. The images indeed show Athenians banqueting but not sitting in an assembly; and although one can find different types of warriors, it is in vain that one looks for the representation of combat, unless it is mythical. Iconographers recognize this and readily speak of the "censorship of the political."[15] At this point, I stop and wonder: if modern researchers could articulate the two ways of imagining the city, at rest and in motion, this broadening of the field of study opened up by iconography would have had great advantages. This would, however, require not only that we acknowledge this remarkable censorship but also that we strive to situate it in the overall functioning of the system of civic representations. There is much to learn from the effort to think about this articulation. Perhaps its time will come. But only if anthropologists-iconographers question their implicit practice of adding a theoretical choice to the choice they discern in their corpus: to exclude the political because the images exclude it; or to be so entrenched in the images — a term we would do well to reflect on — as to overlook the political.[16] Insofar as they are figurative representations, images would supposedly "provide access to mental representations" and would display the "social imagination" of the classical city. Or, in the more precise terms of the preface to *A City of Images*, that of classical Athens (since the representations studied are for the most part from Athens).[17] And here we see that freed from the political — with which classical studies, in their "overly literary idea of the ancient world," had identified it[18] — Athens (or should I say *an* Athens?) is revealed to anyone able to systematize the figurative repertoire of its significant scenes and gestures. Athens avoided, Athens regained outside the time of battles and assemblies, outside the civic space that painters do not depict, becomes something like a finely polished surface. A "flat society."[19] A society that is other, certainly, because it is precisely a question of alterity. But an other in the form of a half, an incomplete *sumbolon*. A "language" said to be autonomous and independent of the discursivity of *logos*. A painted city.

A moment ago I mentioned that Plato considered *zōographia* an immobilization of the living. I would like to quote Plato again as he analyzes the feeling experienced before a model city that has been described — in this case, the one that the *Timaeus* claims to take from the *Republic* — in a passage that carries out a very Platonic movement, an apparent turning back on itself:

49

> I might compare myself to a person who, on beholding beautiful ani-
> mals either created by the painter's art, or, better still, alive but at
> rest, is seized with a desire to see them in motion or engaged in
> some struggle or conflict to which their forms appear suited.[20]

Socrates is there to ask for an account of the city's struggles. One
can imagine the city of images being put through the experiment
proposed at the beginning of the *Timaeus*: a setting into motion.
Or at least (it does not escape me that Socrates's demand will not
be fulfilled in the dialogue, so well does Plato understand the difficulty of seeing such an experiment through to its end), one can
imagine that the inventors of this city of images might set themselves a task: to clarify what it was that prompted Athenian
painters to sort through the complex reality of the Athenian city
and choose "society against the State,"[21] ritual against history, and
to prefer the margins (the marginalized, whom the texts describe
as *akhreioi*, useless, because noncitizens) over the center (the
meson of the citizens).

Yet beyond those who choose Athenian painters, I am interested in what leads anthropologists of Greece to become iconographers. Or, in other words, the perfect coincidence between an
object choice (the investment in images) and an implicit definition of anthropology that identifies it *de facto* with the suspension
of the political.

There are of course many ways of bracketing the political. I have
focused on the iconographic variant not only because of the hege-
monic position it has attained among anthropologists of the
Greek city but also, and above all, because its theoretical implications are, from this point of view, exemplary. But to locate the
first instance of the ellipsis of the political, it may be necessary to
go much further back in the history of this anthropology of

Greece, to its first era, when an anthropological figure of Greek politics began to emerge. In the beginning, the city of anthropologists is indeed political, and political before all else; in this regard, it has probably seduced many Hellenists of my generation who were searching for a new perspective outside the humanities and especially for a model of civic life more civic than any of the tired versions offered by universities in the 1960s.[22]

It was with politics that Louis Gernet began, enumerating the standpoints from which one can speak of the "beginnings of Hellenism," and it is important to note that his text, unpublished for many years, sketched out what later became *The Anthropology of Ancient Greece*.[23] It is important, above all, that such an exposition was proposed by the man anthropologists of Greece consider their founding father, to the extent that they credit him with a representation of "Greeks without a miracle" that may well be mostly their own.[24] Much more could be said about the different ways each of us interacts with Gernet's works; I will not venture to do so here, so as not to upset the balance of these reflections which, as an inquiry into the forgetting of the political, are nothing more than prolegomena.[25] I will only note that displacements occurred. In itself, this is not surprising: there is no tradition without displacements, and we have to take into account the phenomenon of drifting, whatever the field may be; pious regrets are useless, even if, for example, we regret that the anthropologists of ancient Greece never directly tackled the study of law, so dear to Gernet. I come back, then, to what is in my view the essential displacement — the ellipsis of the political in the midst of the political itself — in order to try to understand how this happened and what meaning we can ascribe to it.

I just spoke of the ellipsis of the political. In fact, I am already working at one remove, because I chose as my subject this Greek

51

political existence that has to be reconstructed beyond the documents (textual, epigraphic, archaeological) that bear its mark, and the situation is thus infinitely more complicated than it was with the corpus of images. There is yet another difficulty: iconography seems to postulate the censorship of the political as a whole, whereas in claiming that the political is evacuated from itself, I am constructing an ideality of the political that would be the missing link in existing analyses. Conflict is this missing link, this hidden dimension, which I tend, if not to identify with the political as a whole, at least to see as indispensable to any thought about its workings.

For instance, let us use a very eloquent example: the institution of sacrifice. To transform sacrifice — as Marcel Detienne and Jean-Pierre Vernant's very thorough study once invited us to do — into a "culinary operation" in which one kills to eat amounts to putting the stress on the intermediate stage between the killing and the eating, that is, on the moment of distribution.[26] From this distribution, thought of as egalitarian, a form of ahistorical political existence is born, because the dividing up is strictly regulated and because, above all, it is not certain that power shared by all is still power. But in fact, from this point of view, the sacrificial scheme is only an application of a more ancient model that was truly foundational. I have spoken of the paradigm of the *meson*; following the history of this anthropology of Greek political existence against the course of its development and to its source, we do indeed encounter this center, at once symbolic and real, which is effective for the entire city because it is the place — literally, the middle place — where the distribution occurs. Sharing power in the rotation of duties, sharing *logos* in debate, which is open and contradictory but not conflictual and where the law of the majority requires that the winning opinion at the end of a speech be considered the best one.[27]

Grounded in the *meson*, the political is conceived as having gone beyond conflicts — once and for all, as it were. Vernant explains this in his introduction to *Problèmes de la guerre en Grèce ancienne* by contrasting the political, which "can be defined as the city looked at from the inside," with war, identified with "the same city with its face turned toward the outside."[28] This is certainly a very Greek way of assimilating the political to the city at peace — provided we specify that this city is first of all at peace with itself, as at the end of the *Eumenides* — and of locating conflict only where its existence is legitimate, even desirable: in external war, which sets the city against its outside (in the *Timaeus*, this was the only way Socrates could imagine his model city being set into motion).

The political or the city at peace? We have here a very Greek definition, the most widely shared of all the Greek ideas of the political. It remains to be seen, however, whether to understand Greek categories we must confine ourselves to speaking the language of the Greeks. This is a moment through which we must pass; it cannot simply be eliminated. And yet for all that, I am not certain that modern reflection should find its last word there.

That the city is never completely at peace is confirmed by rereading book 18 of the *Iliad*: there, at the heart of the peaceful city, quarrel (*neikos*) coexists with the festivities accompanying the wedding. This is a legal conflict, to be sure, and is therefore already domesticated; but in this dispute between a murderer and the victim's parent, the scene is immobilized before a judgment is given, at the moment when everything comes to a standstill — between the one who asks to pay the blood price and the other who refuses to accept the least compensation, while the people divide into two camps to support one or the other party.[29] The moment is ripe for someone to intercede and end the conflict. One might object that this conflictual component of the Iliadic

53

city must be ascribed to its pre-political character. I will return, then, to the classical *meson* to test this representation of a form of the political that would be beyond conflict.

It is certainly possible to locate in the *meson* "this purely human choice that measured the persuasive force of the two addresses, ensuring the victory of one speaker over his adversary."[30] But this victory, whether we call it *nikē* or *kratos*, implies a *de facto* acknowledgment of "superiority" — superiority of one orator over another, that is, of one opinion over another, but also, with the tallying of the votes, of one part of the city over the rest. And this is precisely what cannot be taken for granted, because Greek political thought can neither quietly accept — even for the moment of the vote — division in the midst of the city nor agree that the law of the majority has any intrinsic worth.[31] To the first kind of reluctance corresponds the representation of "good" decisions, happy decisions unanimously agreed on; to the second corresponds the recurrent temptation to attribute to human assemblies a tendency to give the victory to the worst decision. The foregrounding of the *meson* thus conceals quite a few reservations....

The second distinctive feature of the *meson*, this locus of a trouble-free political life, is that it gathers together citizens who are interchangeable, because in principle they are all equals (*homoioi*). A great deal could be said about the power, at once conceptual and political, exerted by this isomorphic *meson* — which Vernant first placed in the stark light that projects idealities — over all those who were not satisfied with the official institution of Greek history, with its empirical, or even anecdotal, conception of the city. Yet this model, in its exemplary stability, makes difficult any study of the dysfunctions constituting history: thus it cannot be stressed enough that as the empty site calling for an entirely symbolic power such as the rotation of duties, the *meson* easily becomes, as soon as the symbolic is in default, a site to be effectively occupied, that is, to be taken over by a group or even — and this seems easier — by an individual.[32] It is probably the *meson*, with its convincing authority, that opened the way to the only study of the political as ritual: it was enough to shift the political toward religion, and under the aegis of the politico-religious, we could easily transfer the isonomy of the *meson*, where decisions are made, to sacred sites, where sacrifices are performed, even if this meant rediscovering the political at the heart of the sacrificial distribution — albeit an egalitarian and tension-free form of the political, through which the itinerary closes on itself. The itinerary of discourse: that of the Greeks; and from one discourse to another: that of the anthropologist of Greece, at the risk of confusing the discourse with the thing itself and of effectively thinking the city under the sign of egalitarian distribution (which, even when limited to citizens — as it had to be — was an ideal in all the cities of Greece, including Athens, where, however, democracy required it to be a reality).

Whatever the costs may be, let us resolve to break the spell — for example, by renouncing the idea that we should confine ourselves to the words of the Greeks and by submitting their discourse to the very questions that are silenced in it. If we refuse to speak the Greeks' language to the end, and if we do not deem it necessary to stick to the stories they tell about their own practices, we cannot avoid the hypothesis that the "political" model orchestrated in sacrifice is nothing but a story that the city tells itself. In other words, the isonomic distribution from then on becomes a *figure*. The figure that the collectivity of citizens wishes to project under the reassuring sign of interchangeability. Something like a utopia, covering over what the city wants neither to see nor to think:[33] that at the heart of the political there is virtually — and sometimes actually — conflict, and that division into two, this calamity, is the other side of the beautiful unitary City.

Not taking too literally the Greeks' discourse on the political may also mean recalling that the Greek city is not one of those "cold" societies that, as Lévi-Strauss wrote, "chose to ignore" their historical dimension, so that "a minimal gap separates their ideology from their practice."[34] By lessening the gap between discourse and practice, or rather by interpreting this gap according to what the Greeks suggested it was — nothing to speak of, really — anthropologists of Greece have in fact "cooled off" the object *city*, while simultaneously foregrounding everything that relates this political form to a cold society.[35] This gesture, both essential and rich with consequences, has renewed the study of sacrifice, war, and marriage and will no doubt also renew reflection on other dimensions of the Greek experience. But in every theoretical reevaluation, there is the risk of bending the stick too far in the other direction, and along the way we have almost forgotten that Greek politics was not cold. With this in mind, I would now like to plead a case for the inverse gesture.

To delineate more clearly this figure or utopia of the distribution among equals, I will now use a word, "ideology," that I have so far avoided (until the quote from Lévi-Strauss, who does not hesitate to use it). I have avoided it less because it would be disreputable, due to the current depreciation of Marxism, than because its meaning is often rendered trivial when it is used to designate any system of representation (we speak, then, of the ideology of hunting, of funerary ideology, and so on). Yet I use this word, and I persist in giving credit to this notion. Because "the mask of ideology is made of its silences, not of what it says,"[36] it is necessary to focus on the words that are absent from civic discourse — for example, *kratos*, a word typically missing from the flights of oratory that prefer the word *arkhē*, the name of institutional power, shared and always renewed in the endless succession of magistrates at the center of the city. With *arkhē*, the peaceful *meson* is not far away; but the implications of *kratos* are so dreaded by the city that whenever possible it silences the name that evokes them. Surrounded by silence, *kratos* is one of the key words of civic ideology (which is the ideology of the city insofar as it produces the "city" as ideality).[37]

To argue for a "repoliticization" of the city of anthropologists means taking seriously both the anthropological contribution and the conflictual component of the political.[38] It also means not being content to study conflict (in this case, *stasis*, which I return to here) as "presupposed in what has superseded it" in the civic order.[39] In addition, it means showing that even when civic thought considers the time of conflict a thing of the past, when all the ritual and discursive conditions have been assembled to prove that the city is One, conflict is endlessly reborn as a threat in the very midst of language through the metaphoric use of certain terms — such as *sphagē*, which names the sacrificial throat cutting and, through only a slight displacement, signifies the blood shed in wars between citizens.[40]

Is conflict always superseded? We might believe this if we only looked at, for each city, the "history" frozen in tradition that the citizens tell themselves and in which there is always an oracle to designate the sacrifices that will bring back (are bringing back, have brought back) peace and to name the divinity who, once appeased, will reconcile the two halves of the collectivity. Yet conflict is also something that is always yet to be overcome, on the uncertain border between vote and fratricide, where the law of the majority endlessly attempts to exorcise the threat of division. And, finally, it is constantly reborn in the history of the Greek world, the history of a Herodotus or a Thucydides. How, then, could anthropologists of the ancient world avoid introducing it into their generic city as one of the vital experiences of civic life?[41]

To conclude these remarks and proceed to *stasis*, I will propose a few suggestions. Less a program or the exposition of a few wishes — time has passed, and the interlocutor is no longer the same — than something like a work protocol for oneself.

It should be clear that my aim is not a reversal of the anthropological choice. It is not a matter of going back to the city of the historians, because the problem does not consist in choosing one party over the other: that would only, in fact, renew a Greek division, one that we may well want to think but that we cannot be sure was ever operating in the real life of cities. Because one feature of the Greek city is that it maintained, simultaneously, two competing and complementary representations of itself — one that "accepts history" and one that "is loath to do so and prefers not to know it"[42] — we must strive to bring these two figures together in order to connect them: to think the city of anthropologists historically, but especially to think the city of historians anthropologically.

For an anthropologist, this would mean first of all de-compartmentalizing his own approach, which up to now has sought to separate the spheres of social activity according to broad lines of division (*there is* sacrifice, and *there is* war) in order to avoid uncontrolled overlapping. That there is a time for typological sorting out, and that this is precisely the time of separation, is not in doubt — this is in fact, once more, a Greek moment repeated by anthropological thought.[43] But there also comes a time when, with or without the Greeks, it is necessary to go beyond Greek operations better to explore what goes on behind the scenes. Thus, from the Greek effort to separate war and sacrifice, we can move back toward the major threat to be avoided — namely, "the threat they harbor of the confusion between war and blood sacrifice."[44] For this reason, the only choice is to risk — in a way that is experimental, systematic, and calculated — putting everything back into circulation. This requires that one try out every possible type of cross-checking: sacrifice in war and war as sacrifice. Then, by proceeding to the largest possible cross sections, one can connect war, sacrifice, murder, and execution as practices of bloodshed.[45] In this way, one can also link murder, sacrifice, and the founding of cities as they are recounted, repeated, or executed. In a word, to explore all the zones of superimposition, which require more than simply distributing "representations" on the flat surface of a table of oppositions, where they occupy a fixed, single place; and especially because in these murky zones, ideology — with its clear-cut antitheses between what is beautiful (good, one, legitimate, civic) and what is not — is dissolved. Superimposition and the scrambling or blurring of lines: to work on the borders, we must accept inevitable movement. It is a movement that conflict introduces into the well-regulated machinery of the ritualistic city, a setting into motion of the representations at work in the thought processes that we must follow as they unfold and that we must at times reconstruct.

We must understand the price to be paid for introducing movement: along the way, we might be led to claim that the city *thinks*, which amounts to making the city a subject.

The city thinks: I know very well that this statement is extremely problematic — even unacceptable — to some, and yet I stand by it. First, because it would not have been problematic for a Greek, accustomed to treating the city as a subject that can be invoked as a witness, as in Aristophanes's comedies, or endowed with desires, as in the writings of philosophers (thus Aristotle: "A city wants [*bouletai*] to be composed, as far as possible, of equals");[46] second, because, in everyday political life, a decree voted in the assembly always begins by bestowing feelings or decisions.[47]

I acknowledge, however, that on this point, as on the others, it will not do simply to repeat what the Greeks say, even if it is important to understand the paths of their thought. The ancient historians certainly would not avail themselves of such a delicate utterance as "the city thinks," because they prefer to locate their city in the sphere of action or, if driven to it, to speak of "political ideas" produced in some ethereal region and ready to be integrated into a history — general and without a subject — of political thought. Therefore, it belongs to the anthropologists of Greece to give content to this utterance, especially because their methodology, in its most current formulation, relies on this usage on many occasions — as when they write that the city "averts the threat" or that its defense system is "subtle" — even if they usually do not linger on this point.[48] Linguistically unifying the city as a subject, they open themselves to the criticism of those anthropologists who object to the idea of treating society as a subject,[49] or who, anxious not to flatten social organization by reducing it to its discourse, call for the identification of speakers and addressees in matters of speech.[50] These are general warnings, but they are useful to anyone working in Greek territory, because they can upset long-established habits. We are thus far from underestimating methodological caution, and for two reasons, each of a different order. First, the modalities of the inquiry: because anthropologists of Greece have no other territory than the documents they interpret, the temptation to reduce the city to its discourse is great. Second, and above all, the subject "city": however suspicious we may be of the isomorphic *meson*, where the city projects itself and finds its identity, this figure is too beautiful and often too powerful not to return stubbornly in all its seductive and simplifying charm, awkwardly erasing the gaps between discourse and practice and between speaker and addressee.

Nevertheless, to treat the city as a subject is still the most productive working hypothesis for anyone who wants to escape the motionless discourse of the One and give himself the tools for analyzing the forces behind it. We must, however, accept the consequences of our gesture, with all the uncertain groping, and the advances into terra incognita it implies. We must be willing to reconstruct thought processes that, when confronted with the political reality of the city, look very much like the active work of negation, even denial. Yet in attributing to the city modalities of defense that are so many mediated ways of rejecting reality (or, at any rate, of accepting it only in a neutralized form), we may have to take another step — one more step, and on moving ground — in order to endow this problematic subject with something like an unconscious. I am aware of the difficulties — not to mention the resistance — that this notion, applied to a collective subject, inevitably encounters. Yet even if we see it merely as a word that would help us move forward,[51] it presents an opportunity finally to confront head-on a question too often treated by paralepsis by the very people who — like anthropologists of the city — like to speak of an imaginary or a symbolic.

I will stop here with this wish. A wish formulated in the potential mood, as exhortations to oneself should be when it is uncertain whether the endurance, the means, or the conviction will not be lacking along the way.

To think Greek politics as an anthropologist: to make the city think by listening to the multiplicity of voices and respecting the multilayered instances of enunciation, while refraining from isolating a particular discourse. To do this, we will have to approach the too-perfect model as a historian: to disturb the certainties of the *meson*; to expose the city to what it rejects in its ideological discourse yet lives in the time of the event; and to examine those forces of conflict that found the political at least as much as they destroy it.

To conclude this reflection in the form of a plea for a "warming up" of the Greek city, the last word will go to Lévi-Strauss, whose statement about history and anthropology I quoted at the beginning of this essay and have often followed step-by-step. "The time has come," he says, "for ethnology to focus on turbulences, not in a spirit of contrition, but, on the contrary, in order to widen and develop this examination of the layers of order that it still considers to be its mission."[52]

For the Greek city, may the time of turbulences come.

CHAPTER THREE

The Soul of the City

I have not yet come to the end of the prolegomena. For the purposes of bringing conflict into the city, they are indispensable, because one does not always have the tools, or the courage, to pursue the questions further.

So it is for a historian who cannot dispense with such words as "forgetting," "repression," and "denial" to think the object of her inquiry. These words, no doubt, are meant to help us advance; indeed we do advance, at first, on the tips of our toes — sometimes even on points, like a dancer — and then more and more out in the open.[1]

Simply words, and only to advance: this is at least what the historian tells herself, glad to postpone indefinitely the moment when she must look closely at this way of working in order to clarify it. Yet even while doing so, she is constantly aware that the moment will come sooner or later, maybe more than once. The notions of repression and denial have often helped me to travel further back into the memory of Athens. Indeed, I have spoken a great deal about denial: democracy's denial of its historicity, to anchor itself in an origin that is both noble and natural; the Athenian city's denial of the role women played in the reproduction of Athens, which is erased in favor of the myth of autochthony; the denial of conflict as a constitutive principle, in order to construct the generality "city."[2] I will now revisit all these denials, which, fundamentally, may be only one.

The time has come, then, for me to reexamine this practice, which I like to think took place in the mode of what Michel de Certeau has exquisitely called a "mutual seizure."[3] This mutual seizure implies — and here I rely on the passage at the beginning of Certeau's *The Mystic Fable* in which many historians working on Freud have recognized themselves — less the application of concepts "capable of accounting for" an object than an "awareness of theoretical procedures ... *capable of bringing* [this object] *into play*," whatever "reversals" may result from these procedures.[4] Taking care all the while, throughout this work situated on the borders, not to forget that the borders exist.[5]

What to Make of Stasis

The object, then: what a Greek city called Athens makes of civil war or, more precisely, of *stasis*, the Greek term for what is both a position (a party's position, the upright position taken by a citizen rising against other citizens) and violent insurrection, radical reversal, sequential murders, and political catastrophe. What does the city make of *stasis*? How can it erase it with a gesture and with speech? The gesture consists of the institutional decree that acts committed during *stasis* (which are usually called in Greek the events or the misfortunes)[6] be forgotten, while the speech is national history, which is recounted by concealing as far as possible the fact of *stasis*.[7] In both cases, our project is to estimate the effects, or even the products, of such an erasure: in the text itself and, beyond it, in the memory of Athens.

By using the formula "what a Greek city makes of *stasis*," I also want to suggest that, at a very profound level, it would like to make nothing of it, which means doing everything possible to transform it into nothing: in other words, it becomes very important to deny that conflict has any congenital link to the political. Certainly, the operation is not easy, and two contradictory definitions of *stasis* coexist. There is one for which cities have a distinct preference, because it places *stasis* on the outside: outside the city, perhaps even outside humanity, civil war is a catastrophe that rains down on human societies like a plague (*loimos*), an epidemic, a tempest, or like the nefarious consequences of an external war; battling the storm, the city is weakened, even wounded, yet it waits hopefully for the moment when it will recover its integrity after ridding itself of an evil that has come from the outside.[8] But there is also the much more dreadful feeling, which is rarely expressed — and when it is, always fleetingly, reluctantly, and incompletely — that *stasis* is born from within the city: in Theognis, it is what the city is pregnant with — the terrible gestation of murders between fellow citizens — and, more generally, Greek tradition interprets civil war as a sickness of the *polis*.[9] I have said that in Greek thought on the political the first definition was preferred; there follows from this a series of operations whose aim is to ensure the unequivocal victory of this comfortable definition that amounts to denying that *stasis* is an ongoing condition of the city. Already the temptation is strong to seek in this denial direct access to the city's repressed material. Yet when we see that *stasis* is repeatedly condemned, how can we not evoke what Freud says about condemnation as an intellectual substitute for repression?[10] To the expression "I want to exclude this from myself" we need only give a civic form, which is that of an unreserved blame, uttered by a speaker who would be the city.

Other types of negation follow from this one, of course, such as the negation of hate, which is the very form of relations between individuals in *stasis* but is mentioned only to be immediately denied. "For they did not attack one another out of malice or enmity (*ekhthra*), but they were unfortunate," says one; another echoes elsewhere: "No less ashamed of their disasters [*sumphorai*] than angered against the enemy [*tois ekhthrois orgizomenoi*]."[11]

Here the Greek strategy toward memory as wrath enters into play:[12] this terrible memory whose very name — *mēnis* — cannot be uttered without strict precaution, because it is a word that can actually wound and kill.[13] Whether it is the epic wrath of Achilles or the mutual resentment of citizens after a civil war, the danger is the same, and, Plutarch says, it is just as dreaded as those spirits called "unforgetting avengers" who pursue "the memories of some unforgotten foul deeds of earlier days" (where "unforgotten" translates *alēston*, or in Homeric language *alaston*).[14] Hence the imperative to renounce this memory by an act of denial: "I am making an end of my anger," says Achilles at last — and Achilles has a place in every Greek memory, where his heroic wrath serves as the model for all collective resentments.[15] The city echoes: "It is forbidden to recall the misfortunes." And each citizen, one by one, swears the oath: "I shall not recall the misfortunes," meaning the past, just as Achilles says to Agamemnon: "Still, we will let all this be a thing of the past, though it hurts us."[16] This is the cue for the official exit of memory. Yet we suspect that, in all its deliberateness, such a forgetting leaves traces.

I would suggest that beyond all the denials and the forgetting, what must be forgotten or denied is that *stasis* is congenital to Greek political existence. Forgetting the past would then be to repeat in every civic amnesty a very ancient forgetting: the forgetting of that time long ago — if it ever existed — when conflict ruled life in the community. Unless this primal time, when the human condition was assigned to mortals in the midst of conflict, was never anything but a myth — an origin myth of the political, and therefore something foundational even as it is tirelessly covered over and concealed.[17] In both cases — whether we speak of a primary forgetting or of an origin myth that must be constantly pushed back into the past, the better to rescue the present — the task I have assumed is to uncover (or should I say exhume?) repressed material that contains another kind of thought on *stasis*, a thought that, if allowed to express itself, would take the form of praise. *Stasis*, then, would in fact be something like the cement of the community.[18] In a word, I must *construct* — in the sense in which Freud speaks of a "work of construction, or, if it is preferred, of reconstruction"[19] — a scenario in which hate would be more ancient than love,[20] in which forgetting can be valued only in terms of the unspeakable joy brought by the wrath that does not forget.

Yet it is probably in the nature of this construction always to remain at the project stage. This is because, confronted by a too-perfect erasure, the undertaking does not have the means to realize itself. In addition, there are subjects that historians, lulled by an impression of consensus (all the more powerful because never spoken), simply do not take on, unless it is to provoke guilt in those who transgress the prohibition. A word of warning to the reckless: one cannot without serious consequences work in a direction altogether contrary to the affects driving an intellectual enterprise — a discipline, as we call it — that is as codified as the field of history. Scruples, or suspicions, are there at every step. This is certainly not unfounded: less edifying than archaeological work, which finds reassurance in its positive aim, and lacking the exchange between analyst and analysand, however unequal it may be, that underpins psychoanalysis, the effort to bring to light a dynamics of conflict is sure to encounter resistance from historians, be it personal or professional — and the latter is not necessarily the lesser. In addition, one must deal with the doubts that crop up whenever one moves against the current and with the premonition that everything might end, as it were, in a dismissal of one's case.[21]

Thus, because I must be cunning with my theoretical investments, and because I would like to propose for reflection some sites that are more specific and less threatened, where history and psychoanalysis can engage in a dialogue without too much mistrust and where they can mark off their respective grounds, I shall examine only two symptomatic examples of how Greek political existence functions under the repression of conflict. I shall therefore speak of a forgetting and an undoing. First, I will discuss the gradual and progressive forgetting of a political murder, keeping in mind that any historian who wants to catch Greek memory in the process of repression must learn to work with the blank spaces of history and to focus on those obscure moments when the ways of murder become blurred and names sink into anonymity. (We will see that the victim Ephialtes, killed in 461 B.C., has a "poor" name.)[22] As for the undoing, it bears on a particular word that is essential to Greek political thought, because it is found in the very name "democracy," but that is also essentially ambivalent: *kratos*.

Forgetting, undoing: which subject in the coherence of a tirelessly repeated refusal thus forgets/undoes? I have already suggested that this subject is the city. And I will have to justify this, because in treating the city as a subject, one is bound to provoke objections from historians and psychoanalysts alike.[23] But we must be patient: the moment will arise for posing this question, the most troubling of all in such an inquiry — so troubling that it often threatens to annul our prior intentions.

A Weighty Word

Whoever does research on Athenian democracy has a vested interest in reflecting on *kratos*: on the meaning of the word, on its usage, and on the relation between democracy and its name.

In the Homeric poems, *kratos* "indicates the superiority of one man, whether he asserts his strength over his friends or enemies."[24] Borrowed from Emile Benveniste, this definition is pertinent to the classical period, except that there it is often necessary to replace "one man" with "one party" or "one part" of the city. The essential point is that throughout its history *kratos* always designates superiority and thus victory (hence the word is often associated with *nikē*, victory, both over enemies from the outside, the others, and over enemies from the inside, one's own).

To have *kratos* is to have the upper hand. We may infer from this that it means having "complete power over": thus in a proscription decree from Miletus, the city is described as *egkratēs* with respect to individuals accused of subversive activities; and the authority that Athens effectively exercises over the cities in its maritime empire is regularly described as *kratos* or one of its compounds.[25] More generally, however, *kratos* is a particular type of victory: the verb *kratein* expresses superiority in fighting an external war, and as long as it is used in the active voice, it does not lead to problems in a discourse whose subject is the city. *Kratos* is also used to designate the victory of an opinion in an assembly, as well as the advantage gained by one faction at the end of a *stasis*, when the party that has overcome its adversary "regards political supremacy as the prize of victory."[26]

This is where the problems begin. Indeed, as if the cities refused to admit that there could be a place in political practice for *kratos*—because that would mean ratifying the victory of one part of the city over another and thus having to renounce the fantasy of the unitary and indivisible city—the word is strangely absent from both civic speech and historical narrative, which usually favor *arkhē*, the name of institutional power. Thus Xenophon, recounting the dictatorship of the Thirty, in which only an oligarch—in this case, Theramenes—can dispassionately evoke the

possibility that leaders (*arkhontes*)[27] rule (*kratein*) over their subjects.[28] A democrat would never express himself in such language,
which is perhaps surprising: doesn't the very word "democracy"
signify the *kratos* of the people? And yet this much is clear: it is
better to do without the word *kratos* and even, while we're at it,
the word *dēmos*. Within the city, as we have seen, *kratos* is a disreputable word, and *dēmos* designates both the people as a whole and,
in a more partisan manner, the popular party. This is why, already
in the fifth century B.C., democrats avoided the word *dēmokratia*.
But by avoiding this word, which was perhaps first applied to the
regime by its adversaries as a disparaging nickname,[29] the democrats themselves assumed the oligarchic representation of government,[30] and they implicitly admitted that *dēmokratia* means a
division of the city into two parts and a victory of one part over
the other. As a result, they forgot to give to *dēmos* the sense of
rallying and gathering together that must have belonged — in fact
did belong — to it;[31] and rather than take on the partisan meaning
of the word, they preferred not to give a name to their regime.

Vertigo of the One? No doubt. I see in it above all the trace
of a fundamental denial: the denial of conflict as the law of politics and life in the city. Anything is preferable to recognizing that
in the city power rests in the hands of one group, even if this
group constitutes a large numerical majority. It would be fruitful
to consider the ways in which modern representations of the
political have retained this logic. But we might also ask why there
is such a consensus to make consensus the bond of politics. Or, in
other words, what is it that makes the choice of consensus seem
incontrovertible?

In Plato, we find something like the first step in such an inquiry. Because in his hierarchized universe Plato readily recognizes the universal necessity of *kratos* in the city, as in the body
and the soul of an individual, and because he enjoys revealing to

the Athenians the words repressed in their official discourse, he takes every opportunity to point out anything having to do with *kratos* in the democracy.[32] To make things perfectly clear, Plato insinuates the repeated affirmation of *kratos* into the institutional prose of the funeral oration, indeed, into the very moment when the regime is to be praised, whereas in Thucydides, Pericles only uses *kratos* when discussing military details in his speech.[33]

Plato thus brings to light the operations carried out within the "soul" of the city in order to think democracy as the orthodoxy of consensus: this is the first time we encounter this configuration, but not the last. I will return to it later.

Kratos, then: or the notion that we must work with absent words when their absence can only be the result of avoidance.

Traces of Murder

My second example concerns the forgetting of a murder. In 462 B.C., Ephialtes, the leader of the democratic party whose reputation for being incorruptible made him, as far as we can tell, a "Robespierre *avant la lettre*,"[34] attacked the aristocratic court of the Areopagus, from which he withdrew all rights over political life in the city.[35] Shortly thereafter, he was killed . . . and disappeared almost completely from the Athenians' memory. To be more specific, it would probably be better to say, from the memory of the Athenian *dēmos*, since the oligarchs hardly forgot his deed, according to Aristotle's account of the beginnings of the rule of the Thirty, one of whose first actions in 404 B.C., he says, was to "remove" from the Areopagus Ephialtes's laws concerning the Areopagites, to the great joy of all honest people.[36]

This erasure is all the more remarkable in that we might consider Ephialtes's deed — and I do not hesitate to do so — as marking year one of the Athenian democracy we are accustomed to hold up as a model.[37] By this I mean that it was Ephialtes who

71

first gave democracy — whose "first inventor," according to Herodotus, was Cleisthenes — the effective means for its development.[38] Is it not to him that tradition assigns the role of having
"brought down the law,"[39] in the sense of secularizing its existence and making it more accessible to consultation, when, in
an eminently symbolic gesture, he moved the venerable laws of
Solon from the sacred hill of the Acropolis to the political *meson*
of the *agora*?[40]

Cleisthenes, Ephialtes: two founders of democracy, both "forgotten," or nearly so, by the Athenian *dēmos*, even though it had
solemnly buried them in the official cemetery of the Kerameikos.[41]
Indeed, although it has been said of Cleisthenes that "of all the
great figures of Athenian history, he is without doubt the one least
often recalled," the erasure of Ephialtes may have been even more
complete.[42] Even when we take into account all the information
historians and other Greek writers provide about him, we still do
not know who he was, what the course of his life was, or what the
exact circumstances of his death were.[43] We do know his father's
name — Sophonides — but we are unable to reconstruct a meaningful genealogy. As for his stature as a politician, we know little
more: he apparently served as Themistocles's lieutenant and as
Pericles's adviser. Yet in these subordinate positions, Ephialtes
disappears behind two of the greatest men in Athenian history,
whose biographies were written by Plutarch. There was no *Life*
dedicated to Ephialtes, a man whom ancient sources associate at
most — and very briefly — with the reform that bears his name
(mentioned only in a few succinct phrases) and with his violent
death. But even his death is shrouded in silence: beginning with
Aristotle, who gives the only real information we have (the name
of the murderer and the detail that it was a "murder through
trickery" — or in other words, an ambush), and moving to Diodorus, who simply reports that "he disappeared one night," we

can trace the work of a very remarkable process in which a murder is gradually and progressively erased.[44]

Clearly, such a murder (*phonos*) disrupts the harmony of that irresistible evolution toward a democratic *telos* that the Athenian city, as almost all ancients and moderns believe, is supposed to have followed. There is no need to invent far-fetched scenarios to explain the "disappearance" of Ephialtes, and we should dismiss as fantastic interpretations that, in the manner of the most ancient political history, attempt to reconcile conflicting ancient sources by presuming that Pericles ordered the murder. (They claim that Pericles was jealous of the "leader of the people" and that the murder was committed by the oligarchic party's henchmen because of a secret agreement between ambitious democrats and their adversaries, who were only too happy to get rid of an opponent unwilling to compromise.)[45] I would relate the forgetting of this *phonos* to a completely different logic. In relation to its great figures, from the *tyrannoctonoi* to Ephialtes via Cleisthenes, the Athenian strategy on memory manifests a remarkable consistency. On this basis, I advance the hypothesis that for the democracy confronting its history and eager to recount its harmonious development, the best thing would have been to make it possible to doubt that Ephialtes was murdered. If this was too much to expect, they could at least work to deepen the process of forgetting.

At the beginning of the chain of forgetting, there is indeed an oligarch, Antiphon, who protects his own by forcefully claiming that the killers were never identified; and at the end, Diodorus brackets the murder, places it in parentheses. Between the beginning and end, we must reconstruct the operation by which Athens purges the history of democracy of every act of *stasis*. Rising against the Areopagus, Ephialtes dangerously resembles an insurgent, and it is as such that he is killed by his adversaries.[46] Because all the elements of *stasis* are there, it is necessary to erase conflict

73

at all costs, even if it means failing to recognize that this "insurgent" was in fact the most prominent democrat. Thus, in forgetting the murder, the democracy — so anxious to become for the city a kind of nature and so eager to locate its foundations in an original autochthony — thinks it can escape those moments of tension that constitute the history of cities.[47]

Of course, Greek sources offer another version of this erasure, one that seems weaker but is really more radical in that it does not try to conceal the murder but argues that Ephialtes is not the true father of the reform that bears his name. We find it in Plutarch, in his *Life of Pericles* (as noted above, there is no *Life* for Ephialtes). Pericles is thus the one in charge, and it is "through Ephialtes" that he revokes most of the Areopagus's powers. *Di' Ephialtou*: Ephialtes is here not an active force but only a means to an end, a hired hand used in a ploy devised by Pericles. Then it so happens that Ephialtes is killed by the oligarchs; or rather, to quote Plutarch, his enemies, plotting against him, had him secretly killed by Aristodikos of Tanagra. Thus everything falls into place: Ephialtes is the democrats' hired hand, and he is killed by the oligarchs' hired hand. In this story, there are only underlings. It is left for the reader to make this connection, but without putting too much stress on it, just enough to admire the symmetry, not enough to notice a glaring contradiction: if Ephialtes played only a minor part, why does Plutarch specify that the oligarchs were especially afraid of him because he was "inexorable in exacting accounts from those who wronged the people, and in prosecuting them"?[48] It is precisely here, in this too-obvious symmetry between *di' Ephialtou* and *di' Aristodikou*,[49] that I (stubborn reader that I am) see the trace of a process very similar to the one Freud reconstructs in *Moses and Monotheism*: "In its implications the distortion of a text resembles a murder: the difficulty is not in perpetrating the deed, but in getting rid of its traces."[50]

74

In fact, Plutarch's narrative seems to have one *dia* too many, like a trace it was impossible to eliminate. The first *dia* would have been enough, since it is the agent of what I like to call Ephialtes's second death and pushes him back into the quasi anonymity of a subordinate position. But the second one overburdens the text even as it tells the truth, and no doubt for that very reason: this detail invalidates what precedes by an effect of aftershock, by revealing the oligarchs' fear of a democrat who was as esteemed as he was active and whom it would have been impossible to eliminate out in the open. The second *dia* overflows from the first and uncovers the process of manipulation it puts into play. But who indeed is the manipulator behind the scenes? Plutarch? Athenian tradition? Or is it the repetitive avoidance in the memory of Athens of the law of conflict? With regard to Plutarch, my hypothesis is that he was only obeying the memory of Athens, if Freud was right to claim that "the distorting purposes ... must have been at work already on the traditions before any of them were committed to writing."[51]

In this case, the national tradition of Athens goes too far in its effort to eliminate all traces, to the point that this narrative centered on Pericles indirectly does justice to Ephialtes. And now I can no longer postpone explaining what a political historian can expect to gain by turning to Freud.

Transference in the Form of Analogy

I generally turn to Freud's metapsychological works, and more specifically to *Moses and Monotheism*, to find concepts that may be helpful and inspiring when dealing with the differential gap of analogy and to find the patience and audacity to pursue these problems.[52]

At each reading of *Moses and Monotheism*, I latch on to a few essential points: that we cannot speak of a collective unconscious, because "the content of the unconscious, indeed, is in any case a collective, universal property of mankind," from which it follows — and this is essential to my argument — that "here I am not using the term 'the repressed' in its proper sense"; that Freud confesses he is "not at home" in the subject of group psychology but that it is crucial to "venture on a further step" in order to bridge "the gulf" between individual psychology and group psychology,[53] which means that we should not avoid appealing to repression; and that it is a matter here of a real *transference*, even if Freud speaks more often of "analogy."[54]

The "further step," then, would be from the occasional recourse to the model of the individual and his neurotic symptoms necessary for an understanding of religious phenomena to the open practice of analogy, the only legitimate one or, at any rate, the "only satisfying" one, because it "approaches identity"[55] — a step whose difficulties Freud stressed many times, though he also acknowledged its inescapability as a "postulate," to the point of sometimes taking for granted the analogy between peoples and individuals.[56]

Because I read *Moses and Monotheism* as a historian, I do not fear, as a psychoanalyst might, diverting psychoanalysis outside the sphere of clinical practice, which "would chase what we feel to be at the heart of psychoanalysis toward what we believe is its periphery."[57] To the contrary, and only slightly paradoxically, as a historian, I feel quite comfortable in this periphery, which is, after all, probably not a periphery; it is at most a space opened up by a displacement of the center. It is easy to work in this space because, coming and going between my own field and the Freudian text, I am not afraid of importing concepts from the one to the other. It is as if it were safer because the transference has already taken place.

This hardly means that all the difficulties have been resolved or that it is only a matter of serenely "applying" a theory. To do history with Freud leads to a doubling of the analogical dimension of my analyses: there is not only an analogy between the individual and the group (or between the individual and humanity) but also an analogy — hoped for, assumed, operating — between the historian's field of inquiry and the object of psychoanalytic reflection. This raises many questions that are perhaps destined to remain unanswered. If for Freud the "group" refers in the end to humanity, whose forgotten childhood can be reconstructed on the model of all our individual childhoods, at once singular and interchangeable, what are we to do when our object is a collectivity that is ancient but that we have no intention of considering as the origin of humanity as a whole? Can we ascribe some sort of childhood to the city in order to understand what Athens has repressed? I would of course not venture in this direction except to attempt to cast the myth of autochthony in the phylogenetic mold, a risky undertaking that would no doubt lose its way in an excess of mimetic zeal. Yet something is even more troubling: if only religious phenomena — in this case, Jewish monotheistic religion — can accurately be described as having first "undergone the fate of being repressed,"[58] what will we find in *Moses and Monotheism* when we focus on politics rather than religion, and when, moreover, the politics is *Greek*?[59]

Questions without answers are often badly formulated questions, arising, for example, from attempts to apply problems that are imported without precaution from another field. Thus it is always to the historian's advantage to reexamine his object in an attempt to find his own questions, the only ones he must ask of the Freudian text, acknowledging both the distance and the uncanny feeling of proximity. This, at any rate, is the wager I am making. It is to understand the functioning of political memory in Athens that I often reread *Moses and Monotheism*, not to draw from it limiting schemes but to train historical thought to find in the text the inspiration needed for creating its own processes. In

77

the same way, crediting the Athenian city with repression and denial arises less from an adherence to the text than from an encounter with it.

Adherence is impossible for many reasons — among others, because yielding to the proposition that "we can deal with peoples as we do with an individual neurotic" would lead us to place the entire Athenian definition of the political under the heading neurosis.[60] Yet an encounter is imperative: the Greeks themselves prompt me to attribute to the city a memory that resembles that of individuals because they are the ones who, under the rubric of the political, thought the analogy between the city and the individual.

Of the Individual-City

I shall focus especially on Plato's thought, because Plato most deliberately systematized this analogy and because I hope to understand more clearly what made it possible for the philosopher to go so far in uncovering Athenian democracy's most secret feelings.

In moving directly to Plato, I will have to take a few shortcuts, mentioning only in passing the first steps of the inquiry. First, of course, we should test the relevance of the hypothesis by bringing it to bear on the work of the Greek historian who occupies the paradigmatic position of the rigorous historian for both the ancients and the moderns, namely, Thucydides. Thucydides would provide a very trustworthy testimony that for a historical consciousness, the city and the individual are subject to the same great affects. Not only would we notice in his narrative many occurrences of the phrase *polis kai idiotēs* (the city and the individual)[61] — which is not unique to him, since there are many occurrences in other civic genres[62] — but also we would learn much from a systematic study of the great human feelings that gave rise to history insofar as they set in motion both the individual and the city, thereby giving historiography its explanatory principles. This applies to fear, in which Thucydides sees the true cause of war, and to anger, which, in line with tradition, he gives as the foundation of *stasis*.[63] Next, we would have to gather all the facts, both in language and in everyday Greek political life, that argue in favor of constructing the city as a subject — the subject of every action, of every decision. In terms of language, we can rely on the study in which Benveniste establishes (as a linguist) what Aristotle postulated (as a philosopher) in book 1 of his *Politics*, namely, the primacy of the city over the citizen, of *polis* over *politēs*.[64] Thus in certain official texts — decrees of the city or civic speeches — we would see the *polis* taking on its function as a subject in everyday political life: the city has decided, the city has acted..., such that the city always takes precedence.[65]

This essay could doubtless be long, were I to present the many small examples gathered in the course of my readings. In narratives of *stasis* describing citizens as fighting not "against each other" but "against themselves,"[66] I would readily see a clue that all identity — all civic identity — lies in the subject-city: dependent on the *polis* to which they totally belong, citizens do not have enough autonomy to establish reciprocal relations among themselves; and between citizens, that is between the city and oneself, the relation is always reflexive.

But I promised to go straight to Plato. Closing these barely opened questions, I will be content with a single statement, which is very troubling for us but provides a Greek path for thinking the analogy between city and individual.

Here is the statement: *the city is a subject because it can be attributed with a soul*. Or we can approach it from the opposite direction: the city can be attributed with a soul because it is a subject. Be that as it may, and even if it is only a working hypothesis, let us assume that the city has a soul. The statement is a Greek one, as I have said, and Isocrates formulates it twice, adding that for each city this soul is its constitution (*pasa politeia psukhē poleos esti*).[67] In which case, whenever Athens is the subject, we have grounds to treat the democracy — as I have done — as a *psukhē* having difficulties with itself.... But I will move on to Plato, less because he occasionally confirms this reasoning — as he does, for example, in the *Laws* with the claim that "pain and pleasure are in the soul what the populace or commonalty is in a community" — than because things are both more complicated and more enlightening in his thought.[68]

Like Thucydides, Plato uses the phrase *polis kai idiotēs*.[69] He uses it, however, in the service of a very subtle strategy in which the analogy is reversed several times, from the city to the individual and from the individual to the city.[70] A simple summary of some of these reversals in the *Republic* will make this clear.

First proposition: the individual is both at the beginning and at the end of the city, understood as the ideality on which all inquiries into the political are based. At the beginning, at the source, there were single individuals: "Do you suppose," Socrates says to Glaucon, "that constitutions spring from the proverbial oak or rock and not from the characters of the citizens, which, as it were, by their momentum and weight in the scales draw other things after them?"[71] To say in colloquial Greek that someone is born out of oak or rock is tantamount to reproaching him with concealing his genealogy:[72] "You pretend to be a son of earth" is a way of suggesting that one's interlocutor denies owing his existence to a necessarily sexual human reproduction (and in fact, in book 8, every type of citizen will have a father, a mother, and a family story). If it is necessary to ascribe a genealogy to different constitutions, then we can assume that the citizens' characters "give birth" to each *politeia*. ("Is it not, then, impossible for us to avoid admitting this much, that the same forms and qualities are to be found in each one of us that are in the state? They could not get there from any other source.

It would be absurd to suppose that the element of high spirit was not derived in states from the private citizens [*idiotai*]."))[73]

At the beginning, then, is the individual. Yet the individual is also at the end, like a *telos* (at once end and goal), as the model toward which the city necessarily aims, because the city must be One and because that unity requires the city's being in a condition "most like that of an individual man."[74] At the basis of cities, the *idiotai*; at the end, the isolated individual, or rather the metaphor of man.

Yet we might just as rightly suggest another proposition that reverses the first one: the city is at once the paradigm and the end of the individual citizen. It is paradigm in the sense that it is a very clear example and helps us to understand something more obscure;[75] that is, the city — characterized, like the Homeric gods, by our self-evident perception of it — in book 8 will help us to understand each type of citizen: so many constitutions, so many unique individuals.[76] Forget for a moment that the opposite discourse was just put forth: the city becomes a privileged ground of experimentation for thinking the individual because, in a very Greek way, the city gives a meaning to everything. Thus, if we take Plato at his word, the whole *Republic* — ten books of political reflection — would constitute a simple prolegomenon to understanding the individual. A remarkable passage from book 4 confirms this hypothesis while also complicating its formulation. The passage is about justice, in the city and in the individual:

> But now let us work out the inquiry in which we supposed that, if we found some larger thing that contained justice and viewed it there, we should more easily discover its nature in the individual man [*heni anthrōpōi*]. And we agreed that this larger thing is the city, and so we constructed the best city in our power, well knowing that in the good city it would of course be found. What, then, we thought

we saw there we must refer back [*epanapheromen*] to the individual and, if it is confirmed, all will be well. But if something different manifests itself in the individual, we will return again to the state and test it there and it may be that, by examining them side by side and rubbing them against one another, as it were from the fire sticks we may cause the spark of justice to flash forth, and when it is thus revealed confirm it in our own minds.[77]

Much could be said about this metaphor of friction that produces fire and about the intimate interweaving it suggests between city and individual.[78] Because the fire that Hermes first produces by rubbing two pieces of wood together is a figure of sexuality, we can perhaps deduce that Plato was well aware of the *erōs* at work in the trials and errors of research.[79] But it would be prudent not to press too hard here and to stick to the object of research itself, and thus to the surprising fact that the sexual metaphor par excellence is — enigmatically — located in the close relation between the city and the individual. For now, from this small piece of methodology, let us retain only the idea that the back-and-forth that moves from the intelligible model of the city to the individual is expressed in the language of transport and *transference* (*epanapheromen*, says Socrates). Freud will also use this word, though he does so to move from the individual to the collectivity; the parallel nevertheless deserves attention.

The city, then, would provide a paradigm for understanding the individual. But it is also, and especially, a model of the soul, and a model for the soul. This requires explanation. In the analogy's friction between the individual and the city, Plato gradually substitutes the "soul" for the "individual," just as he readily replaces "city" with "constitution": so many constitutions, so many forms of souls.[80] However that may be, it is clear that the soul is *like* a constitution, which does not yet make a constitution into a soul, or a soul into a constitution — but let us be patient. At the conclusion of this process, the soul has become a city: a city with parties, enemies both within and without, and a council of elders and military leaders.[81] In short, a city prey to *stasis* where it is necessary to impose harmony at all costs and forever. And here comes a dramatic turn of events, although it has been waiting in the wings for a long time: at the end of the *Republic*, the constitution (*politeia*) or the perfect city, is in the soul, where harmony is supposed to rule.[82] But make no mistake: if harmony rules, it is because Plato has firmly installed a *kratos*, that of reason, in the inner city of the soul. Because the soul has parts, it also has parties, and only a legitimate *kratos* will put an end to the rebels' defiance.

Platonizing?

I will break off this survey of passages from the *Republic* and return to a question that has haunted me throughout my work on Greek politics: why is it that in the attempt to grasp the process through which *kratos* is denied or to articulate the modalities in which conflict is repressed, the turn to Plato has so often proved necessary, as if Plato's thought were the most reliable medium through which to reveal the economy of the city's imaginary solutions? Here I find once again the Plato who liked to unmask the *kratos* concealed in democracy's discourse about itself.[83] Why Plato? Now the answer is clear: *kratos* has its place in each stratum of his work, and though he reviles it as every Greek is obliged to do, Plato continually returns to the problem of *stasis* — such that his philosophical reflections present a way of thinking the soul within the regime of conflict that directly informs the questions we must ask of the city when, conversely, we institute it as a subject.

It is no doubt necessary further to complicate the game of analogy and endless exchange between the psyche of the individual and that of the city (analogical for us, though apparently unthought in

Plato, yet in fact fundamental). This would imply that in endowing the city with a soul, we are also endowing the soul with the
conflicts whose figuration Plato borrowed from the city in order
to think the individual soul. As if, in order to think the repressed
within the political, it were necessary to submit the analogy to *all*
possible reversals and, moreover, to all reversals *simultaneously*.
Then we would acknowledge that faced with the fact of *kratos* or
with the reality of conflicts, the city behaves as a subject that is
divided and torn apart, as if — as Plato would say — the inner *stasis*
of the soul prevented the soul of the city from confronting politics in its reality.

I am of course "platonizing." In other words, I am manufactur-
ing myth. Perhaps I am simply fantasizing the freedom of a game
of exchange in which the analogy is endlessly reversed. And at
this late stage, caution returns with the question of this game's
legitimacy. Let us assume nevertheless that there are processes
that define the political in ways that escape the awareness of
human societies and that these processes can be likened to the
unconscious. Then *stasis* is in place, in Freud first of all. I will
quote *Moses and Monotheism* one last time (about the constraining
features of neurotic processes):

> They [the pathological phenomena] are insufficiently or not at all
> influenced by external reality, pay no attention to it or to its psychi-
> cal representatives, so that they may easily come into active opposi-
> tion to both of them. They are, one might say, a State within a State,
> an inaccessible party, with which co-operation is impossible, but
> which may succeed in overcoming what is known as the normal
> party and forcing it into its service.[84]

It is indeed Freud, not Plato, who thus describes psychic conflict
— in this case, the victory of neurotic processes — by using the fig-

ure of subversion in the city. This is the ultimate, and certainly unforeseen, reversal, concerning which I will not venture any further comment. Is this formulation nothing more than an isolated metaphor? Or is it possible to link it more generally to the language Freud uses to describe psychic conflict? Is it merely a result of the back-and-forth movement between individual and group psychology that is unique to *Moses and Monotheism*? If this is the case, the reverse movement of this "transference," which always goes from the individual to the collectivity, would be the movement of the political in its collective dimension as it turns back toward the representation of psychic conflict. These are questions I am not sure I can answer, so I will be content with offering them to Freud's readers. At most, I will suggest that if there is any legitimacy in establishing a "metapsychology of the city," as I have tried to do here by following Greek paths, such an enterprise might well be nourished by the relationship — be it metaphoric — that Freud's metapsychological thought maintains with a conflictual representation of the political.

I have almost reached the end of the itinerary I proposed here, which hardly means that I consider the problems I have raised to be solved; but I hope that by showing the multiple reversals and turns of the analogy, I have more clearly delineated the ways in which it can be formulated. There remains the task of questioning the paths taken in submitting Greek politics to this investigation in which, as if superimposed, Plato encounters Freud.

We no doubt have to return to this word "transference," by which Freud characterizes the work of analogy in *Moses and Monotheism*. To use the word in this way is to speak analogically of analogy, and this derails thought and frustrates translators.[85] In any case, Freud uses the word "transference," and he always intends to use every word with its full semantic force. This applies also to "displacement" (*Entstellung*) as that which erases the traces of murder, and my wager throughout this essay has been that this was also true of "transference."[86]

If there is a transference from individual to group psychology, can the historian who reads Freud completely reject the hypothesis — more than once pushed aside as discouraging or at any rate destabilizing — that "in his work" his own transference is at stake, a transference passing from himself as an individual to the Greek city, the ideal support of all politically charged transferences in that it is supposed to have invented the political?

This is one way, and perhaps the only way, in which a historian of ancient Greece, reconsidering his or her approach, could understand "where the pleasure to write history comes from."[87] It is a pleasure we are often at pains to deny, impressed as we are by the reputation for seriousness of a field that considers itself a science. This is one way, at any rate, in which we can attempt to explain to ourselves the relation, whether distant or close, that we maintain with our chosen object.

This effort to place the city within conflict gives rise to many more questions of method, and the way toward the answers has become more and more uncertain, prompting me to seek shortcuts that lead me more cautiously but perhaps more confidently to the object.

Questions about the divided city: questions for anthropologists, questions for psychoanalysts; modern questions and ancient questions. Or questions the historian asks herself, without the help of any user's manual. Armed with these still-open questions, I decided to press forward into the ocean of Greek discourse on conflict, an ocean as contradictory as that of Alcaeus, which is simultaneously agitated and immobilized by contrary winds.

86

PART TWO

Under the Sign of Eris
and Some of Her Children

Hateful Discord in turn
bore painful Hardship,
and Forgetfulness [Oblivion, Lêthê], and Starvation,
and the Pains, full of weeping,
the Battles and the Quarrels, the Murders
and the Manslaughters,
the Grievances, the lying Stories,
the Disputations,
and Lawlessness and Ruin, who share
one another's nature,
and Oath [Horkos], who does more damage than any other
to earthly
men, when anyone, of his knowledge,
swears to a false oath.

> — Hesiod, *Theogony*

It was never true that there was only one kind
of strife. There have always
been two on earth. There is one
you could like when you understand her.
The other is hateful.

> — Hesiod, *Works and Days*[1]

In setting out on this venture, we may let a poet guide us as he unrolls his catalog of the children of Night, in which the lineage of Eris, the last and most dangerous of the dreaded daughters of Nux, makes up the second generation.[2] After Ponos, who gives to the human condition groaning effort, Oblivion heads the list, and after the various forms of combat and murder have been enumerated, Oath concludes it: a clear suggestion that when Eris is seen as entirely dark — as she is in the beginning, in her very origin,[3] at least before Hesiod realized that there is also a positive side to discord — Oblivion and Oath are for mortals her fearsome offspring.

Yet Eris — whom, were it not for her obviously *feminine* identification as a solitary mother, I would simply call *conflict* — always seems to arise from a thought that is double, as if the dreaded Two were endlessly divided into antithetical pairs of values. Double indeed is the poetic scenario that proclaims the existence of a positive Eris after presenting at great length the sinister catalog of nocturnal powers, just as Oblivion and Oath are double, both in the representations and in the uses the Greeks made of them. Oblivion is fatal when it attaches itself to the deeds of human beings; for this reason, Pindar's poetry and Herodotus's investigations take on the task of combating it. Yet there is also a kind of memory that is dangerous, because it conspires with death or, at any rate, with the mourning that, walled away inside the *penthos alaston*, becomes a refusal to forget; happy then is the forgetting of misfortunes, whether it comes about by the poet's song or by the city's decree.[4] Similarly, if it is the most terrible scourge for the disloyal — and for Hesiod, humanity in its weakness seems to consist entirely of disloyalty — the oath is also the durable cement of civic memory whenever a collectivity attempts to forget hate.

So it is that this double structure governs thought on conflict, which it places, it is said, under the law of antithesis. Very well, but the question here will be: antithesis or ambivalence? Two kinds of Eris divided in their very nature must indeed form a pair of opposites; but who can say whether, in the strong antithesis presented by the *dia d'andikha thumon ekhousi* (these two are not of one mind) the Greek poet does not actually express the constitutive ambivalence of his own relation to Eris?[5]

There are two types of Eris, then, or perhaps only one that is both single and double: "good" and "bad" Eris? Similarly, if we cannot help hearing "amnesty" behind "amnesia," what are we to make of this irresistible assonance in which there is but a single step from consonance to dissonance? After all, if we listen carefully to Aeschylus, even the Eumenides, like the Erinyes, will never cease to be daughters of Night — as attested in Athens by their epithet Semnai, in which respect is grounded in terror — although they are renamed and worshiped as beneficial guardians of the city. The same words, depending on whether they say or unsay them (curse in one case, beneficent wish in the other), will breathe hate and death or civil peace and the fertility of earth, flocks, and women.

Whether we consider Hesiod's palinode about Eris significant or not, we must consider this duplicity constitutive of the powers of Night, especially if we are inclined to think of Eris as less antithetical than ambivalent, and thus as an authentically double Eris, who would be *at once* dark (hateful, terrible) and essential to life in the city.

On the horizon of the path we are to follow emerges a lesson in ambivalence for the historian of the political: to record the recurrent claims that make the oath the cement of civil peace and simultaneously to pay attention to the imprecation that puts *horkos* (oath) in Ares's sphere; to perceive the stifled voice of an *eris* that would be the strongest bond of the civic community and to understand that what the citizens swear to forget — individually and collectively — precisely echoes this voice, more seductive even than the "misfortunes" to which the city would like to reduce civil war.

The most difficult task, however, must be carried out in the other direction. For any historian who, eager to distance himself from a too-recent past, was led to ancient Greece as the most remote past, it is a very loaded task. Because such a historian knows only too well what associations amnesty evokes in national memory, his greatest wish would be to see nothing but amnesia in the Athenian amnesty of 403 B.C., but it will be necessary to resist — if only in the form of a hypothesis — the temptation to ascribe to the Greeks a well-defined opposition between "good" amnesty and "bad" amnesia.

Meanwhile, it is Eris's turn to speak.

CHAPTER FOUR

The Bond of Division

To designate "sedition," revolution in the city, Greeks
use the word *stasis*, which they borrowed from the
root most evocative of ideas of firmness, permanence,
and stability. As if *stasis* were an institution for them!
— Henri van Effenterre

"Let them render grace for grace. Let love be their common
will; let them hate with single heart."[1] Thus do the Eumenides in
Aeschylus express their wishes for the happiness of Athens. After
seeing their accusations against Orestes set aside and after being
won over by Athena's political eloquence, the Erinyes of revenge
and blood accept the goddess's invitation to become "metics" in
the Athenian city. Turned benevolent, they will protect Athens
against the very thing they administered before: reciprocal murders or, at the level of the city as a whole, civil war.

Thus speak the Eumenides: "Civil War [*stasis*] fattening on
men's ruin shall not thunder in our city.... Let them render grace
for grace. Let love be their common will; let them hate with
single heart."[2]

Plato echoes these words in the *Republic* as he seeks a community that truly binds all its citizens into a single whole: "Is not,
then, the community of pleasure and pain the tie that binds, when
... all the citizens rejoice and grieve alike at the same births and
deaths?"[3]

The Strongest Unbinding

If our point of departure is the Greeks, the case would seem clear: the bond of political community, in a tight network connecting each citizen with all the others, gives the city its unity. This bond must be kept very tight, for it supports the city the way that joints support a frame: "When once the original supports have fallen," "the result is a general collapse of one part upon another, substructure and all that has been so admirably built upon it alike." It is a very tight bond or, as in the *Politics*, a very tightly woven fabric: in a word, a *sumplokē*, a kind of perfect intertwining. It is necessary to knot, bind, weave, and regulate civil peace each and every day because the threat of a tear always looms: the slightest loosening of the knot, the tiniest split in the fabric, and the rift dividing the city gapes open. This would be the end of the One, the breakup, the return to multiplicity — in short, a catastrophe. In order to banish the very thought of it, the bond of community must be made ever tighter, so that no disagreement (*diaphora*) may arise and so that no hate and *stasis* can slip through.[4]

This bond was expressed in Platonic language because classical Greece itself *is* Platonic when it comes to this most commonly shared belief on the nature of the political.[5] If, however, we wish to speak of the horror of tearing apart, Empedocles furnishes a vocabulary of division for those occasions when Eris — the discord that splits every being down the middle — slices everything whole into two, in violation of the great law of Friendship.[6] But I will not elaborate here the exploits of the One and the Many: they are too well known and acknowledged, in short, too overly constructed. I would prefer to speak a language that is more secret, one that is still Greek if not Platonic: a language in which the same word is used to tie the knot both of an alliance and of a fight.[7] A language in which reconciliation is expressed as a ruptured bond. A language that is perhaps less "at peace with itself" than the Greeks liked to think.[8]

Luō: I unbind. There is no bond that cannot be subjected to this process, beginning with the social bond. An assembly or a custom can be broken, and democracy can be destroyed. Thus it is not surprising that the poetic name for civil war, in Alcaeus as in Pindar, is *luē*, unbinding.[9] In fact, *stasis* is a principle of dissolution. Nothing surprising in this so far.

With the addition of the prefix *dia-* (dividing), we obtain the verb *dialuō*, and the noun *dialusis*.[10] In the vocabulary of weaving, these words designate what the carder does when she disentangles the raw wool, the opposite of the act of intertwining; they can thus be placed in the category the "art of separating."[11] In the historians' vocabulary, however, *dialuō* signifies the disbanding of an army at the end of a war. In political discourse, *dialusis* expresses every process of dissolution, be it the breaking apart of a community or the breaking of a truce.[12] Of course, it also puts an end to misfortune, such as war, hate, or *stasis* itself.[13] This rubric has by far the longest list of usages in the dictionaries, and this abundance begs the question: because the negative is so regularly subjected to dissolution, does it bind more solidly than socially accepted values? But there is worse to come or, rather, better from our point of view: *dialuō* and *dialusis* are the very words used to designate the reconciliation of two parties after a dispute or civil war. This is true not only in legal speeches and historical prose (for example, in the Athenian reconciliation in 403 B.C.) but also in inscriptions, dear to the modern historian of Greece because he believes he can hear, carved in stone, the present-tense voice of reality.[14]

Dialuō: I untie; *dialuō*: I reconcile. I separate/I weave again what has come undone. Before claiming that this is an example of "antithetical meanings" in a single word, we might try to reduce the anomaly by reconstructing its genesis.[15] Beneath *dialuō* as "I reconcile adversaries" we would find a *dialuō* meaning "I dissolve the conflict." Yet these two readings can be opposed to each other. Some will say that the dissolution is, in fact, only implied or little understood by speakers to whom the socially positive message is the only one that matters. Or, if the reconciliation itself is the act most likely to save the city, as seems clear from speeches and inscriptions, former adversaries very probably understood *dialusis* as reestablished communication. Others — myself included — find much to think about in this way citizens had of referring to the reestablished bond in terms of unbinding, as if one could be reconciled only in the mode of rupture (I reconcile myself: I break with..., I renounce). Or, rather, as if what must be dissolved at all costs — even if it means forgetting that a vocabulary of reconciliation exists within the sphere of exchange (*diallagē, diallassō*) — is precisely what is never mentioned: hatred and division. In other words, the strongest bond is the one that unravels the city, and this bond is so constraining that there is no need to give it a name. To save the community, then, we must attempt *to unbind what dissociates.*

Dialuō: I unbind the citizens from the anger that made them rise against each other. The rest will follow. In this spirit, an inscription from the third century B.C. from the small Sicilian town of Nakone prescribes that "all the citizens who had a disagreement [*diaphora*] while fighting for the community will be summoned to the assembly to make *dialusis* with each other."[16]

Unbinding the disagreement: the possibility of being-with or being-together (*sun*) is reborn in the division of *dia-*. The Greeks, it seems, did not differentiate between *dialuein* and *sulluein*, to unbind by separating or to unbind together, since in the case of *dia* as of *sun*, it is the dividing force at work in the city that is finally unbound.[17] This is, indeed, what historians call conflict resolution. My point is that what separates also forms a strangely powerful bond.

I foresee the repeated necessity of getting used to this contradiction thus quietly opened up. Everything is played out between a few words, sometimes within a single word — pairs of opposites and words that assume the opposition on their own. Returning to my earlier methodological caution, I will speak of a word possessing "antithetical meanings," with the specification that in this case the opposition is derived and not primal. I have already mentioned *sun-* and *dia-*, community and division, *sumplokē* and *dialusis* (though we also know that *dialusis* is opposed to itself, just as retying is opposed to unbinding). I will also consider *stasis*, endlessly caught between rest and motion. Words, then, in pairs or single ones containing two, and some proper names as well — Homer, Heraclitus, Plato, a few others; also some city names, which are not necessarily the most famous, such as the obscure Nakone. A few others could be mentioned that are not included in our vulgate, as if the exchange between opposed meanings took place more easily outside Athens.

Words and names: several scenes of language for a single scenario. Reversing the classical construction of a paradigmatic city whose model is the One, the scenario will uncover beneath the elegant construction the lineaments of thought that the official discourse on community covers over and perhaps represses. Under the excommunication of *stasis* lies the dreaded confirmation that civil war is congenital to the city, that it is even the foundation of the political insofar as it is something held in common.[18] Yet the forgetting of this form of the political — indissociably conflictual and common — is such that in order to bring it to light, we must follow a counter-memory, as it were, and move against the current of memory. Over and against a civic memory that relegates the god of war to a place outside the city, the time will come to

97

do justice to the Ares who settles differences and assembles. But anyone who wants to erect *stasis* in its originary significance need only look to the *meson* — the center of the city, common to all, and the place of sharing that furnishes equal and interchangeable citizens with a space for speech or action on behalf of the *koinon* (that which is common).[19] Conflict, of words and of weapons, dwells in this civic center, which can be described as empty only if one has first emptied it of its inhabitants.

Here the metaphor of the ship of the city can be introduced as Alcaeus first formulated it in Mytilene in the seventh century B.C.:

> I fail to understand the direction [*stasis*] of the winds: one wave rolls in from this side, another from that, and we in the middle are carried along in company with our great black ship, much distressed in the great storm.[20]

Let us assume for a moment that the *stasis* of the winds is a civil war, the one unleashed at Mytilene. The ship-city is there in the middle of the *stasis*, caught between countervailing winds whose adverse gusts fight and cancel each other violently. The *meson* is caught in the storm because the storm takes place in the *meson*.

We will return to Alcaeus and the *stasis* of the winds, but let us stay for a moment with the *meson*.

Of the Meson *and Its Functions*

It all begins in the *Iliad*, with an invitation to distinguish the *meson* of words from that of weapons. Or else it begins with the assemblies, where eloquence shines, and with the fight between equals, which spares no one but for that reason gives all the more glory to the man who excels at it. Or, rather, it begins with the *agora*, where "speakers of words" are found, and with the battlefield,

98

where those who are "accomplished in action" win renown.[21] That Achilles must find his place both in the *agora* and in battle might prompt us to reunite the two "centers." But patience is needed: before trying to superimpose them, we must separate them. Although the *agora* and the battlefield are indissociable, the stance each requires is certainly not the same: the presumed calm of the assemblies in effect compels the warriors to sit down, the same warriors who fight day after day standing upright in the melee (I am here commenting on the verb *histēmi*, from which the noun *stasis* is derived — I will return to this).[22]

Is the *agora*, then, a place of peace? No doubt it would be if the assemblies that gather there could be peaceful, if the place for trials could also be a place of peace. In fact, Homer discreetly erases the distinction between war and the assembly in the first book of the *Iliad*, where he attributes to the assembly a characteristic of war, the *kudos*, which for a hero can be at once a sign of election and a talisman of victory in battle.[23] Peaceful, perhaps, if the scene of political struggles could ever be peaceful — the political struggles that the language of Solon's time, clearly preserved in the classical era in the form of an oath, referred to quite simply as *agorai*.[24] Although *agora* means gathering (from *ageirō*, to gather), it is the conflictual nature of the *agōn* that comes to occupy it,[25] beginning in the first part of the *Iliad*, with its wars of words — struggles of might against might — when two speakers rise against each other.[26] The gap between speaking and fighting may be smaller than it seems there.

Another *agora*, or, rather, a representation of an *agora*: this one, which has been alluded to several times, is engraved on the shield Hephaestus made for Achilles. Two cities face each other, one a victim of war, the other engaged in peacetime activities. In the peaceful city, the *agora* (as its name suggests) swarms with people: the men described as *laoi* (that is — let us not forget — as people in arms) are gathered there.[27] But no sooner has the text gathered them together than we see them divided, still under the name of *laoi*, into two boisterous opposed parties.[28] A trial takes place in the *agora*, or, rather, to quote from Louis Gernet's observations on ancient legal history, an *agōn* — at once contest and combat, a "judicial fight." The quarrel (*neikos*) Hephaestus forges on the shield is paradigmatic (some would even say "archetypal") by virtue of the seriousness of its stakes: one of the two men confronting each other over the blood price — the murderer — risks his own life.[29] Such stakes make for a passionate crowd that shouts and divides into two parties: two men, two camps, two gold talents placed in the middle (*en messoisi*). We might call this scene on Achilles's shield the great scene of the Two.[30]

Conflict, barely domesticated into an *agōn*, is already in the middle of the city. Not every historian of the Greek city would agree with this statement, and some would prefer to replace "already" with "still": the *meson*, then, is *still* conflictual. This would suggest that an irresistible evolution is at work and that there will come a day in the classical city — that is, in Athens — when violent confrontation, regulated or not, will yield to verbal confrontation. As for myself, I resolutely stand by the "already": there was *conflict already*. However disguised it may have been in classical Athens, violent confrontation was not fated to disappear.[31] Let us consider the assemblies and the opposed notions that led the Athenians into an *agōn* during the second Mytilenian debate in the middle of the Peloponnesian War, according to Thucydides's historical narrative.[32] The circumstances are very similar to the ones on Achilles's shield: it is a matter of life and death for the inhabitants of the city that has defected. But let us leave Athens and consider Eresos — which is coincidentally close to Mytilene — at the end of the fourth century. An inscription there bears witness that in Eresos, as in many other cities no doubt, voting in an assembly was called *diaphora*. Voting, then, means dividing up or, rather, disagreeing.

To vote means agreeing to divide up and to choose between. In addition, agreeing to a division implies accepting that one part of the city will be victorious over the other. We can call this victory the law of the majority, which makes everything seem obvious. Yet if some Greeks called voting *diaphora*, Greek political thought was loath to accept majority rule understood as victory (*nikē*) or superiority (*kratos*) as legitimate. It may be surprising that in a Cretan city of the archaic period, trials were won by the party that brought forward the greatest number of witnesses.[33] It is likely, however, that this was more acceptable to a Greek thinker than the law prescribing that in matters of the common good, the dividing up of votes should end in a victory. Victory is upsetting, whether in the assembly or in civil war. That there can be no "good victory" after a *stasis* in which blood was shed is one of the most commonly shared convictions of the classical city. Democritus bears witness to this when, as the spokesman for upright members of the Greek political world, he claims that "civil war is harmful to both parties; for both to the conquerors and the conquered, the destruction is the same," because fellow citizens confront each other from both sides.[34] It is more surprising that victory of one opinion over another is disturbing, even when obtained peacefully in assembly. Because division in two is threatening, as if *stasis* were always latent, the Greeks declare that whenever voters are equally divided, it is inevitably the worse of two opinions that prevails. Thus they dream of unanimous assemblies that make a common decision with a single voice — a decision that would then be unquestionably good.[35]

If we gave sufficient attention to this recurrent scenario, and if we dared to gauge the mistrust of the supposed inventors of the political toward their "invention," the credibility of the geneses of the pacified city — in which voting gradually replaces *stasis* and the conflictual *meson* is smoothly and thoroughly emptied out to make room for the most regulated exchanges of power — would certainly be undermined. Certainly, the Greeks wanted this to be the law governing life in the city, and I will refrain for the moment from any conclusions about the consciousness or unconsciousness of this desire. Indeed, consensus, taken as the essence of the political, shielded their eyes from conflict perhaps at a very early stage. Yet before we take them at their word, before quietly accepting this model that their desire for immortality fashioned for posterity, let us pause in the archaic *meson* to observe Solon. Solon, the "man of the middle," the reconciler who puts an end to the *stasis* between rich and poor, Aristotle's hero.

In Aristotelian thought, the city is led to introduce a middle between its two hostile halves, a middle that becomes the third party of the people in the middle. In the archaic Athenian *meson*, however, where the threat of conflict always looms, Solon alone, standing like a hoplite between the two armies of citizens, like a lone tyrant, keeps at bay the two factions so eager to start fighting again.[36] And after Solon? Aristotle informs us that Solon devised a law for the uncertain future, for the coming conflicts that were only too predictable. And this law states, "If when the city was torn by strife anyone should refuse to place his arms at the disposal of either side he should be outlawed and have no share in the city."[37]

Of course, this law is surprising, even shocking, and many more historians have contested its authenticity than have accepted Solon's authorship. Because we take the man of the middle for a moderate, we are reluctant to attribute to the wise Solon such a prescription for political activism. This law also seems to conflate the very elements that fifth-century political thought seeks to separate, if not to oppose — the glorious combats in external wars and the murders to which civil war can be reduced. In fact, if the

ability to take up arms (*thesthai ta hopla*) is the distinctive criterion of citizenship in the classical city, then the Solonian law is
scandalous in that nothing in it distinguishes the gesture of the
citizen from that of the insurgent, since it is precisely insofar as
one is a citizen that one has the obligation to be an insurgent.[38]
Yet in commenting on this law, I have already anticipated my
interpretation, which renders unto Solon that which is Solon's
due: this is an "emergency law" that takes into account the un-
avoidability of conflict, this *stasis* that Solon's poetry presents as a
"common evil" (*dēmosion kakon*) that is virtually irresistible (it
enters into each house, and no door can stop it; it jumps over the
highest walls and seeks the quiet citizen in the innermost cham-
ber where he has taken refuge). *Stasis* is an evil, and it is better to
guard against its outbreak. Yet when it comes, it invades the city
to the point of substituting itself for the community. The hoplite
is standing (*stas*), ready to die for the fatherland, when *stasis* arises
and leads him to serve it instead: everyone must take a side, for
this is the only way to re-create a totality out of the divided city —
that is, through the remainderless engagement of all its members
— and the only way to glue the antagonistic halves back together.
The apathetic citizen will thus be deprived of his rights as a citizen — he will be politically dead — as if *stasis* had taken on the role
of civic duty.[39] Neutrality does not exist.

We see from the Solonian law that the fundamental modality
of *stasis* is that it affects the entire city. *Pasa polis*: this is ordinarily
thought in terms of the One. Civil war, then, although it is always
put in the category of the two because it divides, would make one
out of two, with the provision that there is a rift in the middle of
this one.

In the game of the one and the two, there is a great risk of losing
the One. Fifth-century Athenians, disposed to venerate Solon,
readily forgot his law and preferred after the oligarchy of 404 B.C.

to isolate the guilty by counting them. There were thirty tyrants, then only ten, plus ten magistrates of the Piraeus, plus eleven prison guards, that is, sixty-one criminals excluded from the amnesty.[40] As for the rest, ah well, they didn't do much of anything and, after swearing to forget the past, will live together once again as citizens, and the community will be restored. The days are long gone when apathy was punished by loss of citizenship.

With this elementary arithmetic, Athenian democracy did its best not to know that conflicts had pitted the two halves of the city against each other. Yet it is a sure bet that by 403 B.C. the Greeks had quite forgotten to ask what *stasis* meant.

Stasis: *A Gegensinn*

Stasis. Noun of action derived from the verb *histēmi*. Synonymous with *kinēsis*, movement or, more specifically, agitation. A Greek dictionary of received ideas might offer such a definition, which is constantly reinforced by tragic and comic poets, historians and philosophers whenever they consider the city.[41] For philosophers interested in characterizing Being, there is another *stasis* as the name of the being at rest and of the standing position in its motionlessness (in fact, *histēmi* means to stand, to set, to stop). Here, between agitation and motionlessness, everything becomes more complicated.

The Greeks, it is said, were able to move from one meaning of the word to another without questions. That may be, but the fact remains that they were always very influenced by their own language and would not have missed an opportunity to explore the possibilities of wordplay offered by double meaning. When Plato, disagreeing with Heraclitus in book 4 of the *Republic*, maintains the impossibility of the coincidence of opposites, he is protesting against the assimilation of *hestanai* (to be at rest) to *keisthai* (to be in motion). He also adds: "So I fancy it is not well said of the archer that his hands at the same time thrust away the bow and draw it nigh, but we should rather say that there is one hand that puts it away and another that draws it to."[42] We can easily detect here a polemical allusion to *palintropos harmoniē* (attunement turning back on itself), to which we will return later. There are, however, many grades in the scale of the unthinkable. When it comes to saying what cannot be thought, Plato himself relies on the notion of *kinēsis stasimos*, a movement at rest, although its inverse — *stasis kinētē* — is never mentioned.[43] Plato takes care not to express it, and with good reason: because he is interested in the city as much as he is in Being, he knows that this phrase is not an *adunaton* (impossible) but rather, in the context of political language, a pleonasm. (To civic ears, *stasis kinētē* would indicate movement twice over, and thought would be powerless against this first perception that for the citizens is both immediate and shared.) Ultimately, the real *adunaton* is not even a phrase: it is contained entirely in the word *stasis* as the noun of agitation/rest.

We could, of course, disregard the opposite meanings of words. We could pretend that nothing of the sort is happening and take shelter behind an etymological dictionary that glosses *stasis* as "stability, place, action of standing, hence insurrection" — in which case, we had better not ask too many questions about this "hence." It is also possible — even as we wonder why in political contexts the word does not retain its neutral meaning of "position" — to claim that the "key to the riddle" is "in Greek society itself." That is the historian's solution.[44]

But I suggest that we complicate the double meaning even further by adding to the above opposition (between movement and rest) the tension between what is upright and of a piece (and therefore unitary) — *stasis*, then — and the representation most commonly associated with *stasis* in daily life, namely, division. I am prompted to do so by a passage from book 5 of Plato's *Laws*, where it is a question of "the most fatal of disorders which might more properly be called distraction [*diastasis*] than faction [*stasis*]."[45] This has also been translated as "dissension rather than faction" or "insurrection rather than sedition." But giving to *dia-* all its distributive value, I take it to mean that the most fatal disorder for the city is "division rather than *stasis*." It is a question of nouns: Plato suggests that *stasis* cannot be used to designate civil war, because he prefers to invalidate the political use of the word by restoring its philosophical value of motionlessness. Only a word in *dia-* (in this case, *diastasis*) can present the duality of division. The intimate link between *stasis* and the fantasy of indivisibility would thus be revealed by a ricochet.

Let me advance a hypothesis without any further ado: civil war is *stasis* inasmuch as the clash between two equal halves of the city erects (just like a *stēlē*) conflict in the *meson*. Thus Alcaeus's *stasis* of the winds, balanced forces holding up the motionless front of air that moves above the ship of state in distress.[46] Above all, it is essential to quote the passage from the *Eumenides* where Athena exhorts the Erinyes to protect Athens from civil war: "[Do not] engraft [*hidruseis*] among my citizens that spirit of War [Ares] that turns their battle fury inward on themselves."[47] Ares often embodies the bloody law of *stasis* during the classical period. *Hidrumai* means either to sit or to found — this is, in fact, also expressed in the Roman *seditio*[48] — and often it means to erect (as a statue or an altar).[49] The image of swift Ares erected as a statue among the citizens thus suggests perfectly how *stasis* functions as a fixed explosive.[50]

Two corollary remarks can help develop this hypothesis. The first one deals with the Greek way of expressing simultaneously the fixity of what is one and the explosion of what is two: whether the two parties are designated as "rich" and "poor" (or as "a great number" or "a small number," and so on) — however differently they may be described — every formulation of *stasis* tends to equalize them on principle, to the point of making them interchangeable both in what they are and in what they say. This is what I call the Greek tendency toward symmetry; that this phenomenon often escapes the notice of modern historians because we have been, in one way or another, formed by Marxist thought and always seek a dissymmetry between conflicting camps is another story entirely and would take us well out of our way.[51]

However that may be, it is often the case that a single description is meant to suffice for both camps, to the point of making the adversaries into abstractions, as in Thucydides's analysis of the insurgents' language.[52] Both parties use the same language and the same words, as if there were only one language possible in the midst of division. And to indicate the reciprocity of violent exchange, Greek writing — whether poetic, historical, or philosophical — uses words that, in order to establish two antagonistic poles, can simply be repeated: whereas we would say "these . . . , the others . . . ," Greek repeats *heteroi, heteroi*. (Similarly, Alcaeus repeats the same word to locate adverse winds coming from opposite cardinal points — *enthen . . . , enthen. . . .*) Also remember that among its other uses, *stasis* can mean faction; thus, according to the same model, it can be used to describe each side of two opposed parties. We may speak of antagonistic factions, but the same process is actually at work in both camps, only intensified or, perhaps, simply divided.

Moreover — and this is my second remark — we need to invent a language that is not Roman in order to speak of *stasis*.[53] We need a language that can avoid referring to the notion of civil war, which I have used and will continue to use for lack of a better term. *Civilis* — as Benveniste observes — first means what "takes place among *cives*," between citizens, that is fellow citizens, within the infinite multiplicity of exchanges that constitute the totality of the *civitas*.[54] In *bellum civile*, the "vast mutuality" of the Roman city is thought within the substance of war. *Stasis* is something completely different — movement at rest, a front that does not yield and introduces into the city the paradoxical unity that characterizes the simultaneous insurrection of two halves of a whole. If we add that substantives in *–sis* are verbal nouns that express action without referring to any agent, *stasis* becomes a self-sufficient process, almost a principle.[55] To say that *stasis* exists is to locate conflict in the middle of the city in the configuration that is proper to it when, by being raised up in the very same movement, two parts become one.

Hence we find this phrase recurring in historiographical prose: "In such and such a city, a *stasis* was taking place." If we wanted to reconstruct the processes involved, we might imagine that there was insurrection first from one side (*stasis*) and then, as a consequence, from the other (*stasis*). The conflict is then generalized — *stasis*. But we can also take the shortcut suggested by the phrase and understand that it is an insurrection of the city. Because with *stasis*, the city as a whole is at stake.

Kukeōn, *Movement and Division*

As an illustration, here is a philosophical anecdote, or, rather, a fragment of Heraclitus and Plutarch's commentary on it. First the fragment: "Even the *kukeōn* separates [*diistatai*], if it is not stirred [*mē kinoumenos*]."[56] The drink of the Eleusinian mysteries, the *kukeōn* derives its name from the verb *kukaō*, to stir up. To be more specific, the word means mixture, and Heraclitus is apparently thinking etymologically when he reflects on the strange law that requires the mixture to be stirred up in order to avoid division (*diistatai*, from which the noun *diastasis* is derived). The statement is very Heraclitean, at once clear and obscure, but so far nothing too disturbing for us.

In Plutarch's story, however, Heraclitus offers no verbal commentary; rather, he gestures in silence and makes signs. Asked by his fellow citizens for his opinion on civic harmony (*homonoia*, the very thing that Greek political tradition opposes to *stasis*), Heraclitus, it is said, remained silent even though the episode occurred during an assembly. Instead of answering, he took a cup and mixed water and barley flour, adding some mint to make a mixture that follows the recipe for the *kukeōn*; then he drank it and went away, still without speaking.[57] In the modest potion Plutarch sees a lesson in political wisdom: by swallowing the mixture, Heraclitus taught his fellow citizens the art of being content with what one has. I want to stress the preparation of the *kukeōn* and the moment when Heraclitus silently stirs it up before the eyes of the stunned Ephesians, translating into gestures for his fellow citizens what he put into words in his writing.

Even the *kukeōn*, however, breaks down if it is not stirred up: the barley flour and the water separate, and there is *diastasis*. It is therefore necessary to shake the potion to make it into a mixture. Before hastily concluding that this is indeed *homonoia*, we should note that for Heraclitus, the safety of the city implies movement.[58] From this follow several interpretations that ought to be engaged simultaneously but that an insufficiently Heraclitean understanding will enumerate discursively:

1. The noun *kukeōn* signifies agitation, and, in fact, it is necessary to shake the emulsion to mix its different elements. Without the shaking, elements will separate irremediably, like oil and vinegar poured in the same bowl, and this division provides Clytemnestra with the perfect metaphor for the unbridgeable gulf between conquered and conqueror.[59] Like the potion, the city is a mixture as long as citizens of all kinds mix with one another. Only the stirring ensures the success of the process: harmony is not static.

2. In Heraclitus's idiom, the real name of this movement is *eris*, and perhaps *polemos*, but we can give the more widely used Greek name *stasis* to movement that is understood as conflict. Think of the uses of the verb *kineō*: though it is synonymous with *kukaō*, *kinēsis* is commonly associated with civil war. And not even *kukaō* is immune to a political reading. To confirm this, we can look at the fate of this verb in Attic comedy: in Aristophanes, for example, *kukaō* regularly refers to the disturbance created by the demagogues sowing division in the city, and it also refers at least once to Polemos's schemes.[60] We can also note — moving back toward Heraclitus — some Platonic examples of the verb: in the *Phaedo*, it is used to denounce the kind of cleverness that enables those who investigate nature (the *phusikoi*) "to muddle everything up"; in the *Cratylus*, the word characterizes the confusion of Heraclitus's followers, who are carried away by the very whirlpool they created.[61] Thus the surprising image of Heraclitus the agitator emerges. Let us close this parenthesis and return to Heraclitus's words and gestures.

3. Heraclitus is not an agitator but a thinker of movement. What exactly does fragment 125 say if we translate *diistatai* and *kinoumenos* into political language? "Even the *kukeōn* separates if it is not stirred." Translation: "There is *diastasis* if there is no *kinēsis*" (and hence, I might add, *stasis*). In other words, if there is no agitation, there is division. We have arrived at a splendid contradiction in terms, which, when it comes to Heracliteanism, is not necessarily a bad sign.

4. If we give *dia-* its full value, then *diistatai* might signify the immobile partition of a bad division that separates instead of confronting with *eris*, an equilibrium with no way out between the two elements of the city, just like water and flour if one does not mix them. Whence the necessity of the movement that some, in a very political mode, call *stasis*, whereas Heraclitus retains the

name that belongs to it. What paradoxically unites (or, rather, mixes) could very well be a certain tendency to conflict.

No one has described the conflict that connects better than Homer. Once more, we will go back to the *Iliad*, if only as a way of returning finally to Heraclitus.

Conflict Suspended

Here is the description of a struggle on the Trojan plain:

> Ares drove these on, and the Achaians grey-eyed Athene,
> and Terror drove them, and Fear, and Discord [Eris] whose
> wrath is relentless,
> she the sister and companion of murderous Ares,
> she who is only a little thing at the first, but thereafter
> grows until she strides on the earth with her head striking
> heaven.
> She then hurled down the quarrel equally between both sides
> [*neikos homoiion embale messōi*]
> as she walked through the onslaught making men's pain
> heavier.
> Now as these advancing came to one place and encountered,
> they dashed their shields together and their spears, and the
> strength
> of armoured men in bronze, and the shields massive in the
> middle
> clashed against each other, and the sound grew huge of the
> fighting.
> There the screaming and the shouts of triumph rose up
> together
> of men killing and men killed, and the ground ran blood.
> As when rivers in winter spate running down from the
> mountains

throw together at the meeting of streams the weight of their
water . . .[62]

This equal confrontation where Eris runs the show is a paradigmatic struggle. Once more, she throws something in the middle
of the *meson*; it is not the apple of discord, but, however subtle
it may be, an allusion to the apple of discord can be found in it —
the fateful golden apple thrown into the middle of the wedding
of Thetis and Peleus that caused the Trojan War. What Discord
throws between the warriors in the *meson* is *neikos homoiion*: equal
conflict, or "conflict that spares no one" — in fact, whoever has
killed will be killed — or perhaps "indecisive conflict," which the
text immobilizes at the instant of equilibrium, as if to delay the
moment when one side will beat the other.[63] For now the confrontation is expressed in the mode of *sun*. They meet (*xuniontes*)
and they clash (*sun. . . ebalon*) their shields together, as two rivers
flow together (*sumballeton*) to become one (*misgagkeian, mis-
gomenon*). This amounts to saying that they experience what Hector claims and Achilles knows: that Ares is *xunos*, common to all,
a traditional saying in Greek poetry, from Archilochus to Sophocles, that Heraclitus appropriates by substituting *polemos* for Ares,
that is, by substituting the war itself for the god who sets it in
motion.[64]

To say that Ares is common to all is to ascribe the power to
equalize the lots and fates of all mortals to a god for whom
Homer has no adjective that is dark enough. Just as the rotation
of duties in the classical city, determined by drawing lots, endlessly transforms leader into servant and simple citizen into magistrate, war is a generalized exchange, except that in this case the
exchange concerns not the distribution of *arkhē*, political power,
but the reversibility of killing and being killed. The divine organizer, whom Aeschylus described as "Ares, money changer of dead

bodies," presides over this equal dividing up, this bloody *isonomia* of combat.[65] This exchange, even if stabilized in its equilibrium, must end in a victory expressed as a decision, with the verb *krinō*, just as in a trial or a debate — for this reason, I call what is at work in combat *the politics of Ares*.[66] By this I mean a politics whose organizer is either deaf or blind and makes decisions randomly, unleashing himself on the two parties equally, and then suddenly giving the advantage to one of them. As Aeschylus observes with respect to Homer: "Ares determines the act with his dice."[67] But men never resent Ares's decisions as they would the decisions of a democratic tyrant, because they know that the god who apportions also dissolves quarrels (he is *lutēr neikeon*).

In short, as strange as the image of Ares the reconciler might be, warriors consider this mediating role his most specific function. As the one who divides up and shares out, Ares assigns each man his *klēros* (his lot). *Klēros* is the undecidable lot that jumps out of the shaken helmet, assigning each fighter a place, a plot of ground — the very thing that tyrants and democrats eagerly redistribute and that Ares generously grants to the fallen hero, whose prone body at last takes possession of the ground — and also the lot of death that is equal for winners and losers. If this dividing up becomes the tearing or even cutting apart of the warrior's eviscerated body, then the egalitarian law of Ares is all the more clearly verified.[68]

In this system, enemy armies find a paradoxical community in *neikos homoiion*. The bond of conflict thus reappears. It is the bond of violent struggle and of war waged on equal terms by everyone, which Zeus and Poseidon, whose opposed plans have convergent effects, stretch alternately for each man in turn in book 13, a bond that cannot be broken or untied but can unbind the lives of the combatants.[69] A bond? Perhaps we would do well to translate it as "knot." Yet the representation of the bond of war in the *Iliad* is complex. If the bond always ultimately encircles its victim, we should, if we are to do justice to the word *peirar*, think of what both ties and stretches itself in a single action: the knot of death, successively fitted around the Achaeans and the Trojans, and the battlefront, stretched like the hide of a great ox — as when people stretch out an ox hide, tugging from both sides, and dividing themselves (*diastantes*) in the process.[70]

One simile is particularly revealing: the battlefront pulled tight like a string. To describe the equilibrium of a war that is too evenly matched, where the most violent charges in either direction cancel and reinforce each other, the string is given the name *stathmē*, just as *stathmos* is used to describe the scale, the other image of *neikos homoiion*.[71] We find ourselves, inescapably it seems, led back to words of the *stasis* family and the representation of motionless conflicts. The string, the scale: symbols of justice, tools for regulating life in a community.[72]

For those burning with the desire to kill each other, the paradoxical feeling of having something in common arises precisely from this stabilized conflict. Here is another relentless fight (for it is clear that the most immobile fights are also the most violent):

> ... now Achaians and Trojans
> cut each other down at close quarters [*autoskhedon*], nor any
> longer
> had patience for the volleys exchanged from bows and
> javelins
> but stood up close against each other, matching their fury,
> and fought their battle with sharp hatchets and axes, with
> great
> swords and with leaf-headed pikes, and many magnificent
> swords were scattered along the ground, black-thonged,
> heavy-hilted,

114

sometimes dropping from the hands, some glancing from
    shoulders
of men as they fought so the ground ran black with blood.[73]

Hena thumon ekhontes: Trojans and Achaeans, all of the same heart.
As if the stakes of the battle were forgotten, erased, in the over-
powering experience of slaughter at close quarters, by both those
who want to set fire to the ships and those who defend them. It
is made very clear that the fighters are not separated from each
other (*amphis*).[74] But in being "all of the same heart," there is yet
more: usually, fighting with such unison reinforces the cohesion
of one camp against the other, and the *Iliad* often attributes to
the Achaeans this single will that, according to Agamemnon, leads
to victory. Similarly, before the battle at Mounychia, which confronts and divides the two armies of citizens for the first time in
403 B.C., Thrasybulus, leader of the democrats, will evoke this
fighting done "with one heart" (*homothumadon*), this unanimous
surge that cements the insurrection of the Athenian *dēmos* against
the oligarchs and gives the advantage to the former.[75] Symmet-
rically, when members of a community divide themselves for
battle, like the Olympian gods in the *Iliad*, they are said to have
"opposed hearts" (*dikha thumon ekhontes*).[76] Yet however remarkable this anomaly is, we cannot escape the fact that in the battle in
book 15, it is the two enemy armies whose hearts beat with the
same rhythm — as if the combat itself were more valuable than its
objectives, which are opposed to each other as the reverse is to
the obverse.

It is also true that hand-to-hand combat at close quarters is described in terms of proximity, *autoskedon*; and at the highest point
of the fighting — in the decisive struggle of book 15 — proximity
seems to get the better of confrontation, such that between these
warriors trying to kill each other, the law of Love (Philotēs) reigns,

this Love that Empedocles defines as the power "to hold elements close together body to body."[77] But when speaking of close fighting in Homer, we must at some point take this word in its precise sense: it is indeed a question of *mixing*, and this is echoed several centuries later in an inscription in Samos describing military encounters as so many forms of *sumplokē*.[78] In other words, if wrestlers grappling in athletic games can be compared to the moment "when rafters lock, when a renowned architect has fitted them in the roof of a high house," Homer also adds that when men are facing each other, the fighting is "fitted" like a joint (*artunthē makhē*).[79]

The Harmony of Ares

"Joining": the word has been used here and there. Yet to formulate this notion explicitly, Homer relies on a word derived from the root **ar-*, the Indo-European expression of order that conveys "the close fitting of the parts of a whole."[80] *Arariskō* is the act of fitting, and *harmonia* is joining in its most concrete forms: the pegs in a frame, the articulation of the bones in the body. It is necessary to restore to the word *harmonia* the close fitting of two halves, two dissimilar halves, like the two parts of a dovetail in carpentry. Philosophers, who like to multiply parts, will name this whole a compound, but Aristotle specifies that its elements are *enantioi*, opposed to each other.[81]

Clearly, the sphere of war is not where *harmonia* finds its most obvious civic acceptance. The verb *harmottō*, which is closely related, describes the contractual dimension of marriage, as well as the correct fitting or application of justice to each citizen, which is the work of the legislator.[82] Often closely associated with *philotēs* — the love that seals the community, just as in Empedocles it cements the world's cohesion — *harmonia* is the pact that presides over the reconciliation of parties. I have mentioned Empedocles, for whom Harmonia is simply another name for Aphrodite.[83]

However great the distance might be between the well-fitted sphere of the *kosmos* and the political world, Empedocles's *harmonia*, with its functional opposition to bloody Discord, is perhaps the figure most apt to suggest what the cities are ready to take from the archaic logic of joining (let us say, *philotēs*) and what they have always already repressed (*neikos homoiion* in all its forms).

The peaceful *harmonia* of Empedocles is so tightly joined together — *harmonia* being at once the principle and the actualization of this joining — that night rules the place where this joining occurs. Differences are assimilated, outlines are blurred, and *harmonia* cements a world from which conflict has disappeared. But if what *harmonia* achieves is in fact, to quote Jean Bollack, "the tight joint that eliminates the gap through which we can discern the world" — in other words, "an absolute darkness, blacker than night" — will it then be necessary — in order to vote, to decide, and to think — to seek the undisguised clarity of disagreement?[84]

It is here that I find what the Greeks of the classical period wished to know nothing about: that there is *harmonia* in fighting; that the legislator, like Solon, fits "force with justice"; that fitting means maintaining a tension rather than confounding. And Heraclitus's *harmonia* of discord, a philosophical figure repressed in the political, returns. The dissimilar that "agrees at variance with itself" is like "the attunement turning back on itself [*palintropos harmoniē*] of the bow and the lyre";[85] a tension of movements at once coming apart and coming together, or perhaps that which is beneficial in opposition — as if *sun* were born of *dia* or even of *anti*;[86] those synapses, *sunapsies*, contacts, or encounters that we "let belong to each other mutually" where the *sun* is the enigma, as Martin Heidegger notes.[87] Unlike unavoidable separation — let us remember the *diistatai* in the formulation of the *kukeōn* — the *sun* of Heraclitus arises, enigmatically, out of this mode of "approach that combat requires."[88] Here we see *dikē* regulated by *eris*

117

— justice as discord — and *polemos* exalted as what is the most truly common to all, which explains the greatness inherent in being killed by Ares. In short, victory of the unseen *harmonia* over the visible one: to announce this law, language is once again very "political," and doubtless we might learn a great deal from Heraclitus's desire always to give the upper hand to the negative term (in this case *aphanēs*) in any opposition.[89] If we return again to the *kukeōn*, we can better assess the boldness of insisting on the moment of the stirring up in the Eleusinian peace and concord.

Between Empedocles and Heraclitus, *harmonia* is both concordant and discordant. It might also be that when it is explicitly a question of the political, "harmony" as a model of civic joining is what is at stake in the confrontation between agreement and discord in Greek reflection on the *polis*, in which the boldness of thinking what is dissimilar in the city coexists with the hurried effort to cover over clashing elements with the discourse of the same — for example, with autochthony. We shall not set out into this territory now, however, because by opening up the rich file of classical discourses on citizenship, we might well find *stasis* again, but only at the risk of losing sight of the root **ar-* as the privileged tool of archaic thought on the political.[90]

Before leaving this topic, I would like to consider two more examples as evidence of the ambivalence of civic order. The first is the adjective *artios*, which for Solon means a perfect fit, the only way of protecting the city against *stasis*; also, the reconcilers who resolve discord in archaic cities are occasionally called *katartistēres*.[91] In mathematics, however, *artion* designates even numbers, insofar as they are equal or well fitted; in Greek speculation on numbers, evenness is called *diastasis*, equal division, on the model of the two, as if a good fitting virtually included in itself tearing, fighting, and opposition. Uneven numbers are thus exalted, because they cannot be divided up completely but always leave something in common (*koinon*).[92] We can clearly see in the word *artios* interference, manifest once more, between civic peace and *diastasis*.

My second example is called Harmony. To crown this development, what better tale than the myth of the wedding of Harmonia? Harmony is the divine power who in the beginning marries Cadmus, the founder of Thebes. Cadmus is a Phoenician who, at the end of his long wanderings, sees autochthons being born and killing each other on the site of the future Thebes. He founds a city based on the autochthony of the Sown men (Spartoi) and on the foreign principle that he himself represents: he is integrated into the city by this wedding, a ceremony that the gods honor with their presence, just as they went to the marriage of Thetis and Peleus, to the great misfortune of humanity. In the national Theban myth, as in the Greek poetic tradition, Cadmus institutes civic order in Thebes.[93] It is still a question of keeping together the two genealogical lines of the bride, who, as the power of marriage, is not an ordinary spouse: Harmony the Gatherer is the daughter of Aphrodite, as the poets like to recall, and of Ares, a fact they rarely mention. She thus brings to Cadmus's city *sun* and *dia* inextricably mixed, symbolized by her necklace, which is both a magnificent bond and an evil gift.

It is time to take leave of the root *ar- and to pass on to other matters. Yet the temptation is irresistible to reveal another word derived from the same family, even if it is only an etymological hypothesis. An etymology, then: the scientifically minded would disapprove of the practice, but under the sign of Heraclitus, we have every reason to embolden ourselves. In fact — perhaps it is easy to guess — I'm referring to the name Ares itself, about which philologists disagree but that some think belongs to the list of words in *ar-. Ares, then: one might well call him the Joiner. He acts as such in war, even if the classical city does not want to

119

remember it — the city that prefers good victories based on merit to the arbitrary dice throw of *kratos* (and that places Ares on the side of *stasis*, understood as the negation of all civic merit). There is, however, also an Ares of city life with whom citizens must make their peace, perhaps without being aware of it: he presides over the armed peace of the trial on the Areopagus. He guarantees oaths and punishes oath breakers. In short, he watches over the city as a well-fitted whole.[94] Ares the killer — a guardian of the social bond? At bottom, this itinerary may have had no other goal than to justify this etymology in the form of an oxymoron.

Greek Questions
In attempting to disentangle civic certainties to recover a discourse that has been repressed — whether originally or little by little — one risks yielding to the drive to construct. It is best to admit that the temptation is inescapable and to add a few more elements to the scaffolding, if only to show that the construction is already a Greek one.

In the beginning, at the inauguration of history and the human condition, there is conflict: the quarrel of Prometheus and Zeus, and the *eris* of Achilles and Agamemnon at Troy, that quarrel whose dimensions are those of humanity itself. When he learns of Patroclus's death, Achilles curses *eris*, which, according to Aristotle, earned him Heraclitus's disapproval, this time perhaps ill inspired.[95] In fact, no text more than the *Iliad* has so identified its subject with conflict, beginning with the first lines, where the Muse is called on to begin her song with the tale of the founding moment, when "first there stood in division of conflict [*diastētlēn erisante*] Atreus' son the lord of men and brilliant Achilles."[96] Once Achilles is in his tent, the story can begin.

We might place Platonic thought at the end of the story of *eris*, seen as a motivating principle, by taking literally what this thought presents as its most obvious content. Having neither the time nor the inclination to instigate such an inquiry, I will just list a few clues in no particular order: the use of *dialusis*, which in Plato never means reconciliation but always designates separation or break;[97] the Platonic pathology of the city that sees in every conflict a form of degradation (in every *diaphora* a *diaphthora*), whereas Alcmaeon of Croton more boldly defines health as *isonomia*, a balance between opposite forces.[98] Then there is much to be said about Plato's anti-Heracliteanism and his refusal to define *harmonia* as a joining full of tension because he thinks that harmony presupposes agreement and thus supersedes opposites as such.[99]

But let me stop here. And not only because Platonic *mētis* is capable of every kind of reversal, whether it is a matter of using the vocabulary of "contact" to evoke *stasis*, as in Heraclitus, or, more seriously, of taking issue with the entire tradition of classical thought by proclaiming that the best fighter is the one who wins renown in civil war.[100] We need only reread book 1 of the *Laws*, in which *stasis* is defined as "the greatest war" (the war that is truly war?). We may also remember, for the sake of comparison, the restored Athenian democracy's hesitations about the status of those who had fought on its behalf and assess how much Plato owes to this archaic view of conflict that he would like to push back to the pre-Socratic past.

Eris as a bond. Is this the first historical state (in other words, the archaic form) of Greek reflection on the political? Or is it a myth of origins, the first fiction of Greek politics, forged in a world where consensus had already won the day? My goal was not to decide between the two — lest I incur the reproach of not having done this — for it is not certain that the Greeks, supposing they would have posed the question in the form of an alternative, would have wanted to offer a univocal answer. At any rate, I shall hold on to one statement, and only one: *in the beginning* (preserving the full ambiguity of the word), *the Greeks instituted conflict* — neither good nor bad, like the human condition, whose form is reflected in the world of cities. At the same time, my purpose was to illuminate indirectly what we call the city, in light of what constitutes it and what it refuses. That, at any rate, is the hypothesis.

Indirect lighting has its advantages: to remind us that Ares is *xunos* (common) and that communities give themselves the title *to xunon* (the Common); to oppose *diastasis*, which irremediably cuts the city in two, to *stasis*, the indivisible insurrection, which is one by virtue of being a totality made out of two; to understand as Solonian the law on taking a side attributed to him, in order better to appreciate the ideological process of 403 B.C., when, after numbering the guilty and denying citizenship rights to those who had fought on its own behalf, the restored democracy institutionally forgets precisely what it had condemned the other half of the city for doing; finally, to hold on firmly to the model of *harmonia* as the joining of the dissimilar in order to question what fostered the autochthonous fantasy of the same at the very heart of Athenian democracy. This history has yet to be done, but it will be done only if we take seriously the thought of conflict. Against the grain, then.

Let us reread Aeschylus one last time on what takes place, or is supposed to take place, in the beginning of the city. The Erinyes are still threatening Orestes with their anger and this bond that "binds the brain [*desmios phrenōn*]" in which they chain their victims.[101] But already the time is near when, vanquished and convinced by Athena, they will be installed at the foot of the Areopagus so that the Athenian city, having placed them where they belong forever, can forget them. From now on, the spirit of *stasis* holds itself back. And we call the Erinyes the Eumenides (the Well-Meaning). Such is the Greek practice of euphemism.

CHAPTER FIVE

Oath, Son of Discord

And Oath [Horkos], who does more damage

than any other

to earthly

men, when anyone, of his knowledge,

swears to a false oath.

— Hesiod, *Theogony*[1]

In the Hesiodic list of the children of Discord (Eris), who is mentioned last among the children of Night, Oath (Horkos) occupies the last place. In both cases, this is a place of honor, and it distinguishes Eris and Horkos in the first and second nocturnal generations, while also secretly uniting them. Still, such a filiation is not exactly self-evident, and before considering civic oaths that swear to forget the past, I will begin by discussing at some length the reasons for and the implications of this filiation. This will slow down the tempo of the inquiry — erudition, even when reduced to a minimum, is slow — but then we will be able to approach the question of amnesty with a sufficient knowledge of what is at issue.

I will concentrate on two points throughout this investigation. First, the close link that Hesiod establishes between the oath and the oath breaker — as if the first had no other purpose than to punish the second and had only been created, in the form of a terrible curse, for those oath breakers who were produced as such by the oath itself. I will come back to this idea, which belongs to a logic different from our own and so seems such a glaring paradox. Yet this issue can be illuminated only by the light of the multiple implications of the genealogy of Horkos.

At first sight it is surprising that in Hesiod's genealogy Eris is the mother of Horkos. One expects oath to be associated with *philia* — or, to use Empedocles's language, with *philotēs*[2] — especially since Horkos seems destined to ensure the continuity of *sun*, in the most widely shared civic practice in which "everywhere they take this oath to agree [*homonoia*],"[3] and thus also to protect the order of the city, embodied in its constitution, from all threats of treachery and *stasis*.[4] Yet we have already seen that in the thought of the civic bond, *sun* has a very ambivalent relationship with *dia*,[5] and we should refrain from deciding too quickly in favor of the strictly positive aspect of *sun*. Is it because an oath always speaks of discord — whether to prevent or to put an end to acts of *stasis* — that its content is perceived as more important than the modalities of its enunciation? It is as if the relationship between oath and *eris*, by its very recurrence, is stronger than all the declarations of hostility toward civil war. It is too early to answer such a question, but before installing oath in the city as the site of the political, it is important to formulate it as the very question the Hesiodic genealogy of Horkos poses.

By placing this question on the horizon of my inquiry, I hope to forestall another prejudicial, so to speak, question, one that anthropologists and champions of the politico-religious will undoubtedly ask: by focusing on the *political* dimension of oath, do we not risk losing the ancient religious dimension constitutive of *horkos* and with respect to which, "ultimately, the pronouncement of a formula can be superfluous"?[6] Indeed, I am more concerned here with the language of the oath than with the matter about which the oath is sworn: I will privilege the utterance — an utterance that "in the historical period" must invoke the gods as witnesses and use an affirmative or promissory formula — to the detriment of its obscure prehistory, when the formulation would be, conversely and by definition, less important than the "'sacred' substance" with which, supposedly, "the man who swears is placed in contact."[7] And because it is here a question of history, not prehistory,[8] it is essential to consider in the study of oath its dimension as a speech act, which is complete only when it includes the imprecation pronounced by every oath taker against himself should he betray his oath. This is where, in everyday political reality, one finds the Hesiodic son of Eris: if it is indeed to the imprecation that the oath taker entrusts the destiny of his solemnly pronounced political message, in this "vocal gesture" by which he forbids himself to go back on his word on pain of death and the extinction of his whole lineage, it is still and always in this complicity between oath and perjury that the essential is played out.[9]

The time has come to focus on this troubling complicity.

Perjury in the Oath

The ambivalence of the oath runs deep, beginning already in Hesiodic poetry, where the oath is both a good and an evil.

A good *and* an evil? Strangely, the positive aspect of *horkos* tends to come second, always to be deduced from the repeated affirmation of perjury's catastrophic character. In the Iron Age, that disastrous era, oaths will eventually no longer have any weight.[10] Thucydides is faithful to this Hesiodic prediction, and he sees the Peloponnesian War as a realization of it in cities given over to *stasis*, where nothing could reconcile (*dialuein*) two hostile camps, "no guarantee could be given that would be trusted, no oath sworn that people would fear to break [*horkos phoberos*]."[11] If, then, the catastrophe of a violated oath bears witness *a contrario* to the eminent value of the sworn word, from Hesiod to Thucydides the focus is on the negativity of perjury. This is only to be expected when it comes to this "misuse of speech" in which Clémence Ramnoux sees "a form of original sin for the Greeks" or this "dissolving of verbal contracts" in which Georges Dumézil sees an error of the "first function," leading the three "Indo-European scourges."[12]

In its essential relation with perjury, however, the oath itself is the bearer of negativity. This becomes clear if we return to Hesiod's presentation of Horkos:

> And Oath [Horkos], who does more damage
> than any other to earthly men, when anyone, of
>   his knowledge,
> swears to a false oath.

A scourge that causes "more damage" (*pēma*) than all the many *pēmata* that afflict men (they are called Pandora, the "race of women," or Helen): such would be Oath when he is born from Eris's solitary childbearing, and this identification is stated authoritatively. Yet uncertainty begins as soon as this point is made: is it a scourge for human beings in general? Or only for oath breakers? Hesiodic diction[13] in fact defines oath as a scourge *in actuality* for humanity[14] before it restricts the object of the verb *pēmainō* to the category of willful oath breakers.[15] Similarly, Styx is described as a *pēma* for the gods when one of them breaks an oath. In both cases, the formulation aims to characterize the entire group as potentially prone to perjury through the one who actually is a perjurer. The formulation of this law is even more striking in its condensed form in *Works and Days*, where Discord is said to have given birth to Oath as "a plague on those who take false oath."[16]

It would be useless to claim to have rediscovered a theory of causes familiar to us — for example, there are oath breakers because there is the oath — because Hesiodic discourse imposes an inverse logic. If the *Theogony* made Horkos into a plague for humanity even before evoking the existence of oath breakers, this time Oath is born *to harm anyone who transgresses him.*[17]

It is as if the finality of the oath is first and foremost self-referential — and in a negative mode, since any good it may do is secondary. Moreover, Hesiod expresses the efficacy of this pledging procedure in his description of Horkos, "who runs beside crooked judgments."[18]

How exactly should we understand the term *epiorkos* in reference to an oath breaker? Philologists debate heatedly the precise meaning of the word. Does *epiorkos* (*epi-horkos*) designate someone who is "subject to *horkos*"?[19] Or — and this is the most widely accepted explanation — does it designate someone who "adds an oath" to lies, because "the fact of adding an oath always assumes, whether explicitly or not, that the person who is swearing will not keep his word"?[20] We could likewise claim under these conditions that just as Clytemnestra is more representative of the race of women than Penelope, humanity as a whole (and with it, the very value of oath) could be judged according to the deeds of Odysseus's grandfather Autolycus, "who surpassed all men in thievery and the art of the oath."[21]

Because it is impossible to come to definitive conclusions in this area, in which the pessimism of modern philologists almost rivals that of Hesiodic poetry,[22] I will only insist that archaic thought is obsessed with perjury, decipherable, as we have seen, in Empedocles when he reserves the same punishment for the murderer and the *epiorkos*. This is all the more remarkable when we consider — as has often been noted — that a legally defined crime of perjury did not exist in ancient Greece.[23] The real punishment, the "silent and sinister pain that silently gnaws at the religious principle of life in the oath breaker,"[24] is a matter "not of the justice of man but of divine sanction."[25] This amounts to saying that the sanction becomes confused with the irresistible effectiveness of the all-powerful imprecation, because the gods invoked at the beginning of the oath are usually mentioned only as witnesses.[26]

Divine vengeance is, of course, slow, and in one plea spoken after the amnesty of 403 B.C., this slowness is quietly assumed. The passage is in Isocrates's *Against Callimachus*. The litigant, claiming that his opponent has disobeyed the amnesty by suing him, praises the *paragraphē*, this "exception [on grounds] of inadmissibility" by which an accused could prevent a trial that violates the oath "not to recall the past." Isocrates says that this procedure had recently been introduced by the "moderate" Archinus and that the purpose of the penalty was:

> That persons who had the effrontery to rake up old grudges [*hoi tolmōntes mnēsikakein*] should not only be convicted of perjury [*epiorkountes*] but also, not awaiting the vengeance of the gods, should suffer immediate [*parakhrēma*] punishment.[27]

To enforce the oath to forget the past, an Athenian from the end of the fifth century B.C. would prefer the "on the spot" (*parakhrēma*) of civic justice to the "on the spot" (*autika*) that in Hesiod signified the immediate effectiveness of the oath. It is nevertheless the case that divine justice, even when mentioned only for the sake of convention, is always supposed to pursue the oath breaker with its vengeance, which is proof — if proof were still needed — that the time had not yet come for the citizen-jurors of the Athenian court when a purely human penalty could be substituted for divine wrath. In other words, this is proof that in the oath *mē mnēsikakein*, the "incantatory force of the oral ritual" was still and always supposed to exercise its punitive action by itself.

If *horkos* is usually seen as a "bond that ensnares" or, as Empedocles put it, "an oracle of Necessity . . . sealed fast,"[28] it is the oath taker who "seals" himself up in this way, when he traps himself in an imprecation against himself. It is because of this imprecation that if he ever breaks his word, "the oath that he has sworn...haunts him and troubles him, for it was his oath...that made his act a crime."[29] I rely on the strength of such a representation, reaffirmed many times throughout the classical period, to locate the power of oath less in the "sacralizing object" touched by the swearer when uttering the curse—the object with which Emile Benveniste would like to identify the oath in its entirety[30]—than in the enunciation of words that cannot be "unsaid."[31] The tragic function of the Erinyes in Aeschylus provides sufficient proof: they are the ones—they who presented themselves as the bearers in the underworld of the name Imprecations (Arai)[32]—whom Athena must convince not to utter a curse against Athens at the end of Orestes's trial:

> ... Be reasonable
> and do not from a reckless mouth cast on the land
> spells that will ruin every thing which might bear fruit.[33]

This amounts to asking them to disavow their linguistic nature: there is no imprecation whose dreaded effects do not weigh on the fecundity of women, flocks, and the earth. It is in fact a plague, harmful to plants and children, that the Imprecations call down on Athens with words that are "reckless" for the city because their fruit would have been death.[34] In this way, by the very attention it gives to the religious power of speech, Aeschylean tragedy brings to light the secret law of *ara*, which in reality the language of oaths conceals by naming the good before the evil. By virtue of this law, mortal sterility is already at work in the words of the curse[35] with such force that, judging from the *Eumenides* and the *Suppliant Women*, every blessing seems always to come second,[36] as a reversal of an imprecation.[37]

A Speech Act and Its Effects

There is, then, the imprecation with which every oath anticipates
the possibility of its transgression and sets the unfaithful oath
taker against himself in advance. Cities and other political and
social groups make frequent use of oaths to found or to reinforce
the community bond. They are careful not to deny the importance of this speech act, whose power is such that a law from
Thasos on the repression of subversive plots explicitly stipulates,
twice over, that if the informer is a member of the conspiracy —
or, rather, of the conjuration (*sunōmosia*) — he will be free from
the consequences of the imprecation.[38]

It would be outside the scope and aim of this essay to enumerate the various civic functions of *ara*. Sticking to the essential, we
may recall that there are two different versions of *ara*: one very
general, the other more complex. The first speaks only of goods
on one side and evils on the other: thus, at Delphi, in the oath
taken by the phratry of the Labyades ("If I respect [this oath], may
things go well for me, but if I break it, may evils be born out of
evils, instead of goods"); or again, more elliptically, in the oath
that seals the pact between Athens and Corcyra in 375 B.C. ("If I
respect [this oath], may I obtain many goods, if not, the reverse").[39]
We find an example of the second version in the imprecation that
concludes the oath of the Chersonesians at the beginning of the
third century B.C.:

> If I respect [this oath], happiness for me,
> For my descendants, and my family,
> but if I do not respect [it], sorrow on me,
> my descendants, and my family,
> and may neither the earth nor the sea bear
> fruit, and may the women not bear beautiful children.[40]

Sometimes the imprecation alone is uttered: this is the oath at its most condensed, when the civic authority disposes with the bothersome sacramental procedure that requires solemn commitment from every citizen and simply reminds the potential offender of the risk to his offspring. In this way do the magistrates of Teos utter every year their solemn imprecation against troublemakers, enumerating all possible transgressions, case by case, and dooming the offender — as well as his offspring — to annihilation.[41] The oath formula is uttered in the name of the city, that impersonal entity, through the sanctioned voice of "those who hold honor," and against an anonymous offender. The imprecation formula in fact "supplies" the law itself, and some have commented on this "penal form with an imprecatory value," underlining the important role of the curse "in the beginnings of law."[42]

Yet, as we have seen, this ritual speech more generally gives force and existence to an oath: this is the case in the *Iliad* when everyone, Achaean and Trojan, calls for disaster on the family of the oath breaker to support Agamemnon's invocation to the gods, which is at once prayer and oath.[43] Thus it is again that Demophantos's decree in 409 B.C., in the Athenian city freed from the first oligarchic government, first utters the formula for the citizens' oath, and then takes responsibility for the conclusion of the formula, promising wealth to those who keep their word but bringing destruction on oath breakers and their race (*eksōle auton einai kai genos*).[44]

Linguists, philologists, historians, and anthropologists are eager to show to what degree "oath as a whole appears as if pervaded by imprecation." They naturally waver whenever they try to account for this between referring to legal language — they claim that "to swear is to impose a law on oneself" or even "to incriminate oneself in advance and conditionally"[45] — and having recourse to the most ancient forms of religion, when they speak of "ordeal," whether the process is defined linguistically or by its anticipatory nature.[46] Beyond all judgments on the aptness of formulas, the essential remains: it matters little whether the wrath (*mēnis*) of gods called as witnesses is summoned explicitly to punish the guilty, as in the oath of Dreros;[47] the imprecation itself suffices — in its "automatic" consequence — and the oath is only as powerful as its imprecation, though the specificity with which it describes the disaster promised to the oath breaker may also be a factor. The identity of the oath taker, outlined by what he risks, is thus delineated in intaglio, as it were, so true it is that one can lose only what one has or, even better, what one is.[48]

What one has: goods, among which the most valuable is land, where one's "house" is rooted, and herds, which are the most highly valued visible asset; thus one dooms oneself to the destruction of these goods, which are extensions of the self for everyone.[49] As for being, one exists only insofar as one will be alive after death through a son resembling oneself. Because no definition is more firmly entrenched in Greek thought, the oath taker threatens the future of his own name, his house, and his offspring with the imprecation he casts upon himself in the terrible anticipation of perjury. Herodotus recounts through the Pythia's inspired voice the edifying story of the Spartan Glaucus, who thought of — and only thought of — taking a false oath in order to keep money that did not belong to him and whose memory was eradicated from Sparta "down to the roots," with no offspring and no house claiming kinship with him.[50] Hesiod had said the same thing when he proclaimed:

> But when one, knowingly, tells lies and swears an
>   oath on it,
> when he is so wild as to do incurable damage
>   against justice,

this man is left a diminished generation hereafter,
but the generation of the true-sworn man
grows stronger.[51]

True, such consequences are not unique to oaths: Hesiod also tells
of kings' decrees having the same immediate effect — universal
fertility for the good king's decisions, and sterility to punish the
bad king's *hubris*. For all that, I will not attempt to offer a genesis
of oath in which it would replace a secularized, and therefore less
powerful, justice. Yet because an oath's effect in *Works and Days* is
confused with that of legal decisions (*dikai*), which it reduplicates,
I will pause for a moment on the consequences of legal judgments
and note an important detail. If disasters sweep down on the
bad king's city ("famine and plague together, and the people die
and diminish. The women bear children no longer, the houses
dwindle"), one man's crime is enough to make the entire city
perish (*xumpasa polis*).[52]

In this lone man "who commits crimes and plans reckless
action," bringing disaster on his city, we must recognize the bad
king, the one whom tragedy will make into a tyrant. But what
happens with a similar man when he is a simple citizen in a city
endowed with a *politeia*? Because such a man does not hold any of
the magical powers of archaic kings, it may be said that he could
not endanger his city.[53] Yet it is not certain that collectivities
think in this way, and in the oath taken by all the citizens, each
swearing — one after the other, in his own name and in the first-
person singular — to practice *homonoia* (*homonoēsō*), I tend to see
the product of a very similar logic: by directing the imprecation
against himself alone, the potential oath breaker distinguishes
between his own person, which he "consecrates," and the city,
which he thus spares — just as (though in a different register, this
time purely political) when the restored democracy counted the

133

culprits in an attempt to save the city, thought of as a totality from which only the "impious" would be extracted.[54]

Arai *and* Ares

I will end the Hesiodic excursus here and return to the close relation between imprecation and fertility found in all the texts. But I return to it only to broaden and to complicate the analysis, because using a single cipher key is never a good method but especially because the imprecation takes on its full meaning only insofar as it implicates other realms — or, as Dumézil would say, other functions — than fertility alone. This is the case in the Panhellenic oath of the Amphictyons of Delphi in which the imprecation is directed at the culprit's entire people (*ethnos*), as we can see in the transcription of the text by Aeschines:

> "Let them be under the curse," it says, "of Apollo and Artemis and Leto and Athena Pronaea." The curse goes on: "That their land bear no fruit; that their wives bear children not like those who begat them, but monsters; that their flocks yield not their natural increase; that defeat await them in camp and court and market-place, and that they perish utterly, themselves, their houses, their whole race."[55]

This imprecation is directed primarily at fertility in its usual threefold register: land, herds, and women. It also specifies that with regard to women, the punishment will be less that they will not be able to give birth than that they will give birth to monsters (which, as the text indicates, means giving birth to sons who do not resemble their fathers).[56] Yet between the evocations of forbidden fecundity and of the destruction of the *genos*, the *agōn* explicitly comes to the surface, in its triple aspect of war, trial, and political struggle.[57]

In this way, the Amphictyons' oath unites the two parts that in

134

the *Eumenides* Athena distinguished within the real. We recall that the goddess saved for herself the "beautiful" war, and she assigned to the Erinyes prevention of *stasis*, which was instantly covered over by the concern for Athens's prosperity.[58] This is a clever division, because it does two things at once: it separates conflict into two parts — one good and valued, the other forbidden — and then hides this opposition under another opposition between war and fertility, as if this would reestablish the simpler image of the two cities on Achilles's shield. Quite to the contrary of this, the Delphic oath does not engage in a strategy of erasure; rather, by aiming simultaneously at wars, legal procedures, and political life as so many forms of one and the same experience, its crowning imprecation recalls at just the right moment that Oath is the son of Eris.

A study of the sacrifice that accompanies oath also leads in the direction of Eris. I say "accompanies" because if sacrifice precedes the oath chronologically, it is in the classical period as an anticipation of the oath, one that reduplicates in gestures the conflictuality spoken in the imprecation.[59] Thus, because it excludes all consumption and requires the complete destruction of the victims, this ritual rejects both cooking and the distribution of meat constitutive of sacrifice in the city at peace.[60] In this, it strictly parallels the oath, where civic peace is usually mentioned only when it is threatened by rebellion and conflict. In addition, the disappearance of the victim, characteristic of all sacrifices offered to the powers below, is also required in order to foreshadow the annihilation of the oath breaker's entire lineage.[61]

The dismemberment of the sacrificial animal during the solemn sacrifice inaugurating every murder trial on the Areopagus can be interpreted in the same way, as can the practice of *diōmosia*[62] according to which the accuser, who must utter the imprecation calling forth *eksōleia* on both himself and his offspring, takes his oath standing (*stas*) on the *tomia*, the cut-up remains of the victim.[63] This gesture probably belongs to the same dominant theme of the *pathos* of fertility: by linking the word *tomia* with the name given to eunuchs (*tomias*), the imprecation sworn over the testicles of male victims that proclaims the obliteration of the oath taker's lineage reduplicates the actual castration of sacrificial animals.[64]

Without question, fertility is solemnly put at stake in these types of sacrifices; yet the nature of the victims — males, often a boar, who is sacrificed alongside a ram and a bull at the Areopagus[65] — seems more important to me insofar as it expresses the close bond among oath and *eris* and war. Is not Mars honored at Rome, along with Quirinus and Ceres, by a similar sacrifice very concretely identified as *suovetaurilia*? I borrow this analysis from Georges Dumézil, who claims that Mars is the chief beneficiary of the *suovetauriles* because he "alone is qualified to restore severe situations" owing to his warrior's strength. Mars has also been wrongly identified as the god of fertility because, as in this sacrifice, he often nourishes his "warrior strength" with the health and fertility that are the "essence of the third function."[66] One might argue that Mars is not Ares, but this connection is strongly suggested not only by the perfect similarity between these two triple sacrifices but also by the Athenian site of the ritual — the Areopagus, the hill of Ares.[67]

This leads back to some of the divine figures associated with oaths, both in religious thought and in ritual. There are the Erinyes, encountered so often in this study, who in the *Iliad* punish oath breakers in the underworld and in Hesiod keep watch like so many Eilithyiai over the birth of Horkos, "whom Strife bore, to be a plague on those who take false oath."[68] These personified Imprecations, whose role is to dry up fertility and who in Aeschylus will protect it only through a complete reversal of their entire being, are at home on the Areopagus under the name Semnai, in their role of *mnēmones kakōn* ("we hold memory of evil")[69] — thus it is by the Erinyes that the two sides swore their oaths at the beginning of a trial.[70]

It would be easy to go from the Erinyes to Ares, with whom they are often associated in the texts. Beside the favored *histores* (witnesses) who are the official sacramental gods, universally invoked as guarantors — Zeus (the Horkios god), Ge (mother of Themis), and Helios (who sees everything)[71] — Ares effectively has his place in those oaths that risk the community's future by means of war but also, conversely, in the protection against war. This happens, not surprisingly, in the ephebes' oath, both at Dreros and at Athens, in which Ares is placed among Enuo, Enualios, and Athena Areia, after Hestia but before Zeus himself;[72] it also happens in oaths accompanying treaties of alliance.[73] It is especially interesting, moreover, to note his presence in the act of founding of a synoecism, such as the one uniting Orchomenos and Euaimon in the fourth century: at the very moment when *sun* must imperatively ward off the dissolving power of *dia*, the destructive god, transformed into an assembler, is as if multiplied in the oath.[74]

Which finally leads me to situate the oath in the city, since that was the point of this inquiry into Oath, son of Discord.

Oath in the City

Because oath involves the reproduction of the city, and thus its continuity, and because it attempts to exorcise conflict by invoking the gods that regulate it, it is omnipresent in any *polis* whenever the question arises of the community's relationship to its own permanence, which is constantly threatened and constantly proclaimed.[75] Hence Herodotus's description of Cyrus's speech and the scorn he feels for the Spartans' demands:

I have never yet been afraid of any men who have a set place in the middle of their city where they come together to cheat each other and forswear themselves.[76]

In these declarations, the Greek historian targets only the commercial functions of the *agora* as a market; and yet I cannot help hearing in them, counter to Herodotus's opinion, a denunciation in Hesiodic tones of the Greek politics embodied in the public square as the civic space par excellence.

Oath taking, as a solemn speech act, is so essential to life in the city that it is sometimes difficult to distinguish an oath — even an imprecation, like the one of Teos already mentioned — from a law.[77] More generally, the place of oath in decrees and other official civic texts should be stressed. In fact, because only an oath, as an unbreakable religious constraint, can seal the citizens' commitment, no public act forming the subject of a decree does not at least mention swearing an oath, if not the actual text of the oath. It is imperative that any modification to an existing document be mentioned in the decree or treaty of alliance from which the modification results.[78] Thus it is that all citizens are invited to swear on peace treaties between cities.[79] The list of the *horkoi kai sunthēkai* known to us is long, and I will not enumerate it; but I will point out the order that governs this phrase, by virtue of which the oath precedes the official agreements themselves because it founds their reliability.[80]

Yet even this essential role in civic life is not at odds with the Hesiodic genealogy that makes Horkos the son of Eris. Because it brings conflict to an end, the swearing of oaths might be characterized as originating in a state of discord — as in the oaths exchanged by Athenians and Boeotians after a disagreement in Thucydides.[81] Likewise, in Hesiod, the gods are invited to swear an oath only after an important *eris* or *neikos*, when Zeus wants to know which of the Olympians is lying; then, for the purpose of the "great oath" of the gods, Styx is summoned to confound the culprit.[82] The imprecation does not have the immediate efficacy in historical cities that Styx has among the gods, but from its role of assigning the burden of proof in trials of the archaic period, the oath remains associated with the adjective *karteros*, which signifies a disagreement.[83]

The adjective *karteros* in itself evokes the notion of *kratos*. We will recall that Styx gives birth to Kratos in the *Theogony*; and Styx, the first to arrive on Olympus with her powerful son to help Zeus, is set up by him in her function as great oath of the Immortals, because in helping him she has given him a decisive *kratos*.[84] And *kratos* is again linked to civic oaths when, for example, to establish the power of its first maritime league, Athens imposed on its allies its "gods of oath" (*theoi horkioi*) and its customary oath (*nomimos horkos*).[85]

These close ties with Eris are no doubt what make the oath the most effective prevention against discord and war.[86] Gustave Glotz observes that oath actually "[prevents] men from being in a perpetual state of mutual hostility."[87] Oath is both born out of discord and a weapon against it. Or, rather: born out of discord, it is therefore a weapon against conflict. We must remember this tension, essential to the representation of *horkos*, in order to reflect on the place of oath in political struggles.

Thus we have civil war, which, as we know, belongs for the Greeks to the realm of *phonos*, murder. To understand the place of oath in *stasis*, we can learn much from *diōmosia*, the contradictory oath ("divergent swearing")[88] before the Areopagus, or from *antōmosia*, the oath sworn by the two sides before ordinary courts at the beginning of the proceedings. Thus historians and legal anthropologists insist repeatedly on the paradigmatic status of this "legal declaration of war" by which opponents, taking sides, also define the disagreement.[89]

Then there is *stasis*: conspirators, whose factions bear the name *sunōmosiai*, are in fact co-jurors or co-swearers of a new kind, set against the *politeia* and its institutional oath. From this perspective, any dissension can be seen, according to Glotz's formulation, as a "struggle of two oaths" until the time comes when "to reestablish a stable unity, the terms of a common oath will have to be defined anew."[90] The oath is exchanged between yesterday's adversaries,[91] and like the oath sworn by the Athenians in 403 B.C., it proclaims the forgetting of the past.[92]

But the time is not always right for an unconditional reconciliation, and whenever the threat of rebellion seems still to hang over political life, the war of oaths goes on. Thus there is the oath secretly sworn by the Athenian oligarchs against the Athenian people before seizing power for the first time.[93] In response to this oath, once the democracy is restored, there is the new oath of struggle that commits all the citizens ("I will slay by words and by deeds, by vote and by my own hand, whosoever shall suppress the democracy at Athens"). It is interesting in its own right that this oath constitutes the essential part of Demophantos's decree in 409 B.C.; yet the final clause of the oath, which annulled all the seditious oaths previously sworn, including those sworn by the present oath takers, deserves even more attention:

> And all oaths sworn at Athens or in the army or elsewhere for the overthrow of the Athenian democracy [*enantioi tōi demōi tōi Athenaion*] I annul and abolish.[94]

"I dissolve them and am released from them" (*luō kai aphiēmi*): only a speech act that has been given its full scope, that has been unwound all the way to the end,[95] can undo the performative power of another, just as Achilles unsaid his wrath and the Eumenides' blessings unsay the Erinyes' imprecations.

Have we come to the end of this trajectory? Not quite. If it is true that an oath, as a positive speech act, precisely delimits each swearer's identity, status, and position in the city,[96] it remains to consider this "I" through which, even in a collective oath, each one personally commits himself.

"I Shall Not Recall the Misfortunes"

One swears in the first-person singular in almost every case, whether it is an oath of civic reconciliation or a treaty of alliance and whether those taking the oath are simple citizens, magistrates or judges, or members of an organization like the *boulē*.[97] Even when a decree specifies that all (*hapantes*) must commit to the oath,[98] it is as an "I" that the collectivity expresses itself, combining, as it were, the sum total of its members' individual commitments. Let us not claim that this is simply "normal." For the historian, normality or banality does not exist. But, more important, there are a few, rare examples of oaths sworn in the first-person plural[99] or alternating between singular and plural,[100] which highlight, by contrast, the prevalence of the "I."

I have mentioned the Hesiodic city that can be ruined by a single man, and I linked this use of the "I" to the always-threatening possibility of perjury. This could explain, for example, the law prescribing that after his victory, the winner in a murder trial held at the Palladium must swear a new oath with *eksōleia*, to confirm that he has spoken the truth and to protect the judges who voted in his favor in case they were misled by a lie ("and he calls down destruction upon himself and his household, if this be not true, and prays for many blessings for the jurors").[101] With this oath, the winner frees the civic court in advance from any responsibility, such that the court is assumed by definition to be making a decision "according to justice and truth."[102] Yet the analysis calls for further specification.

Let us consider again Demophantos's decree. After prescribing that the Athenian citizens regard as "a public enemy [*polemios*]" and "slay with impunity" anyone who overthrows the democracy or collaborates with a seditious regime, this decree of battle orders that a civic oath be sworn:

> And all [*hapantas*] the Athenians shall take oath by tribes and by demes over a sacrifice without blemish to slay such a one. And this shall be the oath [*ho de horkos estō hode*]: "If it be in my power, I will slay by word and by deed."[103]

I will not linger over the clear link between the sacrificial material ("a sacrifice without blemish") and the solemnity of the speech act or over the imperative form *estō* with which the democracy, prescribing the ritual formula, recalls that it has complete power over the performative force of the oath. I am more interested in the complementarity between the civic realm and the individual gesture: the essential point remains that the formula is one and the same for all.[104] Every Athenian is simultaneously citizen and *idiōtēs* (private individual), at once framed within institutional structures — the Cleisthenian tribes and demes into which the whole civic body (*hapantas*) is customarily divided — and invited to swear in his own name (in fact, one might add mentally the formula *kath' hena* [one by one] to the distributive formula *kata phulas kai kata dēmous*). The same analysis could be applied to the oaths sworn by the Athenian civic body in 403 and 401 B.C. In this case, however, it is the form itself of the oath that deserves attention, because to the future tense — standard in all oaths from the historical period[105] — is added a negative statement: "I shall not recall the misfortunes." I have already mentioned that such a statement, to which Thucydides alludes in his description of previous reconciliations between citizens, is not unique to Athens,[106] and after the end of the fifth century B.C., it will be found in this form in many other oaths of civic reconciliation and peace treaties.[107]

We can put into the latter category the oath sworn by the Athenians in 362 B.C., when Athens was regularizing its relations with the city of Ioulis. This oath merits citation because its negative statement is so clearly the reversal of a declaration of hostility:

> I shall not recall the misfortunes that took place in the past,[108] against any of the citizens of Keos, neither shall I put to death any of the citizens of Keos, nor shall I exile any of those who have respected the oaths and agreements.[109]

"I shall put no one to death": thus the Athenian city renounces the *kratos* it exercised over the allied city and commits itself officially through the voice of its magistrates. Yet there is even more in this negative commitment: the negation of the most dreaded utterance, the *ktenō* (I shall put to death) that is reserved for the enemy and that the Athenians had pronounced in 409 B.C. against all citizens who would become enemies of the city.

Containing the hostility it annuls in being spoken, the oath can and must renounce memory, because memory of the misfortunes is memory of hate. Thus it reverses the implicit "I shall never forget" that is the formula of vengeance under the regime of *eris*. Yet such a reversal does not simply substitute one negation for another. In other words, the city forbids each citizen to withdraw into himself out of resentment and also forbids an active recollection of the facts that is directed against others. In amnesty, memory *in actuality* is barred by the efficacy of a speech act born from Eris so that the city may live as one.

143

CHAPTER SIX

Of Amnesty and Its Opposite

The time has come to speak of amnesty. And yet it is clear already that, influenced by the suggestions of a sonorous contiguity, hearing and thinking have succumbed to the irresistible association of this process with amnesia, which leads one directly from an expurgated memory to forgetting. The sequence — amnesty, amnesia — imposes itself with great force: a seductive etymology, an obvious assonance, and a necessity, it seems, when we mistrust both forgetting and amnesty on principle. It could happen, however, that forgetting comes too quickly or is excessive, especially if by this word we mean to designate the shadow cast on memory by the political. Can we truly see something like a strategy of forgetting in amnesty, the institutional obliteration of those chapters of civic history that the city fears time itself is powerless to transform into past events? It would be necessary to be able to forget on command. But in itself such an utterance has little meaning.

There are other difficulties, too. If forgetting is not an irremediable absence,[1] but, as in the Freudian hypothesis, a presence absent only from itself, a darkened surface sheltering what has only been repressed, then the aim of amnesty would be paradoxical indeed. Moreover, to take the language of amnesty literally: What does an amnesty want, what is its proclaimed intention? An erasure that allows no return and leaves no trace? The crudely healed scar of an amputation or an extraction,[2] hence forever memorable, provided that its object be irremediably lost? Or the preparation of a time for mourning and the (re)construction of History?

I will refrain from coming to any conclusions now concerning the problem in general; but at the same time, I can take advantage of the distance between all historians of Antiquity and their object. What about amnesty as it was considered in ancient times, when what we call by that name did not have a name (although the word *amnēstia* was available to this end), but took the syntactic form of two highly restrictive utterances?[3] Thus we will not leave the Athenian amnesty of 403 B.C., whose double utterance adjoins a prescription (*ban on recalling the misfortunes*) to an oath (*I shall not recall the misfortunes*).

Ban on recalling/I shall not recall. The question of memory in Athens takes the form of a prescription and an oath. A rejected memory, but still a memory. Will we lose sight of forgetting, formerly installed in the city?[4] Just long enough, perhaps, to put into perspective what we mean by this word the better to construct the Greek notion: more threatening, more archaic, and apparently originary in that it hides in the shelter of its opposite, this notion will appear only under negation (but in a very different manner from memory in Athens). This points in the direction of a slow decoding at the heart of certain banned utterances that are dissimulated, in a very Greek manner, beneath the reference to memory.

A ban, what is banned. Clearly, the dissonance between the two registers is essential and should not be diminished too quickly.

Two Bans on Memory in Athens

To situate the argument, I will begin with two dated examples of bans on recalling in Athens of the fifth century B.C., one at the very beginning of the century, the other at the very end.

Herodotus is the historian of the first ban. Recounting the Ionian revolt in 494 B.C. and how the Persians subdued the rebels by capturing Miletus, which they then emptied of people and whose sanctuaries they burned, Herodotus lingers on the reactions of two peoples in the Ionian family to this event. Formerly deprived of their fatherland — over which event the Milesians had mourned considerably, as befits parents or guests — the inhabitants of Sybaris did not repay the Milesians in kind. The Athenians, however, expressed extreme, not to say excessive, grief. More specifically, it happened that:

> [W]hen this poet brought upon the stage his drama of the Capture of Miletus, the whole theatre burst into tears; and the people sentenced him to pay a fine of a thousand drachmas, for recalling to them their own misfortunes [hōs anamnēsanta oikeia kaka]. They likewise made a law, that no one [mēketi mēdena] should ever again exhibit that piece.[5]

With this official decree of the assembly of the people, the Athenians no doubt thought they were only forbidding any future performance of the Capture of Miletus, casting Phrynichus's tragedy into oblivion. But I would ascribe an entirely different significance to this decision, eminently paradigmatic of the status of civic memory and the definition of the tragic in Athens. Heavily fined and banned from the stage for having introduced into Athenian theater an action (drama) that for the Athenians is nothing but suffering (pathos),[6] and a family matter — the Ionian family, this family that is also the city, that is, in a word, the civic identity, this collective self that defines itself by the sphere of what is one's own (*oikeion*) — by making them recall "their own misfortunes," the first great tragedian awakens his fellow citizens — for the first time, in my view — to the dangers of recollection when the object of memory is a source of mourning for the civic self.[7]

A long history begins here, that of the Athenian practice of memory and that of tragedy, which we imagine forever marked by this initial check. The Athenian people make it known that they will not tolerate the staging of anything that affects them painfully. The tragedians learn the lesson and find ways of avoiding too-current events, unless those events are a source of mourning for others, a mourning that can always be converted into a hymn to the glory of Athens, as in the *Persians*.[8] One consequence for the tragic genre of this forced untimeliness was the turn to fiction — in other words, to *muthos*.[9] At any rate, it is important to notice that whenever a tragic plot takes place in Athens, the tragedy is characteristically given a "positive" ending, as in Euripides's Athenian plays. Consequently, "real" tragedies, in which *drama* is at the same time *pathos*, take place outside the city, and in the fourth century B.C. Isocrates formulates the law requiring Athens to represent in its own theater crimes originally attached to "other cities."[10]

Thus, at the beginning of the fifth century, Athens commits itself to a well-monitored practice of civic memory.

The second ban, at the end of the century, aims to bar any recall of the "misfortunes" that have befallen the very self of the city, torn apart from within by civil war. After the bloody oligarchy of the Thirty, the ban on "recalling the misfortunes" seals the democratic reconciliation in 403 B.C. Constituting this episode as a paradigm, we call it an amnesty and consider it the first one. Yet Plutarch already used this term when, conscious of a deep affinity, he associated the "decree of amnesty" (*to psēphisma to tēs amnestias*) with the fine imposed on Phrynichus.[11]

The year 403 B.C.: hunted down only the day before, returned now to Athens as victors, the democrats proclaim a general reconciliation with a decree and an oath. The decree proclaims the ban: *mē mnēsikakein*, it is forbidden to recall the misfortunes. The oath binds all Athenians — democrats, important oligarchs, and "quiet" people who stayed in the city during the dictatorship — but it binds them one by one: *ou mnēsikakēsō*. I shall not recall the misfortunes.[12]

"Recall the misfortunes," this phrase — which the compound verb *mnēsikakein* expresses formulaically in Athens and other cities — what does it mean? Once we accept that by *kaka*, the misfortunes, the Greeks mean what we would more readily, if euphemistically, call the "events" (the disorder in the city), we should pay attention to *mnēsi-*, a form developed from the Greek root for "memory." The uses of *mnēsikakein* suggest it was less a matter of bringing back to memory, as when Phrynichus provoked an *anamnēsis* (*anmnēsanta*) among the Athenians, than of recalling *against*. Because *anamnēsis* acts upon the citizens of Athens, the verb requires a double object in the accusative — the content of the recall and the subject who is reminded. At the same time, governing in many contexts a dative of hostility,[13] *mnēsikakein* implies that one wields a memory like a weapon, that one attacks or punishes someone, in short, that one seeks revenge. Thus, from the beginning to the end of the fifth century, the recalling of misfortunes changes from being neutral, as it was (we suppose) before Phrynichus, to being a vindictive act. *Mnēsikakein*: in Plato, this is said of the victorious party that retaliates with banishing and killing;[14] in Aristotle as well as in judicial speeches in Athens after 403 B.C., it more specifically designates the act of initiating proceedings against acts of civil war — an act, typically the democrats' responsibility, once considered both explicable and illegitimate.[15]

Mē mnēsikakein: a way of proclaiming that there is a statute of limitations for seditious acts. The aim is to restore an undisrupted continuity, as if nothing had happened. The continuity of the city symbolized by the *aei* (always, that is, each time) of the rotation of duties that lies beyond any opposition between democracy and oligarchy: the magistrate Rhinon, for example, who enters office under the oligarchy and without difficulty gives an account of his services before the democratic assembly, is a symbol of this continuity.[16] In addition, the clause excluding the Thirty from the amnesty was voided for those who thought themselves faultless enough to go before the people. Yet at the same time, there is the continuity of the democracy of the fifth century with the democracy established after the reconciliation, a continuity more difficult to imagine, short of treating the open wound of the dictatorship as a mere interlude. It was enough to purge this oligarchic interlude, if not of its tyranny (carefully maintained as an anomaly, acting as a foil for all rhetorical indignation), then at least of the civil war in its actuality. Whether the operation was beneficial is another matter: to judge from everything that set the "restored," though toned-down, democracy of 403 B.C. and after against the democracy ending in 405, no operation of memory successfully closed the wound — so deeply did the conflict cut into the city.

It is precisely to purge the history of Athens of conflict and division that it becomes appropriate to evoke the past, where each evocation involves a "letting go of anterior events."[17] They subtract or, rather — this is less apparent — they erase, and from this erasure, and its repetitions, they anticipate the benefits of forgetting.[18]

Further explanation is needed here: by speaking of erasure, I do not mean to turn to a worn metaphor of contemporary idiom; rather, I mean to speak Greek, in this case Athenian. In Greek discourse on writing as the preferred tool of politics,[19] the act of erasing (*exaleiphein*) is first of all a gesture, at once institutional

150

and very concrete. Nothing is more official than an erasure. One erases a name from a list (the Thirty had no reservations), a decree, or a law that will henceforth be obsolete: to ban the deeds of the *stasis* from memory, the restored democracy did this more than once; thus subtraction answers to subtraction. Up to this point, the act of erasure is always very concrete. To erase in the Greek sense is to destroy by additional covering: they recoat the surface of a whitewashed official tablet, and once the lines condemned to disappear are covered up, space is available for a new text; similarly, they insert a correction with paint and brush on an inscribed stone, hiding the old letter with a new one. Erasing? Nothing but banal, run-of-the-mill political life. Not that *exaleiphein* never becomes metaphoric here or there. When erasure does become metaphoric, writing is represented as an interior image, drawn in memory or in the mind and thus susceptible, like inscriptions, to being erased, whether this erasure is beneficial (for example, when thought rids itself of mistaken beliefs[20]), or whether it is harmful (for example, when one must do without an indispensable mourning[21]). It is peculiar to the reconciliation of 403 B.C. that political memory is expressed both symbolically and concretely — not one way or the other but both simultaneously. Erasure then takes place on two levels: some decrees are actually erased,[22] but others effect a symbolic erasure. For instance, when Aristotle claims that the Athenians behaved well by "erasing the charges [*tas aitias*, the reasons for a trial] bearing on the anterior period,"[23] this entirely preventive erasure has no other goal than the ban on *mnēsikakein*, no other aim than to avoid trials to come, and no other effectiveness than that of a speech act such as an oath. Thus it appears that the Athenians equated banning memory with the act of erasing.[24]

Let us go a step further: that there were democrats who wished to erase — symbolically and perhaps institutionally — the agreements between citizens from both sides is confirmed by few sources, no doubt because a democrat rarely expressed himself in this way.[25] But certainly, some wished "to recall the misfortunes," or, more precisely — on this point, Aristotle is explicit — *at least one* among those who "came back" began to *mnēsikakein*. So the moderate Archinus,[26] having come back to Athens with the *dēmos* and having thus acquired prestige, drags this man before the Council and has him put to death without judgment. Whether the story of this unknown democrat, doomed to anonymity because he demonstrated an untimely taste for memory, is historical or whether it serves as an *aition* for Archinus's law regulating the modalities of accusation after 403 B.C., the lesson is clear:[27] the moderate politician made an example (*paradeigma*), and once the promoter of memory had been put to death, "no one afterwards recalled the misfortunes."[28] An expiatory victim has been sacrificed to memory; henceforth, a fine will be enough to dissuade.

At least one execution was necessary because the political stakes governing this entire process were so important. It was a matter of reestablishing the exchange — when they did not speak of *dialusis*, Athenians spoke of the "reconciliation" (*diallagē*)[29] or the "concord" (*homonoia*) — between citizens who, just a few months earlier, had confronted each other, army against army. To this end, and to exonerate those who had not won, the guilty had to be isolated: the Thirty, of course, who in fact were already isolated; designated numerically, as the colleges of magistrates often were in Greece, they were easy to count and were also manifestly promoters of the conflict. One clause of the agreement — modified, we saw, with a significant restriction — made for them alone an exception to the ban on *mnēsikakein*.[30] The responsibility for the bloodshed thus fixed, all the other Athenians were left, destined to be reconciled. Which would make it possible for them not to consider the notion of henchmen (informers in the service of the "tyrants" are exonerated as long as they did not kill with their own hands, and everything goes on as if no one had done it) and allowed them to stick with the reassuring notion of quiet citizens. During the trials that nevertheless took place, scores of *kosmioi*, supporters of order, claimed innocence and blamed themselves for nothing.... At the conclusion of the process, the city will be reconstituted, one and undivided, as it is described in the official praises of Athens.

I have spoken of political stakes. Were I an Aristotelian, I would have to say that *politics* itself was at stake. Consider Aristotle, commenting on Archinus the moderate: "He acted as a good politician [*politeusasthai kalōs*]"; and on the Athenian democrats: "They seem to have used their past misfortunes in the most beautiful and most civic manner [*kallista kai politikōtata*]." Yet Isocrates already gave the real story: "After we came together and exchanged the solemn pledges, we have lived so uprightly and so like citizens of one country [*houto kalōs kai koinōs politeuometha*] that it seemed as if *no misfortune had ever befallen us.*"[31] Everything is said here: politics means acting as if everything were fine. As if nothing had happened. Neither conflict, nor murder, nor ill feelings (or resentment).

An Isocratic-Aristotelian definition of politics: what starts where vengeance stops. Thus, in this tradition, Plutarch will praise Poseidon, once pretender to the title of master of Athens but defeated by Athena, for his lack of resentment (*amēnitos*); that is, the god was "more political" (*politikōteros*) than Thrasybulus, leader of the democrats who returned to the city and to whom his victory afforded an easy generosity. Plutarch adds that the Athenians recorded this divine clemency in two ways: by subtracting from the calendar the anniversary day of the conflict, a grievous memory for the god, and by raising in the Erechtheion an altar to Lēthē, Oblivion.[32] A negative operation — the subtraction — and the installation of forgetting on the Acropolis (the very place Athenians called "the City") in the depths of Athena Polias's temple: erasure of conflict, promotion of Lēthē as the basis of life in the city. And Plutarch, speaking of Solon, the legislator whom men from the fourth century B.C. would make into the paradigm of the politics of the *meson* (that is, of all politics worthy of the name),[33] also gives this as a definition of the political (*politikon*): that it "deprives" hate of its eternal character (*to aidion*) — and such is perhaps its "essential" subtraction.[34]

These are Athenian affairs, to be sure. But how could they be kept completely at a distance? So far I have resisted the demon of analogy, who more than once has whispered to me a parallel with the France of the Liberation and the debates that unfolded from 1945 to 1953 concerning the legitimacy of the purge or a parallel with the repression and forgetting of these events we would like to be certain are behind us, since they took place in Vichy France.[35] To avoid the sin of anachronism, I have even resisted the temptation to quote *Les Oligarques* (although it is an accurate account of the takeover and rule of the Thirty), because Jules Isaac took the opportunity to narrate the first few years of the Vichy regime. As a result, I forbade myself to quote the passage where, meditating in 1942 about the reconciliation of 403 B.C., the historian bitterly asked whether in such circumstances "bad men will be as magnanimous?"[36] But I cannot resist quoting, by way of counterpoint — less contemporary and hopefully more distant[37] — this conversation of July 24, 1902, reported by Isaac:

> Péguy tells me that tolerance leads to degradation, that it is necessary to hate. I asked him: "But what is hate?" — "Non-amnesty."[38]

In 1900, the first turning point of the Dreyfus affair came with the vote of amnesty, but in his anger Péguy did not want the "incident [to be] closed," because he knew that the affair was not an incident.[39] Moreover, in 1902, this conviction led him to break with Jaurès, a move that was decidedly not very "political" in the Greek (the enduring?) sense of the word.

I close the parenthesis for now but ask the question that keeps coming up again and again, like the most forbidden of temptations: What if the word "political" had more than one meaning? Or, more exactly, by appealing to the distinction between politics and the political: What would a Greek form of the political be that did not base itself on forgetting? Does this political, which would take into account the inevitability of conflict and would admit that the city is by definition doomed to divide itself into two — and not simply between "tyrants" on one side and Athenians on the other — does this political, at once inimical and communal, have any existence other than as a construction of the imaginary?[40] If the construction is indeed a Greek one, the inimical community seems to have been thus constructed only as the fiction of an origin always already superseded: in the beginning was the conflict; then came the *polis* . . . And amnesty would then endlessly reinstitute the city against recent misfortunes. Or, rather: against the *muthos* of the origin.

Doubtless, we will not get out of this loop. It is better to begin again with forgetting and with what made it such a crucial issue in Greece.

To Forget Non-forgetting

Let us open up the strategy of Athenian memory onto some of its more generally Greek counterparts. Beginning here, the question of forgetting will be explicit.

It begins with the epilogue of the *Odyssey*. At the news of the suitors' murder, there is a great deal of emotion in Ithaca. People gather in the *agora* with heavy hearts. Eupeithes, father of Antinous,

Odysseus's first target, speaks: *alaston penthos*, "mourning that cannot be forgotten" (mourning that does not want to forget), overwhelms him, and he calls for revenge on the murderers. In response, he receives the wise speech of a wise man — Halitherses, so little heeded during the first assembly of the people in book 2 — who pleads for the rights of the present. Deaf to the arguments of Eupeithes (although this name means the "Persuasive"), the majority may well side — if only this once — with this (good) viewpoint, but the rest of the people run to their weapons. In this emergency situation, Zeus and Athena confer:

> . . . let them
> make their oaths of faith and friendship, . . .
> and let us make them forget [*eklēsin theōmen*] the death of
>   their brothers
> and sons.[41]

Peace will return. For now, the fighting begins: Eupeithes falls; Odysseus and his friends continue fighting. Athena then holds Odysseus's arm. To the people of Ithaca, she says: "Hold back, men of Ithaca, from the wearisome fighting"; and to her favorite, she adds: "Hold hard, stop this quarrel in closing combat [*paue neikos homoiiou polemoio*]."[42] Solemn oaths are exchanged. End of the *Odyssey*. This is an ironic ending, as expected from a poem about *mētis*, in which reconciliation is not desired by human beings but imposed by the gods (in the beginning, as I have said, was conflict . . .); an ending, moreover, that marks the fact that the heroic age is over — but that is another story. End of the *Odyssey*.[43]

As if to echo a response, Alcaeus, a politically committed poet and the first to pronounce in his verses the word *stasis*, puts forth this wish:

may we forget this anger [*ek de kholō tōde lathoimetha*]; and let us relax [*luē*] from the heart-eating strife and civil warring, which one of the Olympians has aroused among us.[44]

Eklēthomai in Alcaeus, *eklēsis* in the *Odyssey*: everything begins with a call to forgetting. To forget not only the bad deeds of others but also one's own anger, so that the bond of life in the city may be renewed. Hence the question: Is it necessary to suppose that between the archaic wish for forgetting and the Athenian ban on memory something like a history intervenes? What could have happened, in the movement from a demand to forget to a prescription not to recall? Because it is necessary to try to construct a history, I propose that between forgetting wrath and recalling misfortunes we place the poetic notion of forgetting ills.

This forgetting of the painful present, which the poet's song celebrating the glory of past men brings, would then be positive when it is conferred by the Muses, daughters of Memory,[45] yet themselves defined as *Lēsmosunē kakōn*, Forgetting of Ills.[46] One must be assured that the forgetting of a very recent bereavement, even if it is imputed to the instantaneous power of the inspired word, is free of all ambiguity.[47]

Already in Homer there is doubt about this "beneficial" forgetting when Helen uses a drug and a story to tear Telemachus and Menelaus away from Odysseus's *alaston penthos* in book 4 of the *Odyssey*. Antidote to bereavement and wrath (*nēpenthēs, akholon, kakōn epilēthon hapantōn*), the drug dispenses forgetting of all ills. And what ills!

and whoever had drunk it down once it had been mixed in
   the wine bowl,
for the day that he drank it would have no tear roll down his
   face,

not if his mother died and his father died, not if men
murdered a brother or a beloved son in his presence
with the bronze, and he with his own eyes saw it.[48]

To weep over father and mother is a duty, and the obligation to
seek vengeance is particularly great when a son or a brother has
been murdered.[49] Its effect being as immediate as it is temporary,
the drug may well replace mourning with the "charm of the tale"[50]
— itself eminently ambiguous — and the pleasures of the feast, but
it nevertheless severs the one who drinks it from society, at least
for a time. Such is the ultimate extreme of the forgetting of ills,
this *pharmakon* that is an antidote to pain but a poison to human
existence insofar as this existence is contractual.

There is an obvious difference between the durable political
ban on pursuing a vengeance that would be hurtful to the community and the charm that temporarily dispels mourning. By
swearing not to recall previous misfortunes, the Athenian citizen
affirms that he renounces vengeance; to place himself under the
double authority of the city that decrees and of the gods who punish, he also asserts that he will maintain control over himself as a
subject. Conversely, sweet forgetting comes from elsewhere, be it
a gift of the Muses or the poet, an effect of Helen's drug or of
wine (in many contexts) or of the sheltering motherly breast —
which in the *Iliad* Hecuba describes as a refuge against cares.[51] If it
is insistently presented as the forgetting of what cannot be forgotten, no approval, no consent is required from the one it befalls,
who, momentarily subjected to this bracketing of misfortunes, is
perhaps deprived of everything that made up his identity.

Without giving forgetting all its power, what is translated pas-
sively as "unforgettable" is also what I would call the "unforgetful": the very thing in the Greek poetic tradition that does not

forget and inhabits the mourner to the point of saying "I" in the mourner's voice.[52] This is what must be canceled by having recourse to the drug the "forgetting of ills"; this is perhaps what the Athenians prefer to avert in their own name by a decree and an oath. Despite the obvious parallels, no word-for-word transposition can transform the political ban on memory into a direct avatar of *lēthē kakōn*. Still, it is necessary to deconstruct this phrase in order to place the unforgetful under the generic designation of misfortunes: *kaka*. In the injunction "not to recall the misfortunes," we see not so much the forgetting of ills (*lēthē kakōn*) in its menacing sweetness as a way of undoing, by avoiding any explicit reference to forgetting, the always-implicit oxymoron hidden under "forgetting of *ills*": the forgetting of non-forgetting.

Let us map out what does not forget (or will not be forgotten). I have mentioned mourning and wrath, which Helen's drug dissolves and Alcaeus's insurgents wish they could forget. Similarly, much later, in a small Arcadian city, wrath will replace the misfortunes not to be recalled during a reconciliation (and *mnēsikholan* will be substituted for *mnēsikakein*).[53] They did not think otherwise in the reconciled Athens at the end of the fifth century. To stick to wrath would be to immortalize the conflict that does not want to be past (the misfortunes), yet, conversely, anyone who wanted to attack the Thirty could advise the Athenian jurors to oppose the tyrants with "the same anger as at the time of the exile."[54]

Mourning and wrath: recall the Athenians' "extreme grief" at the capture of Miletus. It so happens that the verb *huperakhthomai* (by which Herodotus no doubt means excess) is a quasi hapax legomenon; to the Herodotean instance we can add only one use in Sophocles's *Electra*: to Electra, overwhelmed by the thought of a forgetful Orestes, the coryphaeus's advice is to abandon her "grievous anger [*huperalgē kholon*]," and, he adds, "do not be angry in excess against your enemies, yet do not forget [*mēth* . . .

huperakhtheo mēt' epilathou]."[55] On one side, forgetting; on the other, a living memory that bears no other name than excess of grief. In Sophocles, Electra is in fact the perfect incarnation of this living memory, and when she claims *ou lathei m'orga*, she says not only "my anger does not escape me" or "I do not forget my anger" but also "my anger does not forget me."[56] It is as if only anger gives the self the courage to be entirely given to anger, because for the subject anger is uninterrupted presence of self to self.

It is left to the citizen-spectators gathered in the theater to guess what in this anger that does not forget is the ultimate danger for the city because it is the worst enemy of politics: anger as mourning causes the ills it assiduously cultivates to "grow,"[57] and it is a bond that tightens itself until it resists all untying.[58] Dreadful wrath ... And with reason: in this case, tragedy borrows the notion from the most ancient poetic tradition, and particularly from epic, which from the first word of the *Iliad* names this active affect *mēnis*. Wrath of Achilles and, later, wrath of mourning mothers, from Demeter to Clytemnestra. If it were not for Achilles, whose *mēnis* is in all Greek memories, I would say that we have here a female figure of memory, which the cities try to confine within anti-(or ante-)politics.[59] And in fact wrath in mourning, whose principle is eternal repetition, expresses itself by an *aei*,[60] and the fascination of this tireless "always" threatens to make it a powerful rival to the political *aei* that founds the memory of institutions.[61]

Two more words on this *mēnis* that is always perceived as dangerous, to the point that whoever is the seat of it is prohibited from using the very name: it is for this reason that the hypogrammatical utterance of the *Iliad* — *I renounce my *mēnis* — will never be formulated.[62] In *mēnis*, we can understand what lasts — what holds up well, in a troubling parody of the hoplite's endurance — and nevertheless is doomed, as if by necessity, to become the object of renunciation.[63] *Mēnis*: a word that hides the memory whose name it disguises.[64] Another memory, much more formidable than *mnēmē*. A memory that reduces itself completely to non-forgetting. In fact, in non-forgetting, the negation must be understood in its performativity: the "unforgetful" establishes itself. And just as it was necessary to forget the strength of the denial hidden behind the "ills," a recurrent utterance shows the renunciation of memory-anger: it is necessary to deny — assuming that it is possible — the denial that has hardened on itself.

Which takes us back to *alaston penthos*, this mourning that refuses to be carried out.[65]

The adjective *alastos*: like *alētheia*, it is built on a negation of the root of forgetting, and yet it denotes a very different way of not being under the influence of forgetting. It is hardly surprising that in Greek language and thought, *alētheia* has prevailed as the "positive" noun for truth, while in prose *alastos* was forgotten. It is doubtless by virtue of the same euphemizing process that, in place of the verb *alastein*, equivalent to the Arcadian *erinuein*, to be enraged (in which we easily recognize the vengeful Erinys), classical prose substituted the less threatening *mnēsikakein*, the opposite of amnesty.[66]

Mourning, wrath. And philologists wonder: mourning or wrath? But in *alastein*, this choice belongs to the realm of the undecidable. But that does not mean that the verb functions, without reference to its etymology, as a derivative of *penthos* (to which *alaston* is so often adjoined)[67] or of *kholos*. Rather, mourning and wrath naturally associate with each other insofar as they both participate in non-forgetting. *Alast-*: a matrix of meaning to express the *pathos* (or, in Phrynichus's version, the *drama*) of an irreparable loss, a disappearance (*alaston penthos* of Penelope at the thought of Odysseus, of Tros weeping over his son Ganymede in the *Homeric Hymn to Aphrodite*), or a death (*alaston penthos* of Eupeithes).[68] And this *pathos* is piercing: *alaston oduromai*, "I grieve unforgettingly," says Eumaios to Odysseus.[69] Or, rather: "[Never] do I forget to grieve," "I cannot stop grieving." Thus, like *mēnis*, *alaston* expresses an atemporal duration, immobilized in a negative will, that makes the past into an eternal present.

Insomnia of Menelaus, blood of the parricide and of the incest that Oedipus cannot forget:[70] a sense of haunting appears in *alaston*, a ghostly presence that occupies the subject and does not leave. Another example: before the final duel with Achilles, Hector begs his opponent to exchange a reciprocal promise not to mutilate the corpse of the dead enemy. Achilles refuses: "Argue me no agreements [*alaste*], I cannot forgive you."[71] And he adds that there can no more be a faithful treaty between them than between the wolf and the lamb before concluding: "You will pay in a lump for all those sorrows of my companions you killed in your spear's fury." *Alaste*: some translate it as "accursed." And there is something of that: Achilles knows that as far as he is concerned, Hector is unforgettable, like an obsession, just as Patroclus is. Unforgettable in that he killed the one whom Achilles neither can nor will forget.

And so we find the murderer side by side with his victim in non-forgetting. This induces me to evoke yet another derivative of the root *alast-*: *alastōr*, the name of the criminal insofar as he has "committed unforgettable acts [*alesta*], things that will be remembered for a long time," as Plutarch says,[72] but also the name of the avenging demon of the dead victim who tirelessly pursues the murderer.

Non-forgetting is a ghost. *Alastōr*, or *alitērios*: something that wanders, in popular etymology (from the verb *alaomai*), or that must absolutely be avoided, as in Plutarch, who derives this word from the verb *aleuasthai*.[73]

Did the Greeks live, as the often-quoted title of a book puts it, "in the grip of the past"?[74] The fascination that becomes manifest at every mention of "unforgetful mourning" would seem to indicate it. But we must go the whole way. Because they perhaps recognized it and were on their guard, as with many of their fascinations, the Greeks never stopped trying to cast out non-forgetting (starting with the *Iliad* and Achilles's wrath, despite its being so superbly dramatized) as the most dreaded of the forces of insomnia. Ideally, as at the end of the *Oresteia*, it would be neutralized without being completely lost; it would be domesticated by being installed in the city, defused, indeed turned against itself. Thus, by the will of Athena, the Erinyes proclaim that they renounce their fury and agree to keep watch at the foot of the Areopagus while the city sleeps.[75] Yet this is a delicate situation, such as only a divinity can bring to a successful conclusion. And when wrath reclaims its autonomy and *stasis aliteriōdēs* comes in turn, everything must be done to avert the threat of *alaston*: then, unable truly to forget it, they will forget in words, with each prohibition on remembering the misfortunes.[76]

Thus, in the ancient history I am constructing, everything would have been played out between negations. Because the privative *a* of *alaston* will always be more powerful than any verb "to forget," it is better to avoid *alastein* and have recourse to *mnēsi-kakein*, even if it means bringing this memory definitively under negation. All this under the protection of the most inflexible of negations: *mē*, which in itself expresses the ban.

The Power of the Negative, the Force of Negation

Non-forgetting is all-powerful primarily in that it has no limits — especially not those of the subject's interiority.

Let us go back to Hector *alastos*. Or, to use a more common term, *alastōr*. Between the killer and the vengeful demon of the dead victim, non-forgetting is undivided only because it over-flows both; it is between them but also very much before and very much after, and they themselves are absorbed in it. Thus Plutarch can at times use *alastōr* to designate the criminal and at other times treat it under the heading "anger of demons" (*mēnimata*), referring to:

> the wrath of spirits whom men call the "unforgetting avenger" [*alastoras kai palamnaious*], as if they followed up the memories of some unforgotten [*alēsta*] foul deeds of earlier days [*palaia*].[77]

In both cases, Plutarch uses the unforgetful as an explanatory principle. Therefore, it is futile to reconstruct a history of the word, as philologists might, in which *alastōr* would be, for example, first the avenger, then the killer; but neither is it sufficient to invoke a "law of participation" if this means holding on to the notion of a "point of departure" that can indifferently be the defiled guilty one or the "ghost."[78] Unless we ascribed to this ghost the originary figure of non-forgetting: much more than "the polluting act" but also much more than a simple inner state.[79] At once outside and inside, sinister reality and psychic experience, as Louis Gernet said it very well of the Erinys. Except that he was speaking of "supernatural...reality," and I insist on the *materiality* of non-forgetting as indissociable from its psychic dimension.

Let us consider a chorus of Sophocles's *Electra* in which, to multiply still further the negations, affirming non-forgetting gives way to declaring non-amnesty:

> For the lord of the Greeks who begot you will never
> be unmindful [*ou garpot' amnastei*], and neither will
> the ancient brazen axe with double edge that slew him
> in a shameful outrage.[80]

164

No "amnesty" either from the dead victim — who in the *Choe-phoroi* was asked to recall the fatal bath[81] — or from the murder instrument, also believed to be unforgetful: the pair of the deceased and the murderer is replaced by another, apparently imbalanced pair, the victim and the murder weapon.[82] Encompassing all time and space, non-forgetting is everywhere, active at every stage of the process. So much for the materiality of the *alaston* that silently keeps watch against forgetting. Still this list would be incomplete if it did not include the "misfortune" (*kakan*) itself, equally credited with refusing amnesty (but, as we know, "the misfortunes" euphemistically replaces the "unforgetful" in compound verbs).[83] Again, a couple of lines of the *Electra* to bear witness:

> Alas, alas! You have brought to mind the nature of
> our sorrow, never to be veiled, never to be undone
> [*oupote katalusimon*], never to forget [*oude pote
> lēsomenon*]![84]

"Never will sorrow forget":[85] here Electra speaks, yet no Greek hero believes in his inner autonomy more than Electra. It is as if the undivided and silent force in the subject had become a will intent on its endurance: mastery, perhaps, but who is master of whom in this matter?[86]

Electra, of course, believes she is; at any rate, she allows what wants to speak inside herself to speak repetitively. And as if denial was the strongest form of assertion, she uses only negative utterances:

> But amid these dreadful things, *I shall not
> hold back* from this ruinous action.[87]

or again:

For this shall be called insoluble [*aluta keklēsetai*],
and I shall never have respite from my sorrows.[88]

A negation and a verbal form in the future. Refusal and mastery of
time, such appears to be the preferred linguistic formula to assert
Electra's unforgetting existence. But there is also the use of negations in series, accumulations in which a logic that deducts and
cancels threatens to lose itself for the sake of asserting a purely
negative intensity:

> But I shall not cease from my dirges and
> miserable lamentations,
>
> . . .
>
> like the nightingale, slayer of her young,
> crying out loud and making loud proclamation
> to all before my father's doors.[89]

This is only one sentence, but no grammarian could find his bear-
ings in it, as the translation attempts to suggest.[90] Let me wager,
however, that the Athenian public understood in it the intensity
of the refusal. Electra also says:

> yet I am unwilling to give over
> and not to lament for my unhappy father.[91]

Thus the negative formulation becomes a claim for omnipotence
and a plan for eternity. Consequently, we should not look for the
litotes sometimes detectable in statements of non-forgetting.[92] To
the contrary, the reduplication in Electra's sentences reinforces
the negative — as in *ou pote amnastei* ("will never be unmindful")
— or the eternity of a future perfect (*tade aluta keklēsetai*: "for this
shall be called insoluble").[93] It is up to us, listening to Freud, to

hear in these utterances the same negation and the confession, unbeknownst to the speaker, that one shall renounce and disown the wrath to which the future gives assurances of an unlimited becoming; it is up to us especially to understand the confession that the excessive negation will be fought — vanquished, or at least silenced and therefore already forgotten — by another negation. Renunciation, too, is spoken — is accomplished — with the help of many verbs meaning to deny: *apeipon* in the case of Achilles,[94] *apennepō* in the case of the Erinyes compelled to revoke (and unsay) the prohibitions they had uttered against Athens.

Because the Unforgetful must always be the Forgotten.[95]

No detour does not eventually lead straight back to the subject of our inquiry. This brief foray into the world of tragedy has emphasized the proclamation of non-forgetting, and it is time, in order to end the game of double negation, to return to the Athens of 403 B.C., when a decree and an oath proclaimed amnesty.

Expressed directly, like all decrees, in which writing simultaneously presents and subordinates to itself the statement it expresses,[96] the prohibition of memory can be integrated — in the form of a citation — into a historian's narrative or into those paradigmatic recollections of the past of which the orators make use ("then the 'prohibition on recalling the misfortunes' [*to mē mnēsikakein*] came under an oath").[97] The prohibition has been fixed as a *rhēma*, a reified saying, very close to a maxim, or into a definitively noncurrent *exemplum*.[98] As Lyotard notes, "The narrative is perhaps the discursive genre in which the heterogeneity of sentence genres, and even that of discursive genres, is most easily forgotten."[99]

The city bans; it posits its decree for eternity but effaces itself as the instance of speech. There remains the oath, which must be taken by all the citizens, one by one. Or again, by each individual

Athenian, stating in the first person: "I shall not recall the misfortunes." *Ou mnēsikakēsō*: because of the ban, always subordinate to the reminder that there was a decision, the oath has the effectiveness of a speech act.[100] It commits the oath taker, but the subject gains by speaking as an "I" and by endowing his commitment with the power of future negative utterances. I shall not recall: I shall prevent myself from recalling. Thus each citizen makes sure of himself and of the future.

Yet everything can be turned upside down once more. To silence memory, the Athenian oath taker speaks in the same mode (a negation, a future tense) as Electra when she proclaims her will not to forget. But in her speech, Electra is not taking an oath — indeed, what is an oath to oneself? — and, too confident that she can master time, Agamemnon's daughter speaks as if simply proclaiming the existence of the unforgetful were enough to seal the commitment. Conversely, if only the oath allows amnesty to overcome resentment, it is because it owes its actuality to the double guarantee in its language: that of the gods, invoked as witnesses always ready to punish, and that, especially, of the curse, dreadful machine for punishing perjury that the oath taker unleashes in advance against himself as if it were foreseen that he would one day repudiate himself. A more than human guarantee is required to prevent the negation from turning into a denial — which would undo it the moment it is spoken — and to prevent anyone's erasing it by subtraction. To break the *alaston penthos*, one must have recourse to magic;[101] and to push the *alaston* back to the nether side of words, the political needs the religious.[102]

I shall not forget/I shall not show resentment. From one statement to the next, there is all the difference of the ritual of speech, which, one hopes, will give the greater effectiveness to the less marked of the two sentences.

To conclude, I will try to bring the two ends of the story together.

With each Athenian having sworn for himself, the city expects the sum of these individual commitments to reconstitute the collectivity; and at the same time, the city shields itself from the consequences of perjury, which is necessarily individual. By thus making sure of the gods' assistance, political authority can establish itself as the censor of memory, alone authorized to decide what is and what must not be, and the use to be made of it.

Similarly, the *Iliad* can authorize itself only by opening with the Muse, because only the daughter of Memory is able to recount a *mēnis* without the story being affected by the terrible aura of its subject; converting wrath into glory, then, the Muse opens the way to a good *anamnesis*, and the poet is the pure instrument of this transubstantiation.

Restored to its integrity by virtue of the agreement, the community is reestablished and decides. It prohibits recalling the contentious past, displaced because full of conflict, as if Memory appeared in place of Lēthē among the dreaded children of Night as a daughter of Strife (Eris). Each Athenian must forget the *stasis* if he can and, whether he can or not, obey the city by devising for himself a linguistic mechanism against the lucid vertigo of *alaston*.

Politics then will reassert its rights, a civic and reassuring version of the forgetting of ills. The words of forgetting disappear, erased in amnesty's favor, yet the ills remain. But who would still recall that among the "misfortunes" banned from memory lies hidden precisely that which, in the poetic tradition, refused to forget?

Chapter Seven

On a Day Banned from

the Athenian Calendar

What to do with an event that must not be commemorated? One can swear an oath never to recall its painful memory when it is a matter of a *stasis* in which two armies of citizens fought against each other. But what to do when it is a matter of a single day, even if it can be assigned to the distant past of mythical times?

One thing is certain: the solution does not consist in losing all memory of it, as the swift use of negation might suggest. More complex, and infinitely more interesting, is the treatment of the "not" in the context of a negative commemoration. The neutral version of negation, which concerns only the content of memory, is replaced by a marked version of negation, where *the emphasis is on the prohibition itself*. In the first case, one is content with not — with never — commemorating, not even once (because this one commemoration would be the first of a potential series): one simply refrains from evoking the episode that must be erased, and it is likely that the refraining leads to actual forgetting. Yet one can also emphasize the negation as such. This results in an official decree of forgetting: establishing a procedure for not commemorating then becomes essential. Because it concerns a collective practice of memory, the second case will be of particular interest to us; indeed, in the ambivalence of such a procedure, we can best

171

decipher what happens in a refusal of memory when the refusal is itself the object of an orchestration.

Once more, the example comes from Athens, and if the contentious event — in this case, a disagreement between gods — falls under the category of myth, understood in its Athenian sense, it also falls under the categories of both history — or at least of what we may call the Athenian history of Athens[1] — and civic time in its constitutive repetitiveness. But first let us consider the event: Plutarch mentions twice that the Athenians have removed the second day of the month Boedromion so that they will not have to commemorate what happened on the second of Boedromion in the distant past.[2]

The information is surprising: did the date disappear from the Athenian calendar because it was on the second of Boedromion that Poseidon and Athena fought over the first place in Attica? We should not cast suspicion on the value of this information simply because it is unverifiable outside of Plutarch. For once, the reader of texts need not feel guilty for turning to something other than "real" documents (which he identifies with inscriptions alone), because historians of Antiquity, though naturally suspicious, seem to agree and trust Plutarch's word on this point.[3] Not wishing to complicate anything unnecessarily, I shall take seriously this information, which is precious to anyone working on the modalities in which Athenian memory functions.

Two Texts on a Subtracted Day

Twice Plutarch evokes the case of the second of Boedromion. One episode in his *Table Talk* is devoted to the hidden meaning — enigma (*ainittetai*) — of the unwritten law requiring that Poseidon's candidature to the rank of city divinity be dismissed everywhere. Because the text is damaged in the relevant passage, we will never know the meaning of the enigma, but we learn that the god accepts defeat smoothly and without resentment (*ameniton onta*). From here Plutarch goes on to cite the example of Athens, where the event is commemorated twice: with the dedication of an altar to Lēthē (Oblivion), and by the subtraction of the second day of Boedromion.[4] A later exposition in the treatise *On Brotherly Love* endeavors to draw a lesson from the latter practice:

> The Athenians, though they absurdly invented the tale of the strife [*eris*] of the gods, yet inserted in it no slight correction [*epanorthoma*] of its absurdity, for they always omit the second day of Boedromion [*tēn gar deuteran exairousin aei tou Boedromionos*], thinking that on that day occurred Poseidon's quarrel [*tēs diaphoras*] with Athena.[5]

And Plutarch urges the reader to follow the example: it is necessary to treat the day on which we have quarreled with a parent or relative "as a day for forgetting and forgiving [*en amnēstiai tēn hēmeran . . . tithesthai*], and to count it as one of the ill-fated days [*mian tōn apophradōn nomizein*]."[6]

Thus Plutarch does not merely provide a piece of information; he also interprets it. To strike the second of Boedromion from the calendar is to bring a "corrective" to the myth of divine *eris* that is the basis of the city's eponymy: this amounts to saying that Athens's relation to its own memory is at stake and that this memory, even if it begins in mythical time, is *political*. Discord, whatever the occasion may be, must be disregarded. And the comparison, unfortunately interrupted by a lacuna in *Table Talk*, that links the attitude of Poseidon to that of Thrasybulus must turn to the god's advantage, because he is described as more political (*politikōteros*) than the democratic leader and because, without having obtained the *kratos* like the latter, he renounced resentment. This is an explicit reference to the civil war initiated by the rule of the Thirty and to the 403 B.C. amnesty, which, however, was not yet called *amnēstia* but was summed up in its negative command: "It is forbidden to recall the misfortunes." If the gods' quarrel is seen as the paradigm of all *stasis*, not as "a pure anomaly,"[7] then the subtraction of the second of Boedromion begins to make sense for the Athenians as something like a political act of forgetting.

I will return to this dimension, the most easily discernible in the two texts. But first, I will put together the file on the second of Boedromion in all its complexity, beginning with the path, indissociably religious and political, indicated by Plutarch when he likens the day of a quarrel between brothers to an "ill-fated [*apophras*]" day.

A few refinements are vital to assessing the complexities of the journey. Thus it will be necessary to make some scholarly observations. Let us take for granted that "the Athenians . . . always omit the second day of Boedromion." This implies that they would have gone from the first to the third of the month as if it were perfectly natural. (We will see about that.) Always, *aei*: that is how the Greeks define institutional periodicities. We can deduce, then, that the Athenians carried out this subtraction every year. But from which point in their history can we date the practice? Always, *aei*, certainly is also meant to signify from the origins, in the always-renewed *aiōn* of the city.[8] Yet here a doubt arises about the supposed antiquity of this "always." That there is no extant evidence besides Plutarch is one thing; but the existence of at least one contrary, and irrefutable, testimony from the classical period is much more difficult to get around. In fact, if we judge by the accounts of the treasurers of Athena — inscribed on stone and therefore above suspicion — it was still possible for a public deed to be completed on the second of Boedromion in the last years of the fifth century B.C., which implies that at this time the Athenians had not yet struck this date from their calendar.

In addition, Poseidon and Athena's quarrel, which was sculpted on the Parthenon's pediment and doubtless exalted in the official eloquence of *epitaphioi*, seems to have been in classical Athens much more a claim to glory than an episode to be forgotten.[9] Apparently, the time had not yet come to erase this episode, which Plato presents in the *Menexenus* as an essential point in the praise of the city, all the more remarkable in that it is authenticated by the gods themselves.[10] Thus some readers of Plutarch, conscious of this difficulty, have tried to get around it by making the negative commemoration into a positive celebration: they claim that the second of Boedromion was always in the Athenian calendar and that it was the date of the Niketeria, which, according to Proclus, the Athenians celebrated "still in his own time [*eti toinun*]," in honor of the victory of Athena over Poseidon.[11] Yet nothing justifies forcing the texts in this way so as to wring from them the opposite of what they directly state. In *Table Talk*, Plutarch speaks of an ill-fated day, not of a day of glory; and when he describes a practice that he clearly designates as a subtraction, the focus is not on Athena's victory but on Poseidon's defeat, or at least, in his most neutral formulation, on the "disagreement" between the gods. If we accept Plutarch as an authoritative source, then we must accept that things are as he describes them and date the suppression of the second of Boedromion of "later centuries" to the 400s[12] (if not of these years themselves),[13] and very probably to the Hellenistic period, when we know that Athens readily suppressed adversaries who had left a sad memory.[14]

If, therefore, it was truly necessary one day to forget the second of Boedromion to the point of crossing it off the Athenian calendar, then the similarity that Plutarch indirectly posits — by way of the brothers' quarrel — between this date and an *apophras* day deserves attention. I am not arguing that Plutarch actually intended to treat the second of Boedromion as *apophras*. But by assimilating these two days, he at least suggests that there is some affinity between the day that must be forgotten and those that are described as ill-fated (*nefas* for the Romans), which we could more accurately call (I will justify this translation later) forbidden (*apophras: apagoreuomenē*, as the lexicographers gloss it).

The Forbidden Days

If the second of Boedromion belongs among forbidden days, Poseidon's defeat is characterized as ill luck or, more precisely, as a "bad day" (*dusēmeria*), as sinister as Aristophanes's description of the Thebans' life under the reign of the Sphinx.[15] Thus, from the very beginning, Plutarch places the god's misadventure in the category of "lugubrious days."[16]

And yet it is far from certain that making the anniversary of a defeat into an *apophras* day actually was a Greek — in this case, Athenian — gesture.[17] A Roman historian could easily provide examples of a similar practice,[18] beginning with the day of the defeat of Allia, that symbol of humiliation, which opened the road to Rome for the Gauls in 390 B.C.[19] The day of the Allia is a cursed day, what Plutarch translates by *hēmera apophras*.[20] I might note that the Romans are supposed to have spoken of a *dies religiosus*, not of an "ill-fated" day, when they listed this date under the category of days that are "of ill-fame and are hampered by an evil omen."[21]

This is where a crucial and ineluctable problem of translation arises. If the Romans themselves, as Aulus Gellius testifies, confused a "religious" day, on which no one would offer a sacrifice or undertake any business at all, with an ill-fated day, on which it was forbidden to bring a lawsuit[22] — if, that is, a certain approximation had already slipped into the Latin language — how can we expect Plutarch not to amplify this approximation irremediably when he expresses Roman realities in Greek, since there is only one word, *apophras*, to translate two, perhaps even three, other words?[23] Even when Plutarch keeps to purely Greek facts, as he does in the case of the second of Boedromion, how can we expect the word *apophras* to be completely free from Roman contamination? This is a problem that specialists on the Athenian calendar note with chagrin.[24] But I will not resign myself to melancholy for a number of reasons. Doubtless, we can never be assured of the Greek purity of Plutarch's thought and language, but we have no other source on the second of Boedromion: it is with his language and thought, then, that we must work. And if Plutarch does not name this day as belonging to those called *apophrades*, his reasoning at least suggests that anyone who wishes to understand the Athenians' intentions in suppressing this date has much to learn from the Athenian definition of "forbidden" days. Although he at times uses the word *apophras* in his works somewhat vaguely,[25] Plutarch, who wrote a lost treatise on days,[26] — remains the most trustworthy source on a subject that had at least interested him, whereas there are only three references to it by other authors from the classical period.[27] Clearly, we should take him seriously. Whoever is interested in the suppression of the second of Boedromion can escape neither Plutarch nor the *hēmerai apophrades*.

Thus, in relation to this date to be forgotten, and as if to clarify its tonality, we find the notion of forbidden days. Rest assured on at least one point: the word *apophras*, if not the general Greek reality it designates, is purely Athenian.[28] It is in Athens that, according to Jon Mikalson, we can most easily define the characteristics of the *apophras hēmera*, with or without Lucian, who dedicated one work to defining its meaning but seems also to have been seriously contaminated by the Roman model.[29] Such a day is described as *apraktos*,[30] which suggests that nothing can be done with it or that nothing can be done on it. Or at any rate: nothing other than the civic activities — religious and legal — connected with that day. These activities are well defined and not numerous: if we accept Mikalson's count, only the festival of the Plynteria and the extraordinary sessions of the Areopagus for murder trials were institutionally linked with these days,[31] which we still call "impure" and some modern historians of Greek religion designate as "taboo."[32]

On the Plynteria and the meeting days of the Areopagus, I will note only what allows us to ascribe a common tonality to forbidden days. First, there is a religious ceremony, probably a spring ritual,[33] a day unfit for any activity other than those secret rites (*aporrhēta*) of washing and purifying the statue of Athena Polias.[34] It is a moment of temporary freedom from a stain that hovers over the city for an entire day.[35] It is, in short, a lugubrious festival, whose *aition* tells of mourning and of bloody death — in this case, the death of Aglauros, daughter of Cecrops and unfortunate servant of Athena.[36] Then there are the three days at the end of each month on which the Areopagus can pass judgment on murder cases. Consequently, these days are "forbidden" because they are stained.[37] Even the prestigious court only escapes the pollution of premeditated murder because it meets in the open air.[38]

We know how tight the bond is between the Areopagus and the representation of a memory that cannot be erased: there is no doubt that this memory-vengeance is present in the forbidden days at the end of each month, a memory-vengeance embodied by the Erinyes, who, under the name Semnai, keep watch over the most revered of blood tribunals, or by the demons *alastores* or *alitērioi*, whose name, according to Plutarch, recalls the unforgettable character (*alēston*) of the murder committed and the necessity of avoiding (*aleuasthai*) its avengers.[39] And in fact, the Erinyes — we know this from a scholium to Aeschines — do have something to do with *apophras* days.[40] Consequently, it was tempting to add a few more days to this list of forbidden days. Thus Hesiod advises to avoid at all cost (*exaleasthai*) the fifth day of the month, the only one that is completely dark in his list of days:

> Beware of all fifth days; they are harsh
> and angry; and it was on
> the fifth, they say, that the Erinyes
> assisted at the bearing
> of Oath, whom Strife bore, to be a plague
> on those who take false oath.[41]

Because of Hesiod's exhortation, some historians have decreed that the fifth day of every month was *apophrades*,[42] without offering any evidence more convincing than the celebration of the festival of the dead — the Genesia — on the fifth of Boedromion.[43] When it comes to funerary rites, however, everything seems to be linked too easily. The slope is indeed slippery that leads from the Erinyes to the avenging demons and from the demons to the dead: we begin by quoting a gloss of Hesychius that designates days on which sacrifices are offered to the dead as "forbidden,"[44] and while the vast crowd of anonymous dead rushes down into the breach thus opened, the list of rituals that are candidates for *hēmerai apophrades* suddenly becomes much longer.[45]

I will not indulge in this game, because the vertiginous practice of creating chains of equivalences threatens to lead always to more approximation. For example, the claim that the second of Boedromion owes its lugubriousness to the negative connotations of the number two could be considered well founded.[46]

Let us entertain such a hypothesis for a moment. The anniversary day of the divine *eris* then becomes a simple single instance, only a little more marked, of a series including the second day of each month; then we might recall that the second of each month at Athens was considered the day of the *agathos daimon*, "the good demon," obviously so called by antiphrasis.[47] Then, evoking a rare classical instance of the word *apophras*, in the one extant fragment of a speech by Lysias against a certain Kinesias, we will have the satisfaction of believing we have identified a new series of *hēmerai apophrades*: Kinesias the impious is accused of having chosen a forbidden day to have a party with his companions, who gave themselves the provocative name "the society of the bad demons [*kakodaimonistas*]";[48] this appellation destroys the euphemism by revealing the bad demon under the *agathos demon* and seems to designate the chosen date, obviously not appropriate for such festivities, as the second day of the month.

As enticing as this construction might seem, it is unverifiable in the current state of our knowledge, and on top of that, it has the drawback of dissolving the specificity of the second of Boedromion. Thus, leaving the question open, I will also renounce speculations about numbers and keep to the list with which I began (day of the Plynteria, days of murder trials at the Areopagus). The list is short, but it is long enough to allow one to ascertain that the tonality of forbidden days was determined by pollution, bloodshed, and dreaded memory.

A Day Denied

What about the second of Boedromion in all this? The second of Boedromion cannot be a forbidden day because *hēmerai apophrades* by definition appear in the calendar (the problem is to know how to use them: how to go through them safely when one is a simple private citizen, how to perform the secret rites, and how to judge according to one's conscience whether one is a servant of Athena or an Areopagite). We must therefore ask about the second of Boedromion, which, though belonging to the forbidden days, has disappeared from the Athenian calendar.

If Boedromion was the month of glorious celebrations for the Athenians, both because of its name and because of the dates it commemorates,[49] such a day seems out of place in it, since, according to Plutarch, the emphasis was on Poseidon's defeat, not on Athena's victory. The reader wonders about the Athenians' motivations for siding so completely with Poseidon. What bad conscience must have pushed them to surround Poseidon's defeat with forgetting? Certainly, some narratives evoke the consequences of their ancestors' preference for the goddess over the god, but there is no tradition that presents this choice as harmful for the city.[50] How can such a practice be explained?

To understand the erasure of this episode, we should probably stick to the version that stresses the disagreement (*diaphora*). It would be not the victory of Athena or the defeat of Poseidon, then, that must be forgotten but the very fact of the conflict, which in itself presupposes a victor and a victory. It is necessary to forget that there was a defeat but also that there was a victory, for Athena is both *Nikē* and the *polias* goddess, in Athens and elsewhere. Aeschylus celebrates Athena Polias, who is always eager to preserve Athens's prosperity and asks the Erinyes to wish for a *nikē mē kakē*, a victory that is not bad like the one that is won by citizens over citizens.[51]

By setting two gods against each other who will later be closely associated with each other and with the city, divine *eris* seems to foreshadow all other internal Athenian discord. One day, then, the Athenians would have decided to erase its memory, as if better to protect the city against the very idea of *stasis*.

If this is why the anniversary day of the *eris* was subtracted, it must be supposed that the Athenians, either because they were enamored of civil peace or because they were following a path of punctilious religiosity, reasoned about the gods' quarrel in the manner of Plato in the *Republic* and the *Critias*.[52] It is in terms

openly inspired by the *Republic* that Plutarch in *On Brotherly Love*
evokes an episode that he considers the product of mythical ex-
travagance.[53] In this particular case, moreover, to reason like Plato
amounts to manipulating negation as the most efficient operator
of the forbidden. We can see this in a few examples from Book 2
of the *Republic*:

> They are not to be told [*ou lekteoi logoi ... oude lekteon*] ... I do not
> myself think that they are fit to be told [*oude ... epitēdeia einai leg-*
> *ein*][54] ... neither must we admit at all [*oude ge to parapan*], said I, that
> gods war with gods and plot against one another and contend.[55]

Plato also says of the stories of Uranus, Cronus, and Zeus that one
should not talk about them (*di' aporrhēton*) or, if absolutely necessary, only talk about them in front of the smallest number of listeners as possible.[56] It is worth pausing over this prescription. The
formula of the secret is the same one — the substantive neuter [*ta*]
aporrhēta — that is used in other circumstances to name all prohibitions: these are the forbidden words, whose utterance is a crime
in itself and, with no further qualification, the prohibition itself.[57]
This presents an opportunity to go back from another perspective
to what connects the suppressed day of Boedromion with the
notion of *hēmera apophras* and the translation that has been systematically proposed.

Thus the word *apophras*: the etymology implicitly suggested
by Pollux — who derives the word from the verb *phrasso* (to shut
in or to obstruct) because temples, he says, were "barricaded" on
that day — is surely fanciful.[58] Most philologists, therefore, accept
the solution, presented as both obvious and "obscure," that derives *apophras* from *phrazō*, with the prefix *apo-* giving a privative
value to the word. Understood in this way, *apophras* would signify
"that must not be said," as Eustathius suggested.[59]

Hēmerai apophrades: days that must not be said,[60] just as there are words that must not be uttered (*aporrhētai*).[61] Yet more specifically, I see in them days that must not be marked. Even before taking on all the connotations of saying — which it already has in the classical period — *phrazō*, much closer to *semainō* than to *legō*, means to make clear and even to give to see, to show, or to mark.[62] Derived from *phrazō*, the word *apophras* would then designate a category of days that must not be put in evidence. A passage from Hesiod confirms this hypothesis on the use of the verb *phrazō* to denote the taking into account of days. In *Works and Days*, Hesiod uses the aorist infinitive *pephrademen* when he advises his reader to watch over the good use of days, because, he says, they come from Zeus:

> *Mark* the Days that come from Zeus, all
> In their right order.
> Explain them to your workers.[63]

There follows the list of days, "signaled" or "given to be seen" as good or fearsome, and what it is advisable to do or to avoid — in any case, the object of a prescription. Are the *hēmerai apophrades* days about which there is nothing to be made known, days that go unmarked because one has nothing to do on them and everything to avoid and because it is better simply to let them pass by? This connection, which has not been generally recognized, would lead us to think so. But it is true that the classical use of the word, which insists on its negative dimension, invites us to see, rather, days that are negatively marked and thus prohibited for ordinary activities.[64] Suddenly the qualifier *apophras*, effective in itself but in the most negative mode, is enough to characterize a day as "abominable."[65] Vicissitudes of negation between the "unmarked" and the "negatively marked"... Are we so far away from "not commemorating"?

Now we can take one more step toward understanding the analogy suggested by Plutarch between the second of Boedromion and a forbidden day. It is possible that the erasure of the anniversary of the divine *eris*, in relation to its designation as *hēmera apophras*, is equivalent to what Freud called acting out. What is only suggested in language by *apophras*, the Athenians actually carried out, in a sort of radicalism of meaning in which the day that should not be marked is so negatively stained that there is no other solution but to suppress it.

And this gesture is called *eksairein*.

The Act of Subtraction

The verb *eksairein* also opens up other perspectives, for the exceptional gesture is expressed with the same term used for much more ordinary manipulations of the calendar. This is an invitation for us to look closer.

A fierce debate is raging among historians over the Athenian calendar. No one contests the ancient testimony that there were "suppressed" days (*eksairesimoi*) in Greece, and particularly in Athens.[66] Yet the quarrel begins, and two factions form, whenever this practice is used to illuminate the gap between two calendars, the one ruled by the god (*kata theon*), a "lunar" calendar, and the one regulated by the city magistrates (*kat' arkhonta*), the politico-religious calendar of civic life.[67] It is unanimously recognized that in order to coordinate the civic calendar with the lunar one, it was necessary to play with the days (to add some and take some away); if we also accept that the decision to add or to suppress rested with the Archon, the difficulty of what it means to suppress remains: Is there only one manner of "suppressing" by mechanically filling in the disparity with the cosmic order? Or is there more than one means of suppression? This is where Plutarch's testimony in *Table Talk* takes on its full importance, because he himself insisted that if the Athenians suppressed the second of Boedromion, it was "not to suit the moon, but because that is the day on which the gods are believed to have had their territorial dispute [*ou pros tēn selēnēn, all' hoti tautēi dokousin erisai peri tēs khōras hoi theoi*]."[68]

Two parties are set against each other. For some, the whole problem is purely technical, and it involves linking civic life and the movements of the moon. They sum up everything by distinguishing between "hollow" months, from which one subtracts a day, and full months.[69]

In the process, one attempts to normalize the practice of suppressing days, which amounts to limiting its extent or even reducing its meaning. It is enough to claim that what is suppressed is not a day but a date.[70] This date is then situated at the precise moment in the month when the counting of days is reversed, and one concludes with relief that in the civic consciousness of time, there was indeed no solution of continuity.[71] This line of argument leads to a temporality without gaps, certainly different from ours but unperturbed by anomaly. This is the goal: to substitute the idea of extracting a date,[72] painless and without consequence, for the idea of subtracting a day, a very visible, not to say conspicuous, process. Supporters of this reasonable and economical theory — credible, in its coherence, with respect to the everyday life of civic time — may point in passing to other, more remarkable manipulations of the calendar, which suggest a more circumstantial (or political) use of the practice of *eksairesis*.[73] But they willingly pass over them, and they rarely mention the second of Boedromion in their works. And with good reason: the suppression of a second day is not the same as the discrete extraction of a date whose presence at the beginning of the backward count is merely optional; it is rather the very explicit subtraction of a day, whose absence is certainly noticeable, from a brand-new month.

The month has barely begun, and it is already amputated: there is a beginning, but what comes next is missing, and the gap is flagrant and deliberate.

To make sense of Plutarch's statement, we must forsake economical solutions and temporal coherence and speak, with the other camp, of the manipulation of the city calendar. This presupposes that while admitting the existence of another, more regulated category of "suppressed" days (*eksairesimoi*), we will focus less on the invisible operations than on those interventions that drastically modify the organization of the calendar. From this perspective, the second of Boedromion, far from being an exception, becomes the rule, or at least the model that allows us to imagine the Athenian relation to temporality.[74] The verb *eksairein* indeed expresses the suppression of a day, and this suppression, orchestrated as such, is an act. It is a political act, whether its significance is circumstantial or whether — in a less temporal mode — it belongs to the "politics of myth" enacted when the Athenians suppressed the second of Boedromion, "not to suit the moon" but in order not to celebrate the anniversary of the gods' quarrel.[75] And in fact, with the manipulation of the calendar, the origin myth would be corrected (would be expurgated) by reconciling the gods, whom we can no longer describe as rivals, with each other and with the city.

Thus, confronted with the great quarrel over the calendar, Plutarch's text requires the verb *eksairein* to take on the full sense of "suppressing." This is not terribly surprising, because this meaning also is prevalent in other spheres to which the verb is applied: we find it in the *epitaphios* for the Samos dead in Pericles's eloquent orations comparing vanished youth to a spring subtracted from the year;[76] we also find it in reflections on literary genres (where we learn that tragedy "removes" from epic the poet's words, keeping only dialogues), on the materiality of

186

words (to take a letter out of a word is also *eksairein*), and on the censorship practiced in criticism when Aristarchus excised lines from the *Iliad* because they speak of parricide.[77]

Let us come back to days and the use made of them. Clearly, Plutarch designates an actual subtraction with the verb *eksairein*, just as Hesiod uses a compound form in *eks-*, *eksaleasthai*, to describe the radical attitude that must be adopted toward the fifth day, the only one on his list that is utterly bad.[78] The verb *aleasthai*, with its prescriptions of the activity to be avoided, is sufficient for other days.[79] The important thing is to avoid making a mistake, and this can be done by vigilantly refraining from inappropriate acts; the fifth of the month, however, must be avoided in itself and in its entirety. Like the Hesiodic *eksaleasthai* but in a different register,[80] the verb *eksairein* expresses through its prefix an act thought in terms of its radicalism. The linguist will then recall that the prefixes *apo-* and *ek-* both have a privative function and consequently that "the sense of *apo-* is unmarked in relation to that of *ek-*."[81]

One last time, I would like to compare — in order to distinguish them more clearly — the *hēmera apophras*, which must be observed with a behavior appropriate to its negative dimension, with a day such as the second of Boedromion, which is cut from the calendar every year. The forbidden day does not exclude an effective action in the negative sphere of pollution: one washes Athena, one judges murderers, and once the *miasma* has been taken care of, life can go on. The subtraction of a day is entirely different, at once definitive (or perceived as such) and always to be renewed, because it is the act of cutting out that matters for this collective subject that is the city. Let us read Plutarch again: "Every year, the Athenians omit, we omit the second of Boedromion." The second day of Boedromion no longer exists as a date, and yet it has nothing in common with those *eksairesimoi* days that allow civic time to be aligned with lunar time; these are the only days of which we can say that they do not exist at all. On the contrary, the reiteration of the gesture of suppression emphasizes the gap between *amnēstia*, the will to forget, and the random forgetting that erases without thinking.[82]

To sum up: as a date, the second of Boedromion no longer exists; yet one does not suppress the second day of a month without consequences. By going from the first to the third day of this month every year, the Athenians bored a hole in the beginning of the sequence of numbers — a hole that stands like a very visible scar and is the trace of the surgical operation of non-memory.[83] Because all traces call for an *aition*, we will assume that it was necessary to have a story explaining why the second of Boedromion no longer existed, and this meant that one could, after all, speak of the contentious episode of the divine *eris*.[84] Thus a discourse on the damages of *eris* was substituted for the celebration of *eris*, which is a way of rejecting conflict in order to talk about it all the more.

The process of not commemorating is extremely convoluted, worthy indeed of the complexities that characterize the politics of memory in Athens throughout the city's long history. This repeated subtraction takes its place in the city as the most paradoxical form of recall.

Under the sign of Eris, the historian immerses himself in a troubling universe at his own risk — the risk of getting lost, of losing his legitimacy — because the only tools (linguistic, psychoanalytic) he thinks he can use are not his and he is not sure of being able to master them. As for the objects themselves, they are not likely to reassure him: How can we investigate the bond of division without anxiety?[85] And where can we find enough energy to confront the suspicion directed at anyone who dares to show that hate is firmly installed in the *meson*?

Whether or not we assign it to the politico-religious universe —
our guide often being Hesiod, with Aeschylus taking over more
than once — the field of conflict, dominated by the seductive and
unmediated figure of the oxymoron, attracts and paralyzes thought.
Without ceasing to be considered lugubrious, Eris reveals herself
as the most powerful of all bonds, which must be warded off
urgently and repetitively by an act of forgetting, reinforced by an
oath. In other words, she must be warded off by two of her
dreaded children, Horkos and Lēthē.

These are family matters, in a way, in which the Greeks think
they can fight off the daughter of Night with the help of her offspring. Moreover, *stasis* itself, which is often called *emphulos*, is
born of the same lineage — between citizens, or, as we will see
shortly, between brothers — and in and through this *phulon* that
gave birth to *stasis*, it must come to an end, in the name of the fraternity of *politai*.

Eris was the vital thread of this journey into political memory
and the forgetting of the political, a journey whose stopping
points were words and speech rites. Words: *dialusis*, then *menis*,
this pain transformed into wrath, and finally *horkos* and *lēthē*,
between amnesia and amnesty. The speech rite, the vocal gesture,
consisted of the imprecation at the heart of the oath that one will
not revive the memory of misfortunes — except through the act
that negatively commemorates the day of the quarrel. But whether it is in deed or in word, as the judges say, we cannot do without
negative operations in the effort to exorcise Eris. Negation —
whether simple or redoubled and as the strongest substitute for
affirmation when it is made denial — has been ubiquitous throughout this effort to illuminate the prescription *mē mnēsikakein*.
Words with opposite meanings, effective linguistic processes in
the service of politics when a city attempts to ward off the conflictual political element that it would like to forget gave birth to

it. Under the sign of Eris, words, as if endowed with a new depth, turn back onto themselves or become acts of language. And the steady tables of opposition, where the good is on one side and the bad on another, begin to wobble.

And yet, by inviting all the members of the civic body to these negative acts that seal their reconciliation, Greek cities have indeed invented politics. The historian may put his mind at ease: positive procedures are not far away.

PART THREE

Politics of Reconciliation

The Athens of the last few years of the fifth century B.C. demonstrates clearly enough that reconciliation exists. But conflict cannot be forgotten without consequences, and my intention is to show the price to be paid by the restored democracy for this forgetting. But we must be patient. This will be the end of the road. Before that, I will examine some of the strategies that aimed at instituting a lasting reconciliation. Here, the politico-religious sphere so dear to anthropologists of Antiquity must give way to pure politics.

If, from Hesiod to Aeschylus, poetry has given voice to Eris, reconciliation will take place in prose, like the decree that institutes it and is entrusted to a memory of stone when it is engraved on a stela, like the historians' narrative recounting the end of a civil war. Yet two enigmatic lines from Sophocles describe much better than any historian's account what is played out in civic temporality when the time comes to end *stasis* — doubtless because tragedy tests all civic positivities — and it is therefore a passage from *Antigone*, appearing here as a sort of tragic interlude, that will introduce us to the prose of amnesties.[1]

In the Thebes of Laius, Oedipus, and Antigone, the long night of unleashed hatreds draws to a close. The war is over, and with it ends the *stasis* between enemy brothers, of which the war was only a consequence. The chorus then enters to sing the sun, risen at last, and the defeat of the Argive enemy. After celebrating *Nikē*, Victory, who has joyfully come to save the city, the *parodos* adds: "after the recent wars [*polemōn tōn nun*] be forgetful [*lēsmosunan*]."[2] "Recent wars"? Most astute readers of tragedy observe that this is a reference to the wars that were raging just a moment before. Some even go a step further and, with a clear conscience, translate: "the wars of yesterday."[3] This solves the difficulty, but by erasing it: the sun has risen; therefore, at this moment, they are already yesterday. Still, the text remains; it is intact, and in my view it should remain so. If I had to explain why it is "today" that must be entrusted to forgetting, I would say that the chorus of Thebans, more lucid than it believes — or, at any rate, lucid at the moment it utters what resembles a slip of the tongue — denies with this *nun* all the positive certainties that it affirms elsewhere.

Thus, celebrating the victory, it ignores that this victory cannot be assimilated to a *nikē mē kakē*, because victory between equals can only be "bad."[4] What can we say, then, when the "equals" are actually brothers who killed each other? Certainly not, as the coryphaeus just claimed, that the "two accursed ones [*toin stugeroin*]"[5] were exempt by virtue of their shared destinies from the defeat of the Seven Against Thebes, who abandoned their corpses to Zeus, god of trophies. Besides the strangeness of the arithmetic that deducts Polyneices and Eteocles from the group of enemies launched against Thebes,[6] it is also, from a more generally Greek perspective, a fundamental mistake to proclaim the *kratos*[7] of equals who defeated each other at the cost of their own deaths.[8] This is all the more the case because the war, mercilessly persistent, is not over for those who are left of the Labdacid family: the reciprocal murder of the brothers indeed introduces a present that will have to be forgotten, but not until later — that is, outside the tragedy — for the tragedy of the death of Antigone, Haemon and his mother, Eurydice, and the destruction of Creon has barely begun.

The chorus, announcing forgetting in its first song, is doubt-less in too much of a hurry. Yet its contradictory formulation is accurate on one point: as long as they are not warded off by effec-tive procedures, division and hate live on endlessly in the present, a present that is frozen and hypertrophied, absorbing all tempo-rality into itself. Tragedy lives off this presentness of the conflict. Consequently, tragedy knows no realized reconciliation, because it is not possible to go, as the chorus would like to do, from the "now" to forgetting without going through a solution of continu-ity and because, as an extra precaution, the civic formula of amnesty has substituted the prohibition of memory for the ambivalence of forgetting.[9]

Positive politics must break this dreaded spell, and in the cities it is necessary to make *stasis* into a past so that there may be an afterward.

In real cities, a day comes when one works one's way toward rec-onciliation, a day on which the citizens, as if they had forgotten that oath and forgetting are sons of Discord, try to forget conflict by swearing an oath never to mention what is still on everyone's mind, this "today" of hate that must forever be identified as past at all costs. And it is the past that is implicitly designated by the word "misfortunes" in the Athenian version of the oath, which is also the most generally Greek, or by the word "wrath," as in Alipheira, in a less euphemized Arcadian version — and we know how fierce Arcadia nourishes dark wraths and fierce dissensions.[10]

In Athens as in Alipheira, in Megara as in Kynaitha, oaths are sworn not to recall the past. The question whether or not these oaths were kept is perhaps not completely irrelevant. To judge by

Xenophon's or Aristotle's surprise at the loyalty of the Athenian democrats at the end of the fifth century B.C., one can conclude that this was not the usual behavior.[11] Does this mean that the very religious fear of the imprecation's consequences is not enough to prevent perjury in the reality of political practices? Perhaps I should specify that the party of freethinkers was often that of the oligarchs,[12] whereas religious fear was found on the side of the democrats, as the religious "reaction" that follows the democratic restoration shows.[13] It is nevertheless the case, as we will see, that the Nakonians, perhaps taught by the experience of others, did not deem a simple oath sufficient to guarantee the solidity of the reconciliation and added an institutional "brotherhood" to the oath. It remains to be seen if the proclamation of brotherhood actually guaranteed the solidity of the social bond forever, which the ambivalences of the Greek figure of the brother — and, much closer to us, what has been called "the rocky road of brotherhood"[14] — might lead us to doubt.

Are we approaching the end of the road? Not quite if we truly wish to shed light on the strength of the Athenian *mē mnēsikakein* of 403 B.C. To understand what, even more than fear of the gods, lastingly re-creates the bond of community between reconciled citizens, we will have to ask about the positive content of the prohibition, which we have noted in passing had as its target a potential recourse to trials. This is an opportunity to examine more closely the prohibition that prevented civic justice from taking sides in disagreements, which suggests that despite everything, the memory of conflict is awake.

Then it will be time to return to Athens.

CHAPTER EIGHT

Politics of Brothers

You must make a city, that is to say citizens who are
friends, who are welcoming and who are brothers.

— Saint-Just

This inquiry into reconciliation will begin in Sicily, with the
adelphoi hairetoi (the elected brothers) of Nakone. Due to the
appearance of previously unpublished documents, it is known
that a reconciliation (*dialusis*) took place there between citizens
after a disagreement (*diaphora*) that may have been a *stasis*.[1] It is
also known that the reconciliation was carried out in the mode of
adelphothētia (adopting as brothers), by dividing, the better to
combine, the entire civic body into groups of five "brothers" chosen by lots: two "enemy brothers" coming from antagonistic parties, solidly framed by three "neutral" brothers. This, together
with the alchemy of friendship, was meant to constitute in each
case a close-knit group of symbolic brothers.[2]

They were symbolic brothers, but indeed brothers (*adelphoi*)
and not *phrateres* (clansmen), as the editor of the decree would
have it.[3] In fact, the word *phrateres* was not used because in the
third century B.C. Nakonians, faithful to Greek forms of politics,
understood "union between citizens... on the model of blood
kinship."[4] *Adelphoi*: blood relations, but fictitious blood relations,
chosen by lot and yet described as elected (*hairetoi*).[5] In short,
five at a time and all together, the citizens of Nakone became
brothers against the constantly reborn threat of *stasis*.

This invites us to examine Greek representations of brotherhood before we go any further toward an interpretation of the decree.

Brothers Against Stasis and the Stasis of Brothers

Brothers against *stasis*: a surprising figure? Indeed. In fact, this figure, which aspires to the symbolic effectiveness of a festive celebration repeated year after year in Sicily, is surprising only because it is inscribed within the reality of a politico-institutional strategy.

This representation of a brotherhood effective against discord has been identifiable in the texts for a long time. Thus it expresses itself one century earlier as the firmest basis of the Platonic city. Plato invents a brotherhood that is eminently political, albeit in an imaginary mode, as is the case in the *Republic*. The process is accomplished in two steps: first the myth in book 3, a moment of ideology with the "noble lie"; then the construction of the city in book 5. The recourse to myth indeed comes first,[6] as a way of convincing the citizens of their common autochthonous origin, by virtue of which, all born from the earth, they are "all brothers."[7] Accordingly, the political construction will organize a generalized civic kinship, in which citizens are so many brothers, jointly endowed with an impressive number of "fathers," "mothers," and "sisters."[8]

We need only go further back in time, to the last years of the fifth century in Athens, to observe that such a figure already played a role in the city, in the service of the civic imaginary of the *polis* as one and indivisible. At the precise moment, that is, when Cleocritus advances between the two armies of citizens after one has defeated the other and sketches the beginning of a reconciliation. In the speech given in Xenophon by this fighter for the democrats, herald of the Eleusinian mysteries, and spokesman for

198

concord, standing in the no-man's-land between the two armies of citizens, brotherhood is in fact only suggested. Yet who would not hear it in his emotional call in the name of "the gods of our fathers and our mothers"?[9] The Athenians' *patrōioi* gods are of course well known: furthermore, Plutarch tells how participation in the same *hiera patrōia* was enough to define the status of brothers.[10] Yet by linking closely the side of the mothers to that of the fathers, the speaker accomplishes a double operation: he exalts the double lineage that makes a son into a citizen in every Athenian family since the decree of Pericles (451–450), and he reopens the possibility of common civic life for autochthonous citizens united by the same ancestors.[11] If only the Athenians can remember that they are brothers, *stasis* may yield to reconciliation.

Yet there is another, very different model of brotherhood in which, far from leading to concord, the status of brother is inextricably linked with an uncompromising *eris*. If there is the collectivity of brothers against *stasis*, there are also brothers born only to tear each other apart — we know them in pairs, mythical or generic — and Plutarch uses the expression *stasis adelphōn* as if the phrase were self-evident.[12]

Among the foremost enemy brothers, we find of course the irreconcilable pairs of *adelphoi* that Athenian tragedy borrows from the myths of other cities: the Theban paradigm with Oedipus's sons,[13] but also Thyestes and Atreus, and still others.... Let us return to real conflicts.[14] Whether the animosity of brothers comes before civil war or is a result of it, Lysias begins his enumeration of the relatives killed in times of *stasis* with the brother.[15] Moreover, in book 9 of the *Laws*, among familial murders that fall into the legal category of the involuntary, Plato writes: "If brother slay brother in a faction fight or some like case, and the act be done in self-defense and the slain man the aggressor ..."[16] The fact that the brother murderer "shall be clear of guilt, as though the slain had been an enemy in arms," is not what catches our attention: Plato has also piled up extenuating circumstances, among which *stasis* figures significantly, next to self-defense.[17] But in the *Laws*, only the example of brothers is associated with civil war, and this example calls forth two others, where same kills same — citizen killing citizen and alien killing alien.

The insistent theme of brothers for *stasis*, always accompanied by "the terrible couple of brotherhood-and-death," answers to the Sicilian slogan setting brothers against *stasis*.[18] This double and contradictory configuration must be clarified. This requires delimiting the representation(s) of the brother, considering the very Greek tendency to transform blood-kinship categories into merely classificatory categories, and, finally, following the semantic chain that leads from the brother to the citizen by way of the companion.

What Is a Brother?

Hesiod predicts the dreadful days that will bring the Iron Age to an end:

> when the father no longer agrees with the children,
> nor children with their father,
> when guest is no longer at one with host,
> nor companion to companion,
> when your brother is no longer your friend,
> as he was in the old days.[19]

This is a way of recalling that whereas the relationship of father to son and of son to father is asymmetrical, the fraternal bond is reciprocal — and is even the very model of reciprocity, so to speak.[20] How then should we interpret a sentence from Herodotus describing the first kings of Sparta, those twins who, "being brothers [*adelpheous eontas*], were as long as they lived in discord with

each other"?[21] Being brothers: this is often translated as "even
though they were brothers," but in the absence of any adversative
mark, the context could just as well imply "because they were
brothers."[22] Reciprocity would be preserved, except it would
acquire a content very different from *philia*. . . . An examination of
all the occurrences of *adelphos* in Herodotus's works does not
allow us to decide: quarrels and murders between brothers are as
frequent as instances of devotion and loyalty, though quarrels and
murders are usually the deeds of kings and tyrants, whether or
not they are barbarians (but we know that the Spartan royalty was
considered archaic, bringing them closer to barbarians), whereas
loyalty to a brother is common to barbarian kings and simple citizens of Lacedaemonia.[23]

Friend brothers, enemy brothers: the ambiguity, in fact, exists
in Homer between brothers' "vocation" to support each other
and the backdrop of fratricides and family murders; Jean-Louis
Perpillou has shown the singular law of the *kata phrētras* in book 2
of the *Iliad*, where Agamemnon inspects the Greek army, de-
ployed according to organic divisions.[24] There is the fraternal
imperative of mutual aid, effective cement of society, and the discreetly erased reality of heroic fratricides. It is probably unnecessary to go all the way back to Homer to be convinced of the
shared and widespread character of this ambiguity, in which we
can see a Greek problem in general. Yet, notably, the particulars
change so little from Homer to Aristotle when one looks at what
is said about the relationship of same with same (whether it
attracts or repels).[25] At most, the idea gradually becomes clearer
concerning the difficulty of thinking the boundary between the
reciprocal, in which "friendship" (*philotēs, philia*) for each other
(*allēlous*) is expressed, and the reflexive, which from same to
same and self to self is easily transformed into a murderous relationship.[26] The ideal would be to go no further than reciprocity

and to see in the brother not a double but simply the closest of kin, to whom one owes support and help.[27]

Brother helping brother: this is the ideal but also an imperative not to be transgressed.[28] It is a proverb, quoted by Demosthenes and by Plato in the *Republic*, which in many respects is a dialogue about the fraternal bond.[29] On the battlefield, it was for Homeric warriors the experience of their condition as brothers and heroes: a natural ally, brother helps brother, dies with him in combat, or survives to avenge him.[30] If there were time, we could read the beautiful passage in Herodotus where he tells how King Cambyses killed his sister-wife because she had cried at the sight of two young dogs who were helping each other against a lion cub; she was sad because Cambyses lacked the help of a dead brother, and the king knew he was his brother's killer: this was a death sentence for his wife, who was also his sister.[31] In this story of brothers, however, it is the woman — the sister — who is twice loyal to the law of brotherhood.

Yet there are always discordant voices — beginning with Hesiod, who is most certainly thinking of Perses, the paradigm of bad brothers, when he claims:

> When you deal with your brother, be pleasant,
> but get a witness; for too much
> trustfulness, and too much suspicion,
> have proved men's undoing.[32]

Or, even more explicitly:

> Do not put some friend on equal terms
> with your brother;
> but if you do, never be the first to do him an injury.[33]

These words imply that the brother is the least trustworthy of all kin, or at least the one who must be treated the worst.[34] In these maxims in which prudence vies with bitterness, we recognize that fighting between brothers is harsh, as a Euripidean adage, quoted by both Aristotle and Plutarch, claims; yet this adage in the form of an acknowledgment also implies that these fights are frequent. We can put up with them, or we can — and this is the most frequent case — condemn conflict, especially when it turns to fratricide, as it does between Oedipus's sons: for "death dealt thus one to other by two of one blood — of *that* pollution there is no growing old."[35] Yet the *stasis* of brothers resurfaces like the most stubborn of all facts. This explains how Aristotle can go from concord to discord simply by evoking the sons of Oedipus.[36] Yet Aristotle also knows that real civil war can arise in a city because of a dissent between two brothers struggling for power: this happens at Cnidus, Massilia, Istros, and Heraclea, places where only the eldest brother had access to the much-coveted position of public office.[37]

Between *adelphoi*, then, conflict would be as natural as friendship. Of the three Greek words for brother — *adelphos*, *phratēr*, *kasignētos* — I have, apart from a few examples, considered only the first (which in terms of chronology may be last — historians and philologists disagree on this point). The time has come to look at the other terms, which will also lead to an account of the classificatory potentiality at work in the Greek vocabulary of kinship.

Names of the Brother

Plato provided proof in the *Republic* that *pater* is not to be confused with biological father — as Emile Benveniste convincingly recalled — when, imagining a city free from conflict on the model of a family, he distinguished between each citizen's progenitor (*goneus*), forever unknown, and the multitude of "fathers" common to all.[38] With brothers, things become more complicated as soon as we are not limited to the designation blood brother (*adelphos*). Besides *phratēr*, which Greek shares with many Indo-European languages, we find another old Indo-European term of kinship, *kasignētos*.

The word *phratēr* is used in the singular to designate an individual, and in the plural to designate the collectivity of *phrateres*.[39] In the first case, Homeric diction seems to attest the use of this term to designate a blood brother; in the second case, the term is believed to have a classificatory sense going back to the Indo-European **brather*.[40] In the classical period, and perhaps even before then, phraters existed only in the context of the institution of the phratry, which has been characterized as an "intermediate" space between the family and the political.[41] Whether we accept the classificatory sense of "brother" or whether we ascribe a moment in the history of this word to "the elimination of the biological sense," the fact remains:[42] because Nestor's authorized voice claims in the *Iliad* that the man "who longs for all the horror of fighting among his own people" must be "out of all brotherhood, outlawed, homeless,"[43] the word *phratēr* unquestionably speaks of politics, but by means of kinship,[44] which invalidates any Latin translation of *phratria* into *curia*.[45] More than **co-viri*, *phrateres* are, and must be, symbolic brothers. This amounts to saying that their collectivity, a solidarity by definition, is free from all tensions.[46] Because an *adelphos* is a brother isolated in his singularity, he can always rise against another *adelphos*; *phrateres*, on the other hand, like the members of the Homeric *phrētrē*, fight "in divisions [*kata spheas*]" against the enemy, which gives the full sense to the Iliadic statement about the seditious *aphrētōr*.[47] Symbolic brothers, ideal brothers, unfailingly united brothers — the phratry earns its role as described by Aristotle in the *Politics*: the basis of community, essential bond between all those who ensure the city's well-being, a small-scale model watching over the whole, an effective tool in the service of a democratic politics eager to "mix" all the citizens.[48] In short, and to limit ourselves to Athens, no one can be a citizen without being a *phratēr*, and all phratries are equal, just as all citizens — interchangeable, or at least supposed to be so — are equal in a democracy.[49] Is the only positive "brotherhood" to be found in the collectivity of phraters?

This would be forgetting that there is yet another word for brother, *kasignētos*, which is also a classificatory term, although its institutional meaning is much looser. In fact, although the word can designate blood brothers in the classical period and in poetic language (as, for example, in Sophocles's tragedies), *kasignētos* primarily denotes a brotherhood in a wider sense, that of collaterality. If *kasi-* is indeed the equivalent of the Hittite *kati-*,[50] in *kasignētos* we should hear "born with" or "relative," and in fact the scholiasts agree with this interpretation when they gloss the word with *suggenēs* (born with). Born with, relative, that is, collateral, cousin: *kasignētos* is all this and comes to support the constructions of those who dream of the Indo-European "joint family."[51] *Kasignētos*? We could also say *cognatus*. . . .[52] In this sense, the group of *kasignētoi* is the safest of ramparts in Homeric epic when, more than once, the *adelpheoi* are dead, absent, or faltering: this group sometimes has uncertain boundaries, but its legitimacy is equaled only by the intensity of the familial affect that surrounds it.[53]

Kasignētoi: cousins and at the same time the best of companions (*etai*) on the battlefield because they invariably take the correct side in a fight — with and not against. Collateral relatives, always already in arms to assist their "brother" in trouble.[54] The surest of allies because the very idea of betrayal seems to be unknown to them by definition. Surely, from a group of *kasignētoi* a beautiful city could be made. But — and this is not insignificant —

205

if such a group exists, Herodotus places it at the fringes of the Scythian world, not in Greece:[55]

> The Agathyrsi...have wives in common, that so they may all be brothers, and as members of one family, may neither envy nor hate one another [*hina kasignētoi te allēlois ōsi kai oikēioi eontes pantes, mēte phthonōi mēt' ekhthei khreōntai es allēlous*].[56]

Is the city of *kasignētoi*, which knows neither jealousy nor hate, a fiction? Neither more nor less, no doubt, than the Platonic city, where, in similar conditions, the brothers are called *adelphoi*....

Adelphoi, phrateres, kasignētoi: in this series, the first word — the only one that classically designates the brother — is the only one to conceal all the ambivalence of the fraternal bond. Nevertheless, although *phrateres* and *kasignētoi* suggest unfailing loyalty, shielded by definition from all tension, these words do not represent Greek politics in its purest form: the phratry is necessary, but — in Athens after Cleisthenes's reform — it has no real power, and after Herodotus, prose, as the language of politics, forgets *kasignētos*.

And if it were absolutely necessary to deal with ambivalence? Conflict is not far, and we will return to it soon. But we must be patient.

The City of Brothers

Before returning to the question of conflict, I would like to insert another peaceful chapter: the Greek city, as it wants itself to be or as the philosophers like to think it.[57] And when thinking means classifying — placing reciprocal relations, connected yet different, in a progression leading more or less continuously from the family (the basic unit) to the city, at once premise and conclusion of the discourse — for example, with Aristotle, the chain of relations of *philia* clearly comes together, going from the brother to the citizen by way of the companion.

All who are born from the same parents are *adelphoi*; among themselves, *adelphoi* are like companions (*hetairoi*), although this does not mean that all companions should be considered brothers. Caught between the vertical axis of filiation and the horizontal axis of companionship, the brother oscillates from one to the other, without ever filling in the gap between blood kinship and the reciprocity of fellow men:[58] The Aristotelian operation attempts, tendentially, to equate brothers and elective brothers, but the intermediary figure between the two that would realize this fiction does not exist, and one must be content to argue in terms of contiguity — and also, always and somewhat mysteriously, in terms of affinity. It is just as true that there is something of the brother in *hetairos*:[59] do they not both, like the Spartan *kasioi*,[60] belong to the same age-group?[61] Thus they are fellow men who share everything, according to a proverb Plato likes to quote.[62]

"Brother" and companion: the association is frequent in Homer, whether the formula is *hetairos te kasignētos te* or *kasignētoi te etai te*.[63] Greek thought was already busy weighing and reevaluating the comparative merits of the two.[64] Yet if we want to think the connection between social relations that are at once very close and very distinct, from Homer to Aristotle, we must insist on the pivotal role of the *hetairos*: better than a brother for Alkinoos, at best similar to a brother in Theognis's poetry, but always close enough to a brother for the simple utterance of his name to authorize a passage, along the scale of degrees of "friendship," from kinship to sociability.[65]

Brother/age-group companion/companion/citizen: with Aristotle's help, the series is now complete, and, imitating Greek political thinkers, a few shortcuts can be taken from one extremity to the other. If friendship "holds cities together," the fraternal bond might very well be its purest form.

Hence the Platonic noble lie, aimed at making the citizens believe they are all born from the same mother, earth, and are actually *adelphoi*, and hence the *Menexenus*'s insistence on the shared brotherhood of autochthonous Athenians.[66] Hence too many of the slippages in Plato between brother and citizen.[67] But we will focus mainly on everything that from this model of citizenship makes the model citizen, the *politēs* of the best *politeia*: a democrat in the *Menexenus*, he is a timocrat in Aristotle; and in both cases, the friendship of brothers unites fellow citizens.[68] Aristotle even occasionally grants the name *politeia* — valued most of all when, as is the case here, a regime is designated as the regime par excellence because it incarnates the essence of all *politeia* — to "the regime of brothers" [*politeia hē tōn adelphōn*]."[69]

This is a powerful philosophical operation, and we could easily forget that the community of brothers founding a city and the fraternal Good Government are pure fictions, or at least models. It is time to go back to the sublunar world, where the most recognized reality is that of conflict and where, in the city torn apart, brothers confront each other.

Kinship Put to the Test of Conflict

If we can believe Lysias — and in this case, he speaks in his own name — one of the Thirty's gravest crimes was to have forced the citizens to wage an "impious war" against their brothers, sons, and fellow citizens.[70] Under the dreadful constraint of *stasis*, one kills what one holds dearest of all: a brother, a son. The very people whose loss has been considered irreparable since Homeric epic, where it is pictured from the perspective of an older warrior who knows that he is living on borrowed time: it is essential to know how to avenge the murder of a brother or a son but also how to accept fair compensation, which enables the murderer to escape the endless cycle of revenge.[71] A son, a brother: these are also the people, from a citizen's perspective, one tries to hold back when there is a departure for a colonial venture and even when the legislator has ordered that in every *oikos* the son or the brother will leave the father and the brother.[72] A son, a brother: in a word, other selves.[73]

It is precisely those other selves whom one is supposed to kill during a *stasis*. Father kills son, which Thucydides clearly describes as something beyond transgression, and brother kills brother, which I would describe as ordinary civil war, because the brother is also the paradigm of the citizen.[74]

To anyone who objects that this is stating the obvious, because potential adversaries are so few in the sphere of the *oikeion*, I would suggest the always worthwhile — and here also necessary — practice of comparing Greek figures of *stasis* with Roman representations of family murder in civil war. The question is presented as such in Rome, as is attested in Appian or Velleius Paterculus by the real lists of family relations that public hate has transformed into relations of death.[75] Here the historian of Greece, forced to work with scraps — an isolated note, a very general mention of slaughtered *suggeneis* — will no doubt sigh, with relief or envy, when faced with such rich Roman documentation. He will first discover that at least one figure has been substituted for the other: the father (the Fathers) has replaced the son in the role of the favored victim whose murder is a scandal, for in Roman civil wars, the son kills the father.

Frater, then, but also and especially *parens*: such are those who are killed in Rome. Also, to destroy completely the *familia*, in which the slave is a "child," even the slave takes part in the slaughter by killing the master. Among many other texts, Lucan's *Pharsalia* bears witness to this:

The servant drove the accursed sword to the hilt
through his master's body; sons were sprinkled with their
father's blood and strove with each other for the
privilege of beheading a parent; and brother slew
brother to earn rewards.[76]

To kill a brother, just as Romulus killed Remus: if this is indeed
the founding conflict of the city, we would expect it to be the paradigmatic murder of the *bellum civile* in Rome. As a repetition of
the origins of Rome, such a murder often does not, for all that,
appear any less literary and is typically marked by the imitation of
a Greek model (or, more accurately, Theban: to kill each other
among brothers is to act like the sons of Oedipus).[77] Thus, like it
or not, we must accept the following statement: among the in-
numerable horrors of civil war, the palm unquestionably goes to
the sons, at least in terms of intensity if not always frequency.[78]
Because horror becomes the norm in the Roman city as soon
as war, introduced in the midst of families, becomes *plus quam
civile*,[79] it is necessary to claim, with Yan Thomas, that murder
between brothers is only a step — still imperfect, so to speak —
toward parricide as the emblem par excellence of transgression.
The texts often substitute "parricide" for "civil war"[80] because,
understood as murder of the father,[81] *parricidium* names an act of
a nature very different from even the gravest homicide.[82]

It has already been well demonstrated that such a *topos* is determined by reasons that are eminently Roman — the political structure of familial relations, the interweaving of family and city, in a
word, the institution of *patria potestas* — and I do not intend to go
back to this.[83] A few points, however, will shed light on an inquiry
in which it is not enough to compare Greece only with Greece.

Thus, for example, we can learn much from the observation
that civil wars in Rome favored the appearance of a dangerous

contiguity between the term *pater* (or *parens*) *patriae* and the term *parricida*.[84] On the way back to *stasis*, I will measure the gap between the two ways of thinking the city, the family, and the links between them.[85] If the Greek way of integrating the family into the city consists in giving to the son the autonomy that Rome denies him until the death of the father, we should not be surprised that the role of the sons in the *oikeios polemos* is negligible. Despite the recurrence of jokes about parricide in Athenian comedy, the hatred of a son for his father seems never to have had any real political dimension in a city like Athens, where father and son were made politically equal by sitting next to each other in the assembly of citizens.[86] Consequently, the gesture of the murderer son, as reprehensible as it might be, is not considered the paradigmatic monstrosity. Because in *stasis* everything happens between citizens, Greek thought can choose between the murderer son and the father who kills a son; and, in fact, it is the second possibility that is considered unthinkable: unthinkable like *stasis* and more unthinkable, to be sure, than parricide, which, in Athens, can be neither the reverse of some *patria potestas* nor the ghost that haunts Roman historiography.[87]

The father, killer of his son, is only a borderline case in comparison with what I would call the norm of the abnormal. If citizens are brothers in Greece, they are brothers in *stasis* as well as in the city at peace, and the figure of brother rising against brother, intimate enemy transformed into political adversary, constitutes the most elaborate model of political hate.

This stage of the inquiry would be a good time — and the temptation is great — to reflect more broadly on the question of the family and the city, from Athens to Rome and from Rome to Greece. But I lack time and space, and this is not the moment for generalizations, so I will offer just a few brief observations.

1. Because designating any civil war as fratricidal war is commonplace, we could easily forget that the brother is not the inevitable victim of internal wars in all times and in all places. Insurgents in Greek cities, because they are *homoioi*, would probably confirm a basic semantic impulse. May specialists of Rome resist the temptation and be wary of the "fraternizations" and "fratricidal wars" that abound in modern discourse about *bellum civile* even when the Latin texts speak of *parricidium*.[88]

2. If we focus on the notion of *bellum plus quam civile*,[89] we will note that the conflict that strikes the family is more serious in Rome than civil war per se, whose name evokes only the confrontation between armies of citizens. It is as if only the family had value, because there is something primordial in it, something absolutely originary. "War more than civil," war within the family: we will recall that family founds the city in Rome,[90] because of which it is often made into a spectacle — during the aristocratic ritual of public funerals, for example[91] — as the very model of Roman virtues. Yet it should also be added that by itself the family (a family) can lead the city into *bellum civile*;[92] for example, the Gracchi were considered the primary culprits in causing decades of bloody civil wars.[93] Then shall we say that in Rome the family is a reality in thought on conflict, whereas in Greece it is a model, and even a mirror, for the city divided by *stasis*?[94] We should beware, of course, of such a clear-cut distinction. Nevertheless, the claim that "the Greek city is a family" must be understood as one of the most efficacious symbolic figures of the collectivity called *polis*.

3. *Suggeneia* on one side, *parentes* on the other. In Rome, where the fathers (the *patres*) occupy the top of the pyramid, we speak of parents (from which we inherited the late word *parentas* and perhaps the thing itself). In Greece — in this case, Athens — we say *suggeneia*. It is not surprising that in the everyday life of

private trials, the word could become and lose its univocity.[95] Still, in the great majority of cases, *suggeneia*, as one Athenian orator notes in passing, essentially designates — as we would expect — collaterality in its opposition to filiation, which, in this case, is called *genos*.[96]

Suggeneis (Homer said *kasignētoi*): one last time, then, brothers are the Greek figures of those whom we — because we inherited a very Latin tongue — would call parents or relatives. Yet typically, brothers are what make the Greek city, whether it is at peace (when one exalts, with Aeschylus, the political *koinophilēs dianoia*, rampart against the horrors of *genos*)[97] or whether it is consumed by conflict, and there is no stronger hate, at once familial and "political," than that of the sons of Oedipus.[98]

CHAPTER NINE

A Reconciliation in Sicily

At the end of the fourth or the beginning of the third century
B.C., the inhabitants of the small Sicilian city Nakone reached a
reconciliation at the end of a *diaphora* and set in bronze the memory of this event codified in a decree. We will now look closely at
a text to which I have often referred in the preceding essays.

Returning to Nakone?[1] Since 1980—when the document was
first published—the Nakonian inscription has been commented
on by many historians and linguists who were happy to have at
their disposal a new text that is in many ways one of a kind.[2] Now
that the fever has subsided, we can focus on the reconciliation of
Nakone, leaving other aspects aside.

This decree is exceptional both for the symbolic synchrony it
presupposes between its formal composition and the process it
prescribes—indissociably political and religious (summoning an
assembly and a sacrifice)—and for the way it makes an institution
of the brotherhood that is so dear to philosophers' speculations[3].
Yet insofar as it engages a very generally Greek representation
of *stasis* and *homonoia*, the reconciliation of Nakone deserves to
be compared with that of Athens in 403 B.C. or of Hellenistic
Alipheira. This apparently unique text, whose singularity David
Asheri has stressed, ceases to be a *hapax legomenon* as soon as we

see it as one political strategy among others designed to protect the city from conflict. The reader, now accustomed to civic operations of blatant erasure,[4] could even see it as a document that is as exemplary as it is illuminating.

How to Come out of a Diaphora

I give here a complete translation of the text, even though my purpose is not to comment on all the elements:

1 Under the archonship of Leukios, son of Kaisios, and
   of Philonidas, son of [Phil]...,
   the fourth day of Adonios. Decision
   of the assembly as well as of the council: since,
   fortune having made [things] proceed,
   the common affairs

5 of the Nakonians have been set right, that it is
   advantageous that in the future too they live as
   citizens [politeuesthai] in harmony,[5] and that
   especially the envoys of Segesta here, [6]
   Apellikos, son of Adeidas, Attikos, son of Piston,
   Dionysos, son of Dekios,
   have, for the interests common to all citizens
   given advice,
   that it be decided to reunite, the fourth of Adonios,
   the assembly

10 of citizens, and, all those for whom the disagreement
   [diaphora] of the citizens
   happened when they were fighting [agōnizomenois]
   about common business, that, summoned
   [eklethentas] to
   the assembly, they proceed to the reconciliation with
   themselves, by drawing up a list [prograpsanto],

for each of the two groups [*hekateron*], of
thirty. For those who
were adversaries [<*hup*>*enantioi*]
before, that each of the two groups make
the list for the other [*hekateroi hekateron*]. That
15   the archons, after having inscribed on a lot
[*klarographēsantes*][7] the names of each group
separately
and having thrown them into two urns, draw the
lots one of each group [*hena ex hekaterōn*]
and that, about the rest of the citizens, they add
by drawing lots three
to the two, excluding relatives whom the law
requires to be removed
from the courts. That those who have the same lots among
themselves
20   be chosen brothers agreeing
[*homonoountes*] among themselves
[*allalois*],
in all justice and friendship [*philias*]. When the
sixty
lots have been drawn as well as those who
are part of the same lot, that, the rest of
the citizens,
they draw lots by groups of five,
without arranging
25   together the relatives, as it has been
written, and that between
themselves they be brothers, like the
preceding ones,
these who are part of the same lot. That the
officials in charge of the memory of the sacred

[*hieromnamones*][8] for the sacrifice
sacrifice a white goat, and, whatever is
necessary for the sacrifice,
that the attendant provide it. Likewise, that the
magistrates who succeed each other
30   all sacrifice each year on this day to
the Ancestors and to Harmony a victim for each of
the two groups [*hekaterois*], during the *dokimasia*
and that all the citizens celebrate the holiday
with each other,
brotherhood by brotherhood. That this decree,
having had it engraved
on a bronze stela, the archons put
in the vestibule
35   of Olympian Zeus.

All these operations to get out of what the decree describes as a
diaphora among citizens (line 10)? Historians have difficulty accepting such a notion. Some, like Asheri, considering the elec-
toral court cases among important citizens,[9] retranslate *diaphora*
with *stasis*;[10] some try to moderate this analysis without rejecting
it completely,[11] whereas others want to minimize the importance
of the disagreement. If, under the pretext that Nakone was a
"minuscule State," we do understand this word as referring to a
simple local quarrel, it would make no sense for the Nakonians to
invent such an elaborate procedure for the sole purpose of "making excited citizens understand that what unites them is more
important than what divides them."[12]

Doubtless, the word *diaphora*, characteristic of disagreement,
covers a wide spectrum,[13] ranging from general to very specific
uses — thus it can even designate voting[14] — and to instances
where it stands beside *stasis* against a background of violent con-

flict.[15] Yet even if this term is meant to evoke only a disagreement that could lead to civil war,[16] and if its scope is generally broader than that of *stasis*,[17] we may see it as the euphemism par excellence, which reconciled cities used whenever, in invoking their own history, they could not avoid every allusion to a past *stasis*. Such at least seems to be the widely shared practice in civic inscriptions,[18] which reserve the rare occurrences of *stasis* for events in neighboring cities.[19] Similarly, when Plato, in the *epitaphios* of the *Menexenus*, calls the Athenian civil war at the end of the fifth century "our disagreement" — which Xenophon makes into a *stasis* — he undoubtedly means to be ironic about the euphemizing tendencies of official Athenian rhetoric.[20] In addition, when applied to a disagreement between citizens, the verb *diaphero* usually refers to the type of conflict that is ended by a *dialusis*, which suggests that the gap between *diaphora* and *stasis* is insignificant.[21] Consequently, regardless of what the Nakonians' *diaphora* actually was, they clearly considered all these processes necessary to prevent new divisions; the only goal, just as in Xenophon's narrative of the Athenian *stasis*, was to return to normal civic life (*politeuesthai*: line 6).[22]

Thanks to the intervention of foreign "reconcilers,"[23] in this case from nearby Segesta, the Nakonian citizens agreed to be reconciled in order to prevent all division in the future,[24] showing a prudence that was all the more necessary because their city was small. They probably agreed with their contemporary Aristotle that there is no worse danger for a city than division and that small cities are more vulnerable to it than others because, without a *meson* to soften the conflict, it is easier to divide the entire population into two groups.[25]

Some may object that the Nakonians' *diaphora* hardly reached the whole civic body and had only a limited range. That is, some might argue that there were only sixty "adversaries"; that there were only three neutrals grouped with each pair of adversaries; and that other groups, composed exclusively of neutrals, were not counted. But we should not mistake the nature of the number sixty, which is entirely fictitious — or at any rate, merely plausible.[26] First, collectivities ripe for reconciliation usually claim that "only a few at any time are their foes."[27] We know how the Athenians excluded from their amnesty only numbered groups of oligarchs, officeholders like the Thirty, the Ten, the Eleven, and the former governors of the Piraeus.[28] The perfect symmetry resulting in the same number of *hupenantioi* on each side (line 13) clearly does not refer to reality — all *stasis*, in Greek language as well as political thought, typically opposes a group of *oligoi* to a great number (*polloi*) — but reflects the law of symmetry that in every epoch of Greek history structures thought on *stasis*.[29] Surely, once the main insurgents had been identified (and, what is more, identified by the enemy, whose knowledge of its own enemy is always faultless), there remained lower-caliber supporters on both sides, lost in the mass of what the decree calls "the rest of the citizens." Finally, even if the description of the procedure seems to suggest that the entire city was not divided into two camps without remainder, the logic of the decree in itself implies that the division reached the city as a whole: "neutral" citizens must submit themselves to the same "brotherhood" as the others; in addition, the clause inviting to the assembly "all those for whom the disagreement of the citizens happened [*hossois ha diaphora tōn polit[an] gegone*, line 10]"[30] conveys two things: the plan to proceed to an exact count (*hossois*),[31] and the observation that the disagreement, because it took place between citizens, involved the entire city.[32]

The entire city? In this inscription — a new addition to the corpus of civic reconciliation — the reader of texts encounters once again, and with great satisfaction, the very linguistic turns that seem to belong most properly to historians' narratives of *stasis*.

This is true of the "pathetic" use of the reflexive, which historiographical prose often dramatically substitutes for the reciprocal *allēlous* when sedition assails the unity of the city.[33] Similarly, Isocrates will brandish the threat of the Athenians' "destroying" the commitments made "to themselves" against Callimachus, who does not respect the amnesty.[34] In Nakone, the time had come for union, not *pathos*, and the claim that *homonoia* will be reciprocal is duly repeated in the decree (*homonoountes allēlois*, line 20, cf. line 32). Yet echoing this expected use of *allēlous*, the use of the reflexive in *-ta* is quite remarkable,[35] firmly suggesting a relationship of quasi identity and making the "brothers" into a welded block united together by fate (or rather united to "oneself" or to "themselves"). The decree had in fact already prescribed that the *dialusis* among the Nakonians occur "from themselves to themselves [*autous pot' autous*, line 12]," and the groups of brothers, as so many microcosms, can only reflect the indivisible unity of the city's self.[36]

The customary designation of *hekateroi* (each one of the two groups; lines 13–14, 15–16, 16–17) for the two groups, insofar as they are two and are considered interchangeable,[37] also agrees with shared habits of Greek language and thought.[38] As a linguistic tool, this pronoun effectively serves the tendency toward symmetry by erasing every difference between the two opposing parties.[39] It also signifies the perfect reversibility between those who were adversaries in a time that is now permanently past (*en tois emprosthen khronois*) and who are now invited to acknowledge themselves as such only in order to lend themselves to the fraternal mixing. This brings us once more to these "brotherhoods" that the decree institutes as the most unbreakable of bonds between citizens.

Of "Brotherhoods" in the City

One would expect brothers to be united by a very strong bond. Yet this brotherhood is in itself a contradictory notion, because it is completely artificial (being *hairetoi*, the brothers are brothers only by virtue of a political decision,[40] even if this decision is determined by drawing lots rather than by election) and because it presupposes, metaphorically, an originary consanguinity.

Thus the brotherhoods are celebrated on the very day of a sacrifice to the ancestors (lines 30–31), whose title *genetores* designates them as blood ancestors, which might be a way of giving fathers, who are as distant as any fathers can be, to these "brothers" who are not sons.[41] True, the familial metaphor is inextricably linked to political symbolism, because the sacrifice, which is also dedicated to Homonoia, partakes of the city's symbolic celebration of itself.[42] In addition, the figure of brothers easily lends itself to political interpretation: despite obvious cultural differences, we might think of the Roman Arval brothers, the association of *fratres* that sits in the temple of Concord; John Scheid has shown it was composed in large part of former enemies and symbolized the institutional reconciliation of the Roman elite.[43] Moreover, despite the unbridgeable temporal gap, we might think also of the "pacts of alliance" and the "celebrations of oath" with which federations reiterated the fraternal oath of the *Jeu de paume* at the promising beginnings of revolutionary France.[44]

The elected brothers of Nakone were thus metaphoric brothers and not, strictly speaking, classificatory brothers — as the Athenian *phrateres* were within the respected institutional framework of the phratry, which even the Cleisthenian reform may not have undermined very deeply.[45] It is also possible that however solemnly they may have been instituted one day in the month of Adonios, the Nakonian brotherhoods were only a temporary institution, destined to die with the last "brothers."[46] In any case, it would have been a very new institution, one not to be confused with the ancient phratries.[47] In short, the reconciled Nakonians would become *adelphoi*, five at a time and all together.[48]

We are not quite done with the paradoxes of brotherhood. The composition of these groups avoided all intersection with real kinship between the "brothers," a requirement that the decree expresses according to a model based on the legislation regulating judicial proceedings. When the moment comes to add three brothers, also drawn by lots, to the two adversaries chosen first, it is specified that the procedure must take place "excluding relatives [*agkhisteiai*] whom the law requires to be removed from the courts" (lines 17–19; cf. lines 24–25). Whether or not this reference to positive justice, which attempts to avoid familial ties in the midst of law courts,[49] is a simple practical convenience,[50] and whether this exclusion of *agkhisteia* concerns all five brothers or only the three neutral brothers,[51] is of little importance for my argument: what matters is that no real kinship bond must intersect with the bond instituted by the city. It is as if the family — too united and therefore hostile to the outside or, conversely, itself a potential source of conflict — could threaten the cohesion of the group of brothers. In the *Republic*, Plato follows a similar logic — beyond and against the family — when he proclaims a generalized kinship designed to avoid "lawsuits and accusations against one another [*dikai kai egklēmata pros allēlous*]," which invariably arise in the midst of families.[52]

These points prompt me to observe that the contradiction endlessly opposing the family to itself, eternally suspected of bringing both too much cohesion and too much division, is reformed in Nakone, just as in all Greek thought on the city.[53] The kinship at work in these brotherhoods is obviously symbolic, and it would be futile to search for an explanation in traditional procedures or legal models. This was the primary approach of the inscription's editor, who sought the mark of an "adoption in brotherhood" in the *adelphothetiai* mentioned in the text (line 33).[54] Moreover, after observing that such a notion is unknown in the Greek world and explicitly rejected by Roman law, he thought it possible to find its origins in Carthaginian practices.[55] But even if the presence of Carthaginians in Sicily can justify such a step, this explanation does not seem to me necessary, because a journey through the familial imaginary in the city makes it possible to think of this Sicilian reconciliation in purely Greek terms.[56]

For me, the pregnant significance of the fraternal model in *representations* of the unitary city[57] is in itself enough to shed light on the Nakonian invention of brotherhoods, provided we think of the latter as symbolic.[58] To bolster this explanation, I might imagine the Nakonians reading Plato's "Sicilian novel," the *Republic*, but such a fantasized imagined construction is obviously impossible to verify, and I thus will hold on to the idea, infinitely more plausible, of a sort of act that puts into operation certain shared Greek representations.

This takes nothing away from the "extraordinary" character of a procedure linking the brotherhoods with the political celebration of Homonoia in a montage in which David Asheri sees a "mixture of fictitious civic arbitration and religious festival."[59]

Brothers, Arbitrators

Some explanation is necessary if we want to speak of arbitration, whether "fictitious" or not. Although this suggestion by Asheri did not convince me in the past, I will adopt it now.[60] Without a doubt, this hypothesis complicates matters by adding one more dimension to our interpretation of the institution of brotherhoods. Yet we should not be surprised by the proliferation of significations: this is a symbolic institution, which is by definition overdetermined.

If the judiciary indeed provided a model for the first stages of the political, as Louis Gernet has forcefully claimed,[61] the occurrence of terms indistinguishably legal or political in the Nakonian inscription leads us to wonder about the significance of the legal paradigm for this reconciliation at the height of the classical period. We can note, as others have, the use of the verb *anakaleuō*, the technical term to summon someone to appear in court,[62] to call the Nakonians in front of the *halia* (line 11–12).[63] We can also note the use of the verb *prographō* (line 14) to invite the two parties to draw up the list of "adversaries," which suggests something like an accusation, with the difference that the former rebels are summoned not to a trial but to an assembly of all the citizens.[64]

But we should focus our attention on the groups of *five*, though we can only explain them through hypotheses. For example, we could insist on this number's Indo-European harmonics or its political significance, well attested in Athens by the Cleisthenian reform.[65] We could break it up into two plus three,[66] interpreting it as the first odd number that includes an extra "neutral" citizen; thus it would be a way of more securely obtaining a majority.[67] We could also attempt to shed light on the Nakonian decree by way of Athenian legal institutions, in which the number five is the basic unit in establishing juries.[68] In fact, to suggest, as Asheri does, that each group of five is supposed to proceed, even if only fictitiously, to "a mixture of juridical procedures and unofficial mediation" between its members amounts to evoking arbitral-type procedures.[69]

With regard to arbitration, it matters little whether we refer to the general Greek practice of having recourse to private arbitration, in which gaining the majority of votes is a categorical imperative, or to a genuine institution, such as that of public arbitrators in Athens.[70] The essential thing is that all these groups of arbitrators, like the foreign judges who intervene as mediators at the end of a civic *stasis*,[71] aim first and foremost at reconciling (*dialusai*) the opponents.[72]

The reference to arbitration, however, becomes more complicated when we attempt to assign an effective function to the Nakonian institution. We should not be content with claiming that an actual distinction is made in the groups of five brothers between the two initial "adversaries" and the three citizens who would occupy the position of arbitrators between them. We would be forgetting that the whole civic body, including the supposedly neutral citizens — those whom the text describes as the "rest of the citizens [*tous loipous politas pantas*]" (lines 23–24) — will also be divided into groups of five, which excludes all real arbitration, even if we imagine, as I have done, the desire to prevent generalized conflict. Indeed, what kind of arbitrators would they be if they had to arbitrate their own disagreements? As soon as the procedure is generalized, and the whole city is divided into a series of arbitration juries, the city becomes arbitrator of itself, which it could be only fictitiously.[73]

This figure can only be understood as *metaphoric*:[74] arbitrators, perhaps, but symbolic arbitrators who are only recruited so that they will have nothing to arbitrate in reality, because agreement, it is hoped, will reign in the city. Consequently, even though excluding all real kinship within these groups is borrowed from the civic rule in juridical matters, the pregnant metaphor of consanguinity must cover over the problematic one of arbitration. We also know that the chief activity of these brotherhoods, each of which is a microcosm of the city, consisted in celebrating, year after year, the festival of the ancestors and of Homonoia (*hoi politai pantes heortazonto par' allēlois kata tas adelphotetias*, lines 32–33).

Perhaps surprisingly, this decree of reconciliation ends with a festival. Yet it seems that the simple mention of a reunion between citizens after a *stasis* was enough to evoke a festive gathering, as Plato suggests in the *Menexenus* when he celebrates "the very familial joy" with which the Athenians of the Piraeus and those of the city "mixed together" in 403 B.C.[75] Even more remarkable is the official gesture with which the Nakonians inscribed their festival into civic time by assigning to it the periodicity of a regular celebration. In the city at peace, civic time is the time of the always renewed *aei* — repetitive, eventless, and theoretically free from discontinuity — by virtue of which magistrates endlessly succeed each other at the head of the city; in fact, this is how we can interpret the clause assigning to successive magistrates the task of keeping watch over this celebration every year (*hai kata podas*[76] *arkhai pasai kath' eniauton*, lines 29–30). No doubt, the citizens of Nakone thought that the repetitiveness of the festival in the duration without *pathos* of civic time would be enough to separate the recollection of the reconciliation from the memory of the conflict, erasing the past with the present of the ceremony.

Whether or not they were successful we do not know, and it would be vain to speculate — all the more so since we took an interest in the Nakonian inscription only because it presented a remarkable paradigm of civic reconciliation. Beyond the exceptional orchestration of the fraternal theme, beyond even the obvious project of making a clean sweep of the past in order henceforth to master a time free from incident, this reconciliation deserves attention for the elaborate relationship it doubly maintains with judicial procedures: because it refers to the legislation of law courts to explain the exclusion of real kinship, and especially because civic cohesion comes through the implicit yet pregnant metaphor of arbitration.

This decree from an obscure Sicilian city thus leads us back to Athens and the reconciliation of 403 B.C. Indeed, I see it as a means to illuminate one of the reconciliation's constitutive dimensions, an important dimension, though up to now little explored along our trajectory: the Athenian prohibition on reverting to trials as a way of satisfying the demands of a memory that is unwilling to forget the past.

CHAPTER TEN

Of Justice as Division

War is general and jurisdiction is strife
[*eris dikē*]...

— Heraclitus[1]

Will we finally make it back to the Athens of 403 B.C.? Before turning to the catastrophe at the end of the century, let us stop for a moment in fifth-century Athens, an Athens still enjoying its empire and its hold on Greece where, if we can believe the pamphleteering prose of the oligarchs, citizens were engaged in a frenzy of lawsuits.[2] Not surprisingly, comedy finds new inspiration in this, because it is always, and by definition, ready to criticize the democracy. Thus, in Aristophanes's *Wasps*, the old man Philocleon, suffering from an obsession with trials — which his son attempts to cure by giving him cases to judge at home — thinks he sees a very old prediction being realized:

Oft have I heard it said that the Athenians
One day would try their lawsuits in their homes,
That each would have a little Courtlet built
For his own use, in his own porch, before
His entrance, like a shrine of Hecate.[3]

By drawing this feature in such stark outlines, Aristophanes is no doubt merely exercising his trade as a comic poet. Yet even if it never happened that every Athenian organized his own pocket

229

tribunal, it is nevertheless true that all of Athens in the classical period was gripped by the idea of exercising justice. And this was because Athens was a democracy.

This, at any rate, is the link Aristotle postulates between the organization of justice and the *politeia* when he evokes, among the three most democratic features of Solon's constitution:

> permission for anyone who wished to seek retribution for those who were wronged; and third, the one which is said particularly to have contributed to the power of the masses, the right of appeal to the jury-court — for when the people are masters [*kurios*] of the vote they are masters of the state.[4]

The philosopher adds that Solon intentionally made his laws unclear to ensure that the people would always be masters of the decision [*krisis*].[5] I will not linger over this point here, but it should be remembered when we examine the verb *krinein* and the substantive *krisis* as designations of decision in Athenian law courts. It is again Aristotle who, in book 3 of the *Politics*, defines the citizen in terms of his participation in legal decisions and his right to hold office (*krisis kai arkhē*) and who then observes that this definition of the citizen must above all be attributed to democracy.[6] He elaborates this idea in book 6, mentioning among the principal features of democracy:

> that all men should sit in judgment, or that judges selected out of all should judge, in all matters, or in most and in the greatest and most important — such as the scrutiny of accounts, the constitution, and private contracts.[7]

Even Plato, though in the *Laws* he is critical of the workings of Athenian law courts, borrows from democracy the necessarily popular character of justice in matters of public accusation, specifying that even for private matters:

> As far as possible, too, all citizens should take their part in the private cases, since a man who has no share in the right to sit in judgment on others feels himself to be absolutely excluded from the city.[8]

An Insurgent Justice?

Everything is clear and simple — with the exception of one problem which we must now clarify: if the existence of a positive justice in which decisions belong to the people is in itself one of democracy's attributes, how can we explain the persistence with which the same authors — who readily criticize democracy, though they never submit it to a systematic critique — link the Athenian type of trial with dissension (*stasis*), as if there were a bond of necessity between the two?

This is what happens in Plato: the community of property and wives that characterizes the ideal city of the *Republic* aims primarily at freeing guardians from "lawsuits and accusations against one another [*dikai kai egklēmata pros allēlous*]."[9] In the *Laws*, we encounter the image of a blessed age, between the Flood and the time of present humanity, an age ignorant of the arts of war, especially those practiced

> within the city under the names of litigation and party faction [*dikai kai staseis*], with their manifold artful contrivances for the infliction of mutual injury and wrong [*kakourgein te allēlous kai adikein*] by word and by deed.[10]

Thus, with the simple juxtaposition of the substantive *dikē* and the verb *adikein*, the positive justice of trials is suddenly in the service of injustice. As for Aristotle, he occasionally mentions a court judgment among the many possible origins of *stasis*.[11] And if the philosopher does not go so far as to consider it an obvious cause of civil war, a historian such as Thucydides includes trials among the weapons used by the oligarchs eager to overthrow a democracy.[12] However, Xenophon's *Memorabilia* gives this idea its most suggestive form when Socrates scoffs at the Sophist Hippias, who thought he had found an irrefutable definition of *dikē* (justice):

> Upon my word, you mean to say that you have made a great discovery, if jurymen are to cease from voting different ways [*dikha psephizomenoi*], citizens from disputing and litigation, and wrangling about the justice of their claims, cities from quarrelling about their rights and making war [*antilegontes te kai antidikountes kai stasiazontes*].[13]

If justice, *dikē*, understood as a transcendent principle, defines the well-governed city for Greek thinkers of the political — beginning with Hesiod, whom the Greeks consider the official theologian of the *polis* — then is it enough that the same thinkers use this word in the plural, and thus give it the concrete sense of "trials," for the hideous specter of division to rise? Because it emerges so often, I have been intrigued by this theme for a long time. I will therefore attempt to shed light on this contentious point through an inquiry into the notion of the trial.

Of the Trial as a Struggle

Before examining the question more closely, we should briefly recall the most important features of Athenian trial practices, though I do not pretend to offer an exhaustive study of positive justice in the democratic city.[14]

A few essential facts should be recalled: that the great majority

232

of cases, private as well as public, are judged before popular tribunals on the initiative of a citizen — a simple private individual,
although a magistrate seems to have been the accuser in a few
cases;[15] that the trial is preceded by an *anakrisis* (an examination of
parties concerned in a suit, a preparation) before a magistrate and
is often followed by arbitration, private or public (I shall come
back to this); that the adversaries must plead their cause themselves, with the help of witnesses and possibly of *sundikoi* (who
take over for the inarticulate litigant during his pleading time, as
friends or allies but not as lawyers); that the judges — citizens enti-
tled to judge by the fact of their being citizens and having been
chosen by lots to perform this civic task for which they are duly
paid — have no other function besides listening and voting and cannot intervene by questioning the parties any more than the magistrate who has conducted the *anakrisis* and presides over the trial;[16]
finally, that the sentence ends the case, without possibility of an
appeal.[17] Thus the trial is strictly delimited in time and includes, in
good Aristotelian style, a beginning, a middle, and an end. As such,
it organizes — from its opening moments until its final term — a
regulated struggle between two adversaries.

More precisely, as Louis Gernet's impressive study has shown, the
trial is in itself a struggle (*agōn*), whether its agonistic character
was inherited from a distant past, as the great historian of Greek
law believed, or whether it was a structural element of the Athenian trial, in opposition to arbitration procedures.[18] Open struggle,
then, between two adversaries made rigorously equal: the same
speaking time (equally limited) for each and, from the beginning
to the end of the trial, the same gestures for the plaintiff and the
defendant — for example, recourse to the oath (speech act for
speech act) — so true is it that before the silent judges everything
takes place exclusively between the two parties. This is how

233

"agreeing with the spirit of *agōn*, the proofs, and especially the proof of the oath, are directed at the adversary: they are meant to compel and *convince* him."[19]

Thus the vocabulary of division occurs frequently, characterizing a procedure in which the judge's only function is to be a "divider into two [*dikhastēs*],"[20] because he decides between two arguments and because the members of the tribunal divide themselves by voting. (Recall how the judges "voted different ways [*dikha psephizomenoi*]" in Xenophon, as well as the word *diaphora*, the name for the vote, so close to *diaphoron*, disagreement.)[21] The vocabulary of division is recurrent, as attested by the abundance of *dia-* terms,[22] particularly to designate the judges' decision: for example, *diairein* (to divide into parts, hence to decide) and *diagignōskein* (to judge between two contradictory claims); likewise, *krisis*, the word for decision as choice, is intensified by the addition of a *dia* into *diakrisis*.[23] In and of itself, *krinein* remains the essential verb of the decision conceived as division.

It is *krinein*, not *dikazein*, even though the Athenian judges are traditionally called *dikastai*. The difference between *krinein* (a kind of *discernment* that in its most ancient uses suggests the idea of conflict)[24] and *dikazein* (the application of the appropriate formula [*dikē*] in an archaic phase of justice where sentence by proofs is, so to speak, mechanically determined)[25] has been the focus of many authoritative commentaries.[26] I will not elaborate this point, except to recall that "in Attic law, the judge does not apply the law to concrete cases but must resolve a disagreement, . . . a conflict between two irreconcilable arguments."[27] This means that he judges in all conscience, the word *gnōmē* describing both the intellectual process in which he engages — the bringing into play of his "discernment," the highest quality of the citizen in Thucydides — and his judgment on the crime. This judgment is at once his individual "feeling," which the city trusts completely,[28] and the resulting decision,[29] which, by virtue of the majority rule, expresses in the end the judgment not so much of individuals as of the majority, as Aristotle notes.[30]

Because all struggles lead to the victory of one of the two adversaries over the other, the judges' sovereign vote at once proclaims and constitutes this victory. Or, to take things in the reverse order: the judgment ends the struggle but is also its faithful and perfect expression. The judgment decides, but in a certain way also gives the fight its completed form by consecrating the result of the *agōn*, to which "the city remains in a sense foreign."[31] Should we go so far as to add: and, in a way, a spectator? However that may be, we can no longer avoid the question of the judges' passivity.

We know that plaintiff and defendant appeared before Athenian judges in succession, each pleading his case;[32] and then, immediately and without deliberation, the court voted, without any magistrate or public officer expressing an opinion.[33] The judges' silence is so essential to Athenian *dikē* that we can legitimately consider the trial for high treason of the generals of the Arginusae (406 B.C.), which took place in front of the *Ekklēsia*, with many citizens pleading for or against the accused,[34] less a trial, strictly speaking, than a debate of the assembly.[35] It is as if, in speaking about the issues involved in a trial, one ceased to occupy the position of judge.

Without a doubt, such a distribution of roles indicates once again that "the legal reality of the trial . . . is exhausted by the idea of struggle." The court itself does not "criticize or investigate"[36] — because the management of proofs is left entirely to the parties. And in trials in which the punishment is not fixed in advance by the law, it does not assess the penalty; it merely chooses between two adverse proposals made by the litigants.

There is much to say about the paradoxical situation that usually leads the defendant to propose for (that is, against) himself a penalty greater than what he would like in order to escape the heavier sentence always requested by his adversary.[37] This would be a good moment to appreciate, inversely, the extent of Socrates's challenge when he suggests a "punishment" that is in fact the quintessence of civic honors instead of the death penalty sought by his accusers. We could then understand how the Athenian judges, because they could not accept this request that openly mocked civic justice, had no choice but to accept the accusers' request by condemning the eccentric who proposed to be fed at the Prytaneum as his punishment.[38] This is an unusual case, to be sure, but legal thought feeds on unusual cases,[39] and the trial of Socrates, often considered from a purely ethical point of view, sheds a peculiar light on Athenian legal procedures, vividly illustrating the passivity that constrained the judges in popular trials.

But make no mistake: far from being exclusively Athenian, this constraint is very generally Greek, and, in fact, it is the *communis opinio* on the margin of initiative allowed to judges. A passage in Aristotle, who always heeds the shared opinions of common sense, will offer the proof. In book 2 of the *Politics*, Aristotle examines the constitution of Hippodamos of Miletus, which placed trials under the category of judgments and granted to judges the right to assess the punishment. The philosopher severely denounces this clause: such a practice would not only transform judges into arbitrators — and arbitration is not a judgment — but also mean that judges would then confer with each other about the sentence as arbitrators do, and:

> in courts of law this is impossible [*ouk estin*], and, indeed, most legislators take pains to prevent the judges from holding any communication with one another [*mē koinologōntai pros allēlous*].[40]

How can we interpret "this is impossible" if not as "this is not done"?[41] Thus, renewing the postulate of common opinion according to which "the only way to decide the trial by a judgment is to choose one or the other of the two parties," Aristotle transforms fact into necessity: if the judges do not deliberate, it is because they must not deliberate.[42] Perhaps, beyond Aristotelian conservatism in legal matters, we should wonder about the implications of this strange trust granted to the vote of judges who cannot ask questions, either of parties or of witnesses, and who have not shared (*koinologeisthai*) their personal questions in any discussion.[43] This would entail reflecting on the wager by virtue of which the decision resulting from the sum of individual *gnōmai* will be — by what kind of alchemy? — necessarily the good one.[44] We have come to the most difficult question, usually so poorly formulated or always supposedly solved, of the link between the individual and the collective in Athenian democracy. But I will not try to answer it, because such an endeavor goes beyond the scope of this essay — not to mention the means at my disposal.

In this case, it is better to oppose Aristotle's conservatism to Plato's boldness in the *Laws*. There Plato reflects on the possibility of a justice that would be characterized by activity, and he criticizes the Athenian trial methods — from the judges' silence during the *anakrisis* to their silence during the legal action, as well as the very principle of the secret vote.[45] Denouncing in particular the rule stating that the judge, alone of all magistrates, need not give an account of how he carries out his functions, Plato is not satisfied with the Aristophanes of the *Wasps*, who ironically shows Philocleon's pride in acting without being "called to account, something no other office holder can claim."[46] In order to conceive another administration of justice, Plato states the inverse rule, according to which no judge and no magistrate in the city of the *Laws* can render justice or exercise power without giving a full account of it.[47] This, of course, requires that judges be specially qualified — and here the whole edifice of popular justice collapses.[48] But in the meantime, Plato invents the interrogation of the parties by the judges who "shall review any omissions or errors," an interrogation that will be repeated three times before the vote takes place.[49] And, of course, the Platonic judges also intervene in the determination of the punishment.

I will not comment at any length on this very Platonic mixture of imaginative boldness and criticism of the democracy that, by reversing the Athenian reality, hopes to secure the good of the city. I would like to return to the Athenian trial to determine the extent to which its entire coherence presupposes that *dikē* — justice, but also a trial — is first and foremost a joust between two adversaries before a civic court.

We are not quite done with this definition of the trial as struggle. In the light of such a representation, we can now return to the starting point for these remarks: the bond that Greek thinkers of life in the city persistently establish between *dikē* and *stasis*, between the positive organization of justice and the "dissension" that gives its name to the worst calamity that can befall a city in Greek thought on the political. This is the point where we finally meet up once again with the Athens of 403 B.C.

Dikē, *Arbitration, and Reconciliation*

The process of arbitration keeps emerging in this account, like the very figure of the alternative to the trial. A figure all the more important in that recourse to arbitration seems to have been genuinely popular in Athens, to judge by the many allusions to it in the speeches of Athenian orators. Yet I will not be referring here to private arbitration, despite the Athenians' apparent preference for such a practice, at once discreet and unencumbered, when it came

238

to disputes that were easily resolved[50] — which actually confirms Plato's claim in the *Laws* about the "truest court [*kuriōtaton*]," defined as "that which the various litigants appoint themselves for their own cases by an agreed choice,"[51] or the Aristotelian notion according to which "the arbiter is always the one trusted, and he who is in the middle [*mesos*] is an arbiter."[52] Instead, I will be referring here to the "institution of public arbitrators in Athens,"[53] whose principle is presented in the *Athenian Constitution*:

> The arbitrators [*diaitētai*] take the cases over, and if they are unable to bring about a settlement [*dialusai*] they give a verdict [*gignōskousi*]. If both parties are satisfied with the verdict and abide by it, the case is at an end [*ekhei telos hē dikē*]. If either of the litigants appeals to the jury-court, the litigants place the testimonies, challenges and laws in jars, those of the plaintiff and those of the defendant separately; the jars are sealed, with the verdict of the arbitrator, written on a tablet, fastened to them, and handed over to the four members of the Forty who act for the tribe of the defendant. These men take over the case and introduce [*eisagousin*] it into the jury-court.[54]

In the guise of factual presentation, this text expresses the deep ambiguity in a procedure that is indeed institutionalized yet that oscillates, by its very definition, between a private arrangement and a trial: *diaitētēs* is the word for both public arbitrator and private arbitrator, and though the distinction established by Aristotle between the search for conciliation (*dialusai*) and the fact of the verdict (*gignōskousi*) seems to refer to two very different levels of jurisdiction, in reality things are not that simple. Not only can public arbitration be the preliminary phase of a trial that it helps to prepare, by defining the state of affairs and gathering proofs[55] — somewhat like an *anakrisis* — but also, because it can end in a verdict, it is already something of a trial.[56] The procedure is therefore at once flexible and rigorously codified and — I will return to this in a moment — it first appeared "in the years or the months that followed the restoration of the democracy" in 403.[57]

Whether or not arbitration represents, "in relation to the justice of law courts, a different conception that is more ancient[58] and ever renewed," as Gernet put it, the essential thing is the emphasis on conciliation in the present — to the point that when the arbitrator decides in the end, he is supposed to judge not by law but by "equity."[59] Yet in the evocation of verbs of conciliation — *diallattein* and *dialuein* — how can we not think of these other procedures that are not legal but political and that in Greek cities effect the solemn reconciliations between citizens at the end of a *stasis*,[60] reconciliations precisely called *dialusis* and *diallagē*?[61]

Here I arrive again at my initial question about the close link between *dikē* and *stasis*: if in fact we can rightly "feel, in the institution of public arbitration, the desire to put a stop to as many trials as possible before they reach the law courts" — and whether or not we see, with Gernet, this institution as a "resistance to the taking over of justice by the state"[62] — how can we not see that its creation is rooted in the politics of amnesty that characterized the restored democracy in the last years of the fifth century B.C.?

Let me venture a hypothesis. As if disgust for heavy-handed legal procedures had inspired all the city's decisions, in its effort to achieve as complete a reconciliation as possible between the citizens Athens banned recourse to trial when it implied recalling the intense pains of a too-recent past. From the same impulse, it created for the future an institution of arbitration, thereby actualizing the interest it always had in a suitable treatment of private litigations.[63] Thus all disagreements, private or public, that pitted Athenians against each other had to be channeled through, or at least diverted toward, negotiation.

Once we realize that the concrete object of the slogan *mē mnēsikakein* enjoining citizens "not to recall the misfortunes" (a euphemism for the Thirty's oligarchic dictatorship and the hate between citizens of opposing camps) was the prohibition on initiating legal proceedings related to these events that the city wanted to erase from its memory,[64] we understand better everything that associates an act of civic reconciliation, whose conciliatory essence is artificially maintained, with a procedure of arbitration,[65] but a "pure" or purified arbitration that never leads to a trial.

By forbidding all the *dikai* that could rekindle old resentments, the city no doubt sought to avoid awakening "anger" unnecessarily — the anger that sets factions against each other in a civil war,[66] but also, and this is not only an Aristophanesque *topos*, the anger of the Athenian judges against the accused.[67] In this way, the city attempted to protect itself against the threat of a continuation or a reopening of *stasis* in other quarters. And the sources support this idea of a dual purpose to the prohibition when they credit Archinus, moderate politician and great victor of the democratic restoration, both with ensuring that the amnesty be respected by inviting the Athenians to put to death without judgment a recalcitrant democrat who wanted to recall the past[68] and with being the inventor of the *paragraphē*, the "exception on the grounds of inadmissibility," illustrated by Isocrates's speech *Against Callimachus*, with which an accused could prevent a trial initiated against him by an adversary in breach of the amnesty.[69]

Thus the existence of the institution of arbitration bears witness to the Athenians' resistance to the state taking over justice. Yet the Athenians also exhibit a very different kind of resistance when two camps solemnly renounce their privilege of judgment by trial as a means of redressing their grievances and satisfying their rights: this is the resistance of a reunited city facing the

241

possibility of trials that would pursue by other means the struggles it wanted above all to forget.[70]

Stasis, Dikē: *The Case of Phlius*

Let me conclude by leaving Athens once more, to verify *a contrario* the logic thus reconstructed.

In book 5 of his *Hellenica*, Xenophon evokes the Peloponnesian city of Phlius, which in 382 B.C. experienced, to its chagrin, the difficulty of bringing a civil war to a painless conclusion. The first act of what initially seemed to be a satisfactory reconciliation consisted in deciding to allow the (pro-Spartan) exiles to return and to restore to them their property, even though this meant compensating the buyers of the property at the community's expense.[71] When the historian adds that "if any dispute should arise in any case between these purchasers and the exiles, it was to be settled by legal process [*dikēi diakrithēnai*],"[72] the reader familiar with Athenian history wonders: Do we have here a counterexample, at last? Was there at least one Greek city that was not afraid of having recourse to trials to solve disagreements following a reconciliation? But is it really a question of reconciliation? In fact, such a resolution implies that counter to all traditional practices of reinstating civic peace, no oath of amnesty was sworn between the citizens and those they had banished.

Subsequent events soon demonstrate that what seemed to be an economic solution actually was not. According to Xenophon, the inhabitants of Phlius — those anti-Spartans who were in charge of the city — refused to recognize the former exiles' rights (*tōn dikaiōn*). Using the agreement,[73] the latter asked that the disputes be settled by a tribunal but specified — or rather added — that it had to be "equal" (*en isōi dikastēriōi krinesthai*), which Jean Hatzfeld translates as "neutral."[74]

Neutral? The following sentence sheds light on what we

should understand by this word: "Their policy was to compel them to plead their cases in the city itself [*en autēi tēi polei dia-dikazesthai*]."[75] Whence it appears that appeal to a "neutral" tribunal by definition excluded recourse to a city jurisdiction; in the plaintiffs' logic, this equitable entity could only be composed of citizens from other cities,[76] those "foreign judges," arbitrators, in fact, whom Hellenistic cities would later ask to resolve their disputes, thus reviving an archaic practice.[77] And Xenophon lets the exiles speak, objecting: What kind of justice is this in which the guilty pass judgment? The "guilty" (*hoi adikountes*): this is how, in their biased language, they designate those deprived of city and property by the political order. We can well imagine that those in power were deaf to this argument, so that the others, taking the path of exile once more, went to Sparta to complain.

The solution to this problem offered by Agesilaus when Phlius finally surrendered after a long siege is drastic but also instructive. Under the pretext of introducing a new legal procedure, it actually ratified and perpetuated the division between "those from the city" — condemned by the king because of their anti-Spartan sentiments — and the others, whose sole aim was to hand the city over. Agesilaus in fact decided that "fifty men from the restored exiles and fifty from the people at home should, in the first place, make inquiry to determine [*anakrinai*][78] who ought justly to be left alive in the city and who ought to be put to death, and secondly, should draw up a constitution under which to conduct the government."[79]

Such a decision needs no comment. Obviously, the sinister selection between those who will be saved and those who will be put to death concerns only those whom the exiles designate as guilty: people from the city, who opposed Spartan maneuvers in the Peloponnese. Equally obviously, the constitutions established by Sparta are generally pro-Spartan. At the very most, we may observe that the ostensible numerical equality[80] — fifty on each side — was a delusion, because the same number of "wise men" was supposed to represent the civic body of Phlius, which was numerically great — as the historian himself, friend of Sparta and Agesilaus but even more of truth, takes care to inform the reader — and the group of exiles, which was numerically small.[81]

Phlius: a lesson in the inherent danger of entrusting the resolution of conflicts between citizens to civic tribunals? Such seems to be the Greek interpretation of this episode, and by lingering a little longer over the woes of the Peloponnesian city, we cast a stark light on the Athenian prohibition against any recourse to justice when it comes to deeds of civil war. This is a way of confirming, along different lines, the idea that the trial is perceived as a struggle, especially when the properly political struggles have ended.

If in Greek ways of thinking the trial is indeed a form of conflict, the complexity of the Athenian strategy in matters of justice is particularly interesting insofar as it simultaneously acknowledges and seeks to thwart the implications of such a state of affairs. Consequently, we can measure more clearly the stakes involved, once the democracy was restored, in maintaining distance between the safeguard of a political "agreement [*homonoia*]" and the exercise of a justice whose very working is a criterion of democracy but which democracy prefers to be minimal and private, even if it reserves the right to supervise its organization.

Such are the conclusions suggested by a historical approach that confronts the everydayness of the trial as it verges toward the timeless, in those exceptional moments that remind the citizens, against a background of powerful tensions, that politics is conflict.

CHAPTER ELEVEN

And Athenian Democracy

Forgot *Kratos*

Although not the first one in Western history, an amnesty in Athens — far removed from the present — nevertheless takes on the paradigmatic function of an origin. An amnesty in Athens, and what followed from it.

Far removed from the present? Certainly, if we count up the twenty-four centuries that separate us from the restoration of democracy in Athens in the last years of the fifth century B.C. Yet we only need to open up ancient Athenian history to the complex interaction between near and distant in the historian's theoretico-political investments to realize that we cannot give to this episode the simple frame of a purely linear and chronological temporality: short circuits between past and present are as multiple as they are necessary, and the historian must take them into account. If Marc Bloch can write that "without studying the present, it is impossible to understand the past," it is also possible, conversely, that the far-off history of the Athenian democracy constitutes a valuable experimental terrain for helping us think this present full of uncertainties, if only for the way in which such a subject forces the historian too immersed in his own present to take some distance.[1] As for myself, at the conclusion of this purely Greek journey, I would like to see in fifth-century Athens an opportunity for a "distant gaze" onto very contemporary concerns in the hopes that this methodical distancing might allow us to dissociate what is very near from the excessive clinging to the self.

An Amnesty in Athens

Let us consider the Athenian city in the years 403–400 B.C. The bloody oligarchic dictatorship of the Thirty crumbled after a battle won by the exiles' troops. Two governments in transition, the belligerence of the democrats and the active intervention of the Spartan king Pausanias end in a reconciliation with an oath of amnesty:

> I will harbour no grievance [literally: I will not recall the misfortunes] against any citizen, save only the Thirty, the Ten, and the Eleven: and even of them against none who shall consent to render account of his office.[2]

The orator Andocides, from whom I borrow the formulation of this oath,[3] hastily adds the following comment to emphasize the oath's importance:

> After swearing to forgive even the Thirty, whom you had to thank [*aitios*] for suffering untold [literally: the greatest of your misfortunes], provided that they rendered account of themselves, you can have been in very little hurry to harbour grievances against the ordinary citizen.[4]

Andocides knows what he is talking about because he was deprived of his citizen rights some time before, and he has many reasons to be happy about a politics of forgetting as deliberate as it is all encompassing. Let us now turn to the orator Lysias, a very well integrated "metic" who took the side of the exiled democrats but did not gain citizenship, as he might have hoped. Not surprisingly, he adopts a very different discourse, insisting, when he speaks in his own name, on the irreversible character of the wrong inflicted on the *dēmos* by the oligarchs:

> And whereas these men put people to death untried who were guilty of no wrong, you think fit to try according to law [*kata ton nomon*] the persons who destroyed the city, and whose punishment by you, even if unlawfully devised [*paranomos boulomenoi*], would still be inadequate to the wrongs that they have committed against the city. For what would they have to suffer, if their punishment should be adequate to their actions? ... Since therefore, whatever you might do, you could not exact from them an adequate penalty, would it not be shameful [*aiskhron*] of you to disallow any possible sort of penalty that a man might desire to exact from these persons?[5]

Lysias's position, like Andocides's, can probably be explained by his recent history: it is in the democratic orator's interest to plead for vengeance, because he is suing one of the Thirty,[6] whom he considers responsible for his brother's iniquitous execution. By initiating a lawsuit (*dikē*) — one of those trials that the oath of amnesty specifically tried to prohibit (whence the allusion to the eventual illegality of the punishment) — he is demanding justice and punishment, indissociably and under the name of *dikē*, repeating to the judges that they "now have reached the moment in which [their] thoughts must have no room for pardon or for pity."[7]

In another speech, Lysias repeats that the democrats have much to lose because of this prohibition on recalling the past, whereas the "people from the city" have gained by it; in fact, he claims that "the latter have received no less honour from the city than those who marched on Phyle and got possession of the Piraeus."[8] He also insists more than once, in the context of other trials, on how justified the democrats would be in manifesting their resentment in deeds (*mnēsikakein*).[9] Yet I find confirmation of this notion in another orator, precisely because he does not share Lysias's democratic convictions. I'm speaking of Isocrates, who notes that the people coming back from the Piraeus — meaning the democrats — would have to assert their rights, even if no one "has had the audacity to introduce such a suit."[10] Of course, in a speech on behalf of a man from the city, Lysias makes a very different argument, claiming that some "consider that their perils in the Piraeus give them license now to do just as they please."[11] But in this case, the undemocratic logic is attributable to his occupation as a logographer, by definition expected to side with his client, who will defend himself during his trial with the speech composed for him by the orator.

In short, the behavior of the *dēmos* in this amnesty brought the Athenian democracy widespread praise, which, repeated countless times, is a major addition to the already thick chapter of eulogies of Athens: thus Aristotle will oppose the behavior of the Athenian *dēmos* to that of the *dēmos* of other cities, who readily took much more radical measures in similar cases.[12] Yet everything indicates that in those last few years of the fifth century B.C., an entire century of democracy — the democracy of Cleisthenes, Ephialtes, and Pericles, which I consider the golden century of *dēmokratia*[13] — tumbled into the past.

It is a past that the city wants to be certain is really past and that nevertheless does not pass so easily. But let us not anticipate. First, I would like to return to the behavior of the democrats, victors who immediately bound themselves by an oath of amnesty.

How to Obtain Pardon for a Victory

Almost all authors of the fourth century B.C. affirm that the democrats were indeed the victors in these struggles at the end of the fifth century. There is, first of all, Aristotle's pithy account of the events in his *Athenian Constitution*, where he not only mentions the democrats' military victory over the army of oligarchs (*epekratoun tōi polemoi*) but also the political legitimacy of the people's reconquest of power, the people who "have made themselves masters [*kurios genomenos*] of everything, and control all things by means of decrees and jury-courts, in which the sovereign power resides with the people."[14] Moreover, after listing every change of regime the city has undergone since its origins until this return of the *dēmos*, Aristotle again describes the people as "sovereign" (*kurios*), repeating that they "have made themselves masters of everything."[15] Such an interpretation is certainly consistent with the teleological perspective of the *Athenian Constitution*, in which this episode marks the beginning of the fulfillment of the *politeia*, and when Aristotle specifies that from now on they "control all things by means of decrees and jury-courts [*ho dēmos estin ho kraton*]," we should see a comment on the very name — *dēmokratia* — of the regime that has finally reached its *telos*. Yet this interpretation of the facts is not unique to Aristotle; other fourth-century writers,[16] including Lysias and Isocrates, also speak of the *kratos* of the people when they write about civil struggles, but it is a less political *kratos* than that obtained through the use of weapons. Thus Isocrates refers to a moment "after the Thirty had been expelled, the Piraeus had been taken, and when the democracy was in power [*ekratei*]"; but we might as well quote Lysias, for whom the democrats won (*nikēsantes*) and have "superiority [*kreittous*] to the city's foes in [your] fighting."[17] I shall rely on this interpretation of the facts because it was the contemporary interpretation, although it will certainly awaken some skepticism among modern historians of Greece.[18]

Let us consider *kratos*. One still has to come to terms with it. With all the negative connotations of any claim to a "victory" or a "superiority" internal to the city, the word *kratos* is in itself risky.[19] The same is true of its derivative *dēmokratia*, which the democrats used only reluctantly or with reservations throughout the fifth century B.C.,[20] perhaps because, as Aristotle does in book 2 of the *Politics*, they made a distinction between constitutions worthy of that name, grounded in the common welfare, and those that existed only by superiority (which is what "democracy" literally means),[21] and they were therefore afraid that *dēmokratia*, with a name that says the "victory of the people," was not on the right side. Now we have to recognize an unexpected truth: far from seeking to obscure the *kratos* of the democrats, their contemporaries, from all political leanings, seem to have insisted on it, and such a consensus is troubling.

To explain such an insistence, I propose a hypothesis: are not those who favor the version that grants full victory to the people trying to weigh down the *dēmos* with a crushing responsibility? Some, like Lysias in *Against Eratosthenes*, have no second thoughts and incite the *dēmos* to punish its adversaries by recalling the wrongs inflicted; moreover, they exalt the regained power, which the people owe it to themselves to use in order to punish the guilty. Yet others, whose declarations are infinitely more troubling, also insist on the *kratos* of the people but argue that they must seek if not the goodwill, at least the neutrality of the democrats, because they stayed in the city under the dictatorship of the Thirty.

These latter are interesting to me because, as Isocrates's *Against Callimachus* attests, they did not hesitate, when they were being pursued in court, to obtain the favor of popular judges by assigning to the victors' generosity the most troublesome obligations, beginning with the duty of clemency.[22] I hear in this a late echo of Plutarch's rhetoric in a passage of *Table Talk* where he compares the mildness of Thrasybulus, the leader of the Piraeus democrats, toward his fellow citizens with that of Poseidon toward the Athenians after they had chosen Athena as their protecting divinity,

and he infers the superiority of the loser over the winner in matters of generosity.[23] It is as if nothing were easier for the winner
in a civil war than to be generous.

This is a strange idea, to be sure, but without a doubt a Greek
idea on the best way to come out of a *stasis*. Thus, when Thucydides claims that during the Peloponnesian War, civil wars were
lacking in that elegance of the winner in victory, the very formulation of the sentence — "if an opponent made a reasonable speech,
the party in power, so far from giving it a generous reception, took
every precaution to see that it had no practical effect" — seems to
indicate that the loser did not find in the winner the "nobility"
(*gennaiotēs*) appropriate in such a case according to the implicit
code of reconciliation.[24] Is congratulating Poseidon for having
renounced his resentment despite his loss a way of suggesting that
the *dēmos* should have been grateful to the people of the city, the
losers, for having agreed to the return of the winners? We can
imagine the extremes to which this paradoxical logic could lead.

According to my hypothesis, this is how, through a reversal of
what seemed evident, one would never cease to remind the democrats of their victory, the better to suggest to them that they had to
forget this victory, since they had won it by forgetting how great a
wrong they had suffered. The administration of justice is considered a species of sovereignty:[25] what better proof of their *kratos*
can the people give than to renounce administering justice by forbidding themselves to initiate lawsuits? Forgetting victory in
exchange for forgetting resentment: one forgetting for another, it
would seem. But who could not see that the same camp was
required to face the consequences of this double forgetting?

The fact remains that the people, thus endowed with *kratos*, internalized the lesson so often repeated to them. Not only did they
not use this *kratos* to "take over" the city, as victorious factions

251

often do when they are actually superior,[26] but, proceeding to a fair division of civic rights among "all the Athenians" — that is, with the other Athenians — the democrats managed to transform the behavior that had been so insistently suggested to them into a title of glory.[27] Such behavior, they say, was necessary to reassure respectable citizens and thus to maintain, perhaps even to "save," the democracy. Not surprisingly, the speeches of city people most often elaborate on this argument in the form of discreet blackmail.

Thus, appearing before a popular tribunal, one of these quiet Athenians who had turned a blind eye to the Thirty's abuses generously begins — like Poseidon in Plutarch — by forgiving the judges for the anger that could be awakened in them by recalling the past.[28] After this, taking refuge behind the Piraeus fighters, the most prestigious of whom "had often before exhorted your people to abide by their oaths and covenants," he claims that these same leaders "held this to be the bulwark of democracy."[29] Isocrates's *Against Callimachus* similarly exhorts the Athenians to "save" (*diaphulattein*) the current regime by their moderation.[30] And finally, according to Aristotle, the moderate Archinus also invited his fellow citizens to "save the democracy [*dēmokratian sōzein*]" by respecting the oath of amnesty when he put to death the first recalcitrant democrat.[31] It is as if the democrats would have made democracy fragile by taking up their *kratos* too openly.

It was thus that moderate politicians, through a remarkable process, diverted this very victory they did not cease solemnly to recall. This is how a cult of *dēmokratia* was established, as well as a festival of freedom in honor of the return from Phyle.[32] It is particularly relevant here that Phyle is celebrated under these circumstances. Phyle, a fort in the north of Attica, was actually the point of departure for the reconquest and not the more reprehensible Piraeus, where the troops subsequently gathered, troops that we know were "mixed" with democrats.[33] In fact, it seems that in this case the choice of appellation was a matter of political leaning, with the moderate Archinus's allies reducing the democrats to a small group of "men of Phyle,"[34] whereas Thrasybulus's party spoke of "the men of the Piraeus,"[35] and the same Lysias who referred to the Piraeus when speaking in his own name readily put all the weight on the "return from Phyle" when he composed a speech on behalf of a "good citizen."[36]

Setting Phyle against the Piraeus initiates a fruitful ideological operation. Clearly, this was a way of dispossessing Thrasybulus, who seized Phyle, of the glory attached to the first phase of the reconquest and of benefiting Archinus, great political winner of that time and an uncompromisingly loyal guardian of the oath, the same one who secured public calm and recovered legality with the blood of the first democrat bold enough to disobey the prohibition on remembering.[37] Thus it is easy for Hermes, in Aristophanes's *Ploutos*, to call on the spirit of Phyle to caution the insolent Carion: "Don't bear malice [*mē mnēsikakēseis*], if you've Phyle got!"[38] Let us take one more step, since many texts permit us to do so, and observe that behind the moderate democrat Archinus, the moderate oligarch Theramenes was actually rehabilitated.[39] With this, we have reconstructed the main points of this ideological operation.

This is how the people who were only lukewarm toward the Athenian democracy were able to praise the moderation (*metriotēs*),[40] and even the "correctness,"[41] that characterized the behavior of the *dēmos* in this period. And those who, like Lysias, offered a bitter diagnosis were few:

> The people, after recalling them [the exiles], restored your city to you, but did not venture to participate in it themselves [*autos de tautes ouk etolmēse metaskhein*].[42]

We can no doubt return without delay to the treatment of memory in this matter. Before doing so, however, one question, which I will not avoid, emerges: what happens to *dēmokratia* at the conclusion of this process?

Where Dēmokratia *Loses* Kratos

Under the praise, the embalming. Despite the establishment of a cult of *dēmokratia*, nothing indicates that *dēmokratia* — the thing, but also the word — has become acceptable. *Kratos* is more audible than ever, but not until the Hellenistic period, or even Roman uses of the word,[43] will *kratos* cease to reverberate in *dēmokratia*. For the time being, several strategies of avoidance are at work.

The first, and simplest, consists in substituting *politeia* for *dēmokratia*, the name of the constitution for that of the democracy. Isocrates excels at this, from the *Panegyricus*, where he repeatedly evokes the "Athenian constitution" without using its name,[44] to the *Panathenaicus*, in which, after opposing the "present constitution" to the old one at great length, he claims that neither the word "oligarchy" nor the word "democracy" existed in the time of the old constitution.[45] And perhaps the thought of Aristotle also belongs under this category of avoidance through substitution: when he defines what he considers the best government in the *Politics*, he gives it the name *politeia* despite all its similarities with a democracy — just as we might speak of a government named "the government."

The second strategy consists in avoiding not the word "democracy" — it is even pronounced with a certain emphasis — but its historical reality, since something very different from democracy is expressed in the term "ancient democracy." Isocrates again stands out, and if he opposes "badly constituted democracies" to those that are "well-ordered"[46] in the name of the "excellence of government,"[47] it is only to cast the first category into the most distant past — a thousand years of democracy, from Theseus to Solon?[48] But also: what could be more *hic et nunc* than the dazzling memory of this radiant past?[49]

The third strategy is less complex in that it does not try to use the word that must be neutralized, and in this refusal of an oblique approach, one might see in it a version of the two preceding strategies for the use of democrats. At any rate, I see it as the discourse through which the restored democracy sought to master time by smoothing out the vicissitudes of its history. Because all constitutions are subject to changes and reversals (*metabolai*), it is best to anchor them in the perpetuity of the city: *polis* then becomes the operative word in discourses on the City, which is presupposed untouched in its essence by all the upheavals that affect its constitution because it has time on its side, a time that looks strangely like eternity.[50] Consequently, it cannot be modified by the "misfortunes" (*kaka*) that the Athenians swear one by one to forget. The city is no doubt the subject that once underwent the misfortunes, but now that it is time to put them in the past, it comes to terms with them, with the strange responsibility of one who was not responsible for them, on the condition that the good version be the official one[51] — the "political" version, in the sense of the term that implies the erasure of conflict.[52]

We could doubtless find many indications in Athenian writings on political theory that *polis* became the most important word of the democracy in the fourth century B.C., much more important than *dēmokratia* and even *politeia*.[53] Yet what interests me are the narratives of the 403 reconciliation, especially when they speak of the reimbursement of the debt incurred by the Thirty.

The story is well known: after the Thirty borrowed money from the Lacedaemonians "for the war," as Aristotle puts it (that is, the war against the democrats), the winning *dēmos* shared in the reimbursement of the borrowed money, even though the agreements stipulated that the two sides would repay their own debts separately.[54] This is a revealing episode, which fed the orators' patriotic rhetoric for a century: by choosing to share the debt of the people of the City, the democracy, they say, put itself in the service of the City, one and indivisible, beyond the rifts of history and the conflicts among citizens.

Notably, the principal aim of this evocation of an idealized City is in fact forgetting; the narrative allows the erasure of everything that precedes it, especially the actual modalities of the political takeover. In what language, indeed, could they recognize that the Thirty were magistrates in the real city of 404–403 B.C., exercising the power (*arkhē*) that the Athenians had handed over to them through fear or despondency?[55] We can understand why silence was acceptable on this decisive moment when the democracy let itself be divested of itself, and why there is something like a consensus in favor of evoking the finer hours of the reconciliation. This brings me back to the edifying episode of the debt.

Considering the reimbursement of the debt as an even more remarkable act than the prohibition against trials bearing on the recent past (*ou gar monon tas peri tōn proterōn aitias exeleipsan alla kai*) — because this gesture was the first step toward establishing concord between the citizens (*homonoia*)[56] — Aristotle says that the Athenians, individually and collectively, "reacted to their previous misfortunes ... better and more public-spiritedly than anyone else at any other time" [*kallista kai politikōtata*].[57] He adds that "when democracies come to power in other cities, however, far from making voluntary payments out of their own property, the democrats redistribute the land."

In other words, whereas in other cities the *dēmos* forgets nothing of the harm done and proceeds to redistribute the land, a practice that ever since the archaic period has been a symbol of subversion, in Athens the people behave *politikōtata*. That is, not only were the democrats in a sense Aristotelians long before the term existed,[58] because they ensured the continuity of the *polis* beyond "misfortunes" and "changes" of constitution, but also they defined politics as the practice of forgetting, forgetting less their grievances than the very content of the word *dēmokratia*, which presupposes an active presence of the people in their *kratos* — this active presence that the Homeric poems simply call "memory."

Thus is inaugurated the *topos* of the praise of Athens as the city of *homonoia*,[59] or rather, of the Athenian democracy as the paradigm of the City, an ideological construction that we have inherited and from which I dare say we have not escaped. Yet how could we escape it when the entire tradition took it up *ad nauseam*? The words Demosthenes uses to evoke the episode of the debt attest to this. Although Demosthenes accurately names the adversary fought by the Thirty ("those of the Piraeus") and emphasizes the people's initiative on the reimbursement,[60] he justifies this attitude in terms of the reunification of the city (*epeidē hē polis eis hen ēlthen*), not of the democracy, and, like Aristotle, he considers this gesture "the first sign of reconciliation."[61]

If to deserve the title "political," it is advisable to have been linked to a nondemocratic government — for no democrat receives such great praise from Aristotle as one Rhinon, who, after becoming a member of a body of magistrates who succeeded the Thirty during the oligarchy, gave a satisfactory account of his acts under the democracy[62] — there is no doubt that in speaking of Athens, *polis* is a much more satisfying word than *dēmokratia*. The restored democracy sought to distance itself from *kratos* to such a degree that, putting the common interest first, it was on the verge of asking the citizens to forget that the oligarchy ever existed.

In fact, it would be simplistic to assign responsibility for such a policy to the "moderates" alone.[63] The figure of the *polis* as the unique subject of Athenian history was adopted as a rallying point by the democrats because, pained at having fought against their fellow citizens, they identified more readily with the recovered unity.

Here I return again to my point of departure: the question "why do you wish to kill us?" in Xenophon's account of the democrat Cleocritus's speech at the conclusion of the battle of the Mounichia; and this entire speech, centered on the values of communal life, with which the winners recall that they never shirked their civic duty and seem to seek from the losers a recognition of their status as citizens.[64] Of course, this speech expressed only one of many sentiments of the time: we can ascertain this by comparing the *pathos* of Cleocritus's speech with the much harsher tone of Thrasybulus's harangue before the fight.[65] It is all the more interesting, then, to realize that in his speech to the assembly after the official return of the men of the Piraeus, Thrasybulus, who had been very firm in his speech to the people of the town, now simply reminds the democrats of their necessary allegiance to the oath and still adds an explicit recommendation to avoid all "trouble."[66]

Shall we say that once the people have shown themselves to be the city, they must espouse communal life? I would answer that an appeal to the *polis*, however justified it may have been in its time, later became very effective in neutralizing *dēmokratia*. Or more precisely: in neutralizing *kratos* as an integral part of the word. From then on, Athenian orators, like Isocrates in the *Areopagiticus*,[67] praised the democracy for its "mildness" (which they had no difficulty in opposing to the excesses of the Thirty).[68]

Yet after noting the very selective treatment of the memory of the oligarchy, we still wonder about what happens to the memory of Athens.

A Memory in the Service of Forgetting

If we are to believe the Athenian orators, then one thing is clear: the break introduced by what is conventionally called "the misfortunes" of the city was so violent that never again, absolutely never, would Athens know any other constitutional change. Thus a proposal made by the moderate party to limit access to the civic body exclusively to landowners was rejected. Lysias, in the speech he composed for this occasion, was already incensed at not being able to count on the unerasable intensity of the memory of misfortunes:

> We were supposing, men of Athens, that the disasters that have befallen her have left behind them sufficient reminders [*hikana mnēmeia*] to the city to prevent even our descendants from desiring a change of constitution.[69]

Is this the result of the recall to memory ("it is not at them that I wonder, but at you who listen to them, for being the most forgetful of mankind.... What, I ask, was the object of returning from your exile, if by your votes you are to enslave yourselves?")?[70] In any case, the proposal was rejected. This was a way of proclaiming that after the disastrous interlude of the oligarchic government, the history of the Athenian constitution was definitively closed. Aristotle bears witness to this: for him, the evolution from the return from the Piraeus, considered the eleventh, and last, *metabole*, up to the constitution "in force today" (*hē nun katastasis*) is the government's progression toward the full completion of its *telos*, by granting ever-greater powers to the greater number.[71]

Should we say that here the philosopher is content with giving a theoretical dimension to the Athenian representation of the internal history of Athens? Do not be deceived: distinguishing between a "before" and a "now," as Aristotle does throughout his

259

narrative,[72] amounts to recognizing the importance of this break, which the democrats would rather erase insofar as their goal was to exorcise the effect of the rift. Consequently, they presented the period of the Thirty as a violent interlude that in no way prevented their constitution from being inherited from that of their fathers, with, so to speak, no solution of continuity.[73]

Whether we like it or not, this meant thinking the future in the past. This is how Thrasybulus, in his first speech to the assembly of all the Athenians, will advise them to "live under the laws that had previously been in force [*tois nomois tois arkhaiois*]."[74] Because *arkhaios* means "ancient, that which goes back to the origins,"[75] one might well recall that in the eyes of a fourth-century democrat, the democracy by definition goes back to the origins.[76] Nevertheless, Thrasybulus carries out his inaugurating gesture by associating himself with the current that grounds *arkhē* (legitimate power) in *arkhē* (the beginning of history).[77] This movement is certainly powerful, feeding as it does on the desire to have a history without shadows, and this is how we can explain the inclination perceptible in fourth-century Athenian writers, even those least suspicious of democratic leanings, to look toward the Athens of the previous century. This is what happens with Plato, who never ceases to think of Athens in terms of the past.

But in reality, the dialectic between past and present is complicated, because we can only accept the present, which we acknowledge with so many difficulties, on condition of transferring it to the past. This is how credit for "having brought back the people," according to a formulation belonging, strictly speaking, to Thrasybulus,[78] is retrospectively attributed to Cleisthenes,[79] otherwise credited, like Thrasybulus, only with restoring the democracy — that of Solon.[80] Thus a double ideological operation is carried out: by being projected into the past, the democratic meaning of Thrasybulus's deed, losing all relevance in the present, is attenuated, if not hidden, while Cleisthenes, usually pushed aside as founder of the democracy in Athenian memory,[81] becomes an acceptable figure as restorer of the "democracy of Solon,"[82] just as Thrasybulus was an acceptable figure of the actual democracy of Pericles. It is as if the present were thinkable only in the past, on condition, however, that the past, stripped of all potentially subversive value, only be used as an edifying model.[83] To disarm, one by the other, the present and the distant past: this is political memory's great strategy for forgetting the most recent past.

This hardly means that the *trauma* of the recent past was definitively overcome. In legal speeches during trials that did take place, the history of the last years of the fifth century was tirelessly remade. Yet it was made under the surveillance of the prohibition of memory. This brings me back one last time to the formulation of the prohibition.

Mē mnēsikakein: although the negative formula in itself suggests that the prohibition of memory actually sealed the past, it was up to the Athenian judges — each one alone with his conscience, just as he was when he swore his oath not to recall the misfortunes[84] — to decide with their *gnōmē*, case by case, whether a particular trial went against the prohibition. Paradoxically, it became necessary to focus more on the recall than on the forgetting, on the *mnēsikakein* more than on the negative prescription *mē*. "Please forget": this utterance is about as viable as the "please ignore" implicit in the subtraction of a contentious date from the Athenian calendar,[85] or the "please keep your eyes closed" in Freud's famous dream.[86]

I wonder: what if banning memory had no other consequences than to accentuate a hyperbolized, though fixed, memory? It is thus that from the end of the fifth century on, the Athenians, in order better to control their most recent past, never ceased to

261

keep watch over the narrative of this past. In fact, by studying speeches from the first two decades of the fourth century, we could draw up a very complete typology of the variations found there on the topic of memory.

Some speeches, such as Lysias's *Against Eratosthenes* and *Against Agoratus*, explicitly struggle against forgetting:[87] they are addressed to the judges' memory, and they ask this memory, in the form of judgment (*gnōmē*) on the recent events,[88] to turn into a decision of justice (*gnōmē*).[89] *Dikē* is here associated with vengeance (*timōria*), and the appeal to the anger of the judges — or to that of the democrats among them — must have been very persuasive. Other speeches, written on behalf of someone from the city, insist, as we have seen, on the necessary loyalty to the amnesty. Another speech, written for Nicias's nephews, who were attempting to get their father's property, which had been confiscated by the *dēmos*, emphasizes this same sense of loyalty.[90] The argument about memory in this speech, paradoxical in itself, deserves further study. After having claimed that "*homonoia* is the greatest boon to a city" whereas conflict (*stasis*) is the source of all evils, the orator adds:

> This was your conclusion [*egnōte*] shortly after your return, and your reasoning was sound; for you still remembered the disasters that had occurred [*eti gar emēmnesthe tōn gegenemēnōn sumphorōn*], and you prayed to the gods to restore the city to unanimity rather than permit the pursuit of vengeance for what was overpast to lead to faction in the city [*tēn polin stasiasai*] and the rapid enrichment of the speech-makers. And yet it would have been more pardonable [*pleion suggnomen*] to show resentment [*mnēsikakein*] shortly after you had returned, while your anger [*orgē*] was freshly kindled.[91]

In other words, although the Athenians had excellent grounds to be severe, it is precisely because they remembered the past that

they forbade anyone to recall it. Thus the orator tactfully addresses his two audiences, who are sitting next to each other in
the court: Thrasybulus's companions, among whom the allusion
to the legitimacy of their anger aims at rousing sympathy for the
plaintiff, and the people from the city, including Archinus's allies,
who like to hear the amnesty praised.

This is certainly a complex strategy for a discourse that resembles an *ainos* in its attempt to communicate two messages at
once.[92] But there may be more than one strategy at work in the
claim that memory alone can decree forgetting: the prohibition of
memory may affect the very definition of memory; and the will
to memory may take refuge in recalling why memory limited its
own existence. Still, the fact remains — and this will be the conclusion of this too-short study — that the "people of the city," who
wished that all memory of a conflictual episode would disappear,
were clearly more at ease in a situation in which the *dēmos*, while
well aware that they had been wronged,[93] paradoxically saw
themselves repeatedly driven to provide proof that they were not
at fault.[94] Thus just after the battle of Mounichia, Cleocritus's
conciliatory speech to those adversaries who are his fellow citizens claims, "We never did you any harm,"[95] whereas Thrasybulus, who had reminded his men before the battle that they had
done and were doing no injustice,[96] repeats, when addressing the
people from the city during his intervention before all the Athenians at the first full assembly, that the people "never did you any
wrong [*ho dēmos ... ouden pōpote ... humas edikesen*]."[97] If the
democratic leader is eager to evoke "this unjustly treated people"
as he notes that their allies, the Spartans, have abandoned the
Athenians to their victims' anger, it is only the better to remind
the *dēmos* to be loyal to their oath of amnesty.[98] It is as if, in this
language of the just and the unjust that the people chose over
kratos, the winner could only claim his right in the problematic

263

mode of the double negation, endlessly repeating that he has not been unjust.

I here conclude this journey through a history that is very ancient yet whose overtones ring in our ears, in 1994, with a certain familiarity. Whether one is French or German, if we want to ensure that the memory of the 1940s does not disappear with the death of the last eyewitnesses, we must know how much energy, even how much daring, it takes tirelessly to recall that there is no prescription for war crimes before justice or vigilantly to disturb the public peace that is easily satisfied with monuments raised "to all the victims of the war."[99] This does not mean that collectivities, like individuals, should not know the slow work of mourning — which is the incorporation of a painful or conflictual past, not a rejection or distancing of it.[100] Whoever speaks of mourning does not speak of forgetting, and we know that in individual psyches, the unconscious watches over the past — the unconscious that Lacan superbly defined as being in man "the memory of what he forgets."[101] Is it expecting too much from our contemporaries and from ourselves to wish that in each collectivity, an analogous memory, all the more forceful for not being domesticated, would — in order finally to think the future — make a place for the "misfortunes" that we would like not to be ours and that we say are past?

Notes

Preface

1. Loraux here uses the term "le politique," which is to be distinguished from the more common "la politique," meaning politics. "Le politique" is a more conceptual term than "la politique" and designates less political activity or a particular political position than, more broadly, that which is political, or, in a sense, the political form of human social life in general. To maintain this distinction, I have translated "le politique" as "the political" whenever doing so did not require overly awkward English constructions. — TRANS.

CHAPTER ONE: TO FORGET IN THE CITY
A first version of this essay was published in the "Recherches" section of *Temps de la réflexion* 1 (1980).

1. Plutarch, *Table Talk* 9.6741b. vol. 9. The key term throughout Loraux's arguments (and in the book's subtitle) is the noun *oubli* (from *oublier*, to forget), which can be rendered as "oblivion," "forgetfulness," or "forgetting." In this translation, the last of these is the most frequently used by far, except in cases where the meaning seems closer to one of the others; but it should be noted that all three of these terms render the same French noun. — TRANS.

2. See below, Chapter 11.

3. This does not mean that it was either the first reconciliation in Greek history or the first instance of the oath "not to recall the misfortunes." But as far as

Western historiography is concerned, this Athenian episode is paradigmatic and, like Aristotle's city, logically if not chronologically prior.

4. See below, Chapter 2.

5. Thus, to limit myself to a single example already old but meaningful, the same Glotz of *La Cité grecque* forgets that he wrote a dissertation titled "La Solidarité de la famille dans le droit grec" (1904).

6. See Nicole Loraux, "Thucydide n'est pas un collègue," *Quaderni di storia* 12 (1980), pp. 55–81. On the specificity of Greek historical writing, see also Catherine Darbo-Peschanski, "L'Historien ou le passé jugé," in Nicole Loraux and Carlos Miralles (eds.), *Figures de l'intellectuel en Grèce ancienne* (Paris: Belin, 1998).

7. See, in general, Detienne and Vernant, eds., *Cuisine of Sacrifice Among the Greeks*.

8. Neither Hartog, *Mirror of Herodotus*, nor P. Payen, "Les Iles Nomades: Comment résister à la conquête chez Hérodote" (Ph. D. diss., Ecole des Hautes Etudes de Sciences Sociales, 1994), denies this obvious fact, although both of them, rightly, want to show the deep unity of Herodotus's work.

9. Not unlike the way François Furet wishes to "cool off" the object of the French Revolution in *Interpreting the French Revolution*, trans. Elborg Forster (Cambridge, UK: Cambridge University Press, 1981), p. 10.

10. Since 1980, when these pages were written, things have notably changed among historians, if only because a large number of them have internalized anthropological questions.

11. Thrasybulus, in Xenophon's *Hellenica* 2.4.14.

12. To borrow this notion from Marcel Detienne, who readily theorizes it.

13. See, for example, Aristotle, *Politics* 5.1.1301a28ff. About Aristotle's interpretation of *stasis*, see Loraux, "Corcyre 427, Paris 1871."

14. This is how one anthropologist of ancient Greece understands *stasis*; see Frontisi-Ducroux, "Artémis bucolique," and my critique of this stance in "La Guerre civile grecque."

15. See Detienne, *Dionysos mis à mort*, pp. 143–44, and Marcel Detienne and Jesper Svenbro, "The Feast of the Wolves, or the Impossible City," in Detienne and Vernant (eds.), *Cuisine of Sacrifice Among the Greeks*, pp. 156–58.

16. Aristotle, *Athenian Constitution* 25.4.

17. Lefort and Gauchet, "Sur la démocratie."

18. Vernant gives an excellent definition in *Origins of Greek Thought*, p. 42. On vote counting as a Greek invention, see J.A.O. Larsen "The Origins of the Counting of Votes," *Classical Philology* 44 (1949), pp. 164–81.

19. See A.E. Raubitschek, "Athenian Ostracism," *Classical Journal* 48.4 (1953), pp. 113–22, as well as E. Vanderpool, "Ostracism at Athens," *Semple Lecture II 1966–1971, University of Cincinnati Classical Studies* (1973), pp. 217–50.

20. See Loraux, "La Majorité, le tout et la moitié."

21. Pierre Vidal-Naquet, in the article about Greece in *Encyclopaedia universalis* (Paris: 1970), vol. 7, p. 1019. This sentence is restated in "A Civilization of Political Discourse," in Vidal-Naquet, *Black Hunter*.

22. See below, Chapter 2; and see below, Chapter 10, about justice as division.

23. Homer, *Iliad*, 18.502.

24. *Ibid.* 18.508.

25. *Ibid.* 18.490–510, with commentary by Gernet, *Anthropology of Ancient Greece*, pp. 188–90, and especially Benveniste, *Vocabulaire des institutions indo-européennes*, vol. 2, pp. 240–42. About the good king's words, see Hesiod, *Theogony* 89–90; Aeschylus, *Eumenides* 858–66.

26. It would be appropriate to quote the entire page of Finley's book, *Economy and Society in Ancient Greece*, p. 94. About the "natural" character of the condemnation of *stasis*, see, for example, C.W. MacLeod, "L'unità dell'*Orestea*," *Maia* 2 (1973), pp. 274–75.

27. Hesiod, *Works and Days* 29–30; Hesiod, *Theogony* 86–90; Lysias, *Funeral Oration* 61; Aeschylus, *Eumenides* 903.

28. Thucydides 3.73–74.1. About the women, see Loraux, *Experiences of Tiresias*, pp. 227–48.

29. See Loraux, "Corcyre 427, Paris 1871," p. 188.

30. In Glotz, *La Cité grecque*, compare pp. 113–14 and 66–69.

31. See the brief but suggestive remarks of C. Ampolo, "Commentary," in Molho, Raaflaub, and Emlen (eds.), *City States in Classical Antiquity and Medieval Italy*, pp. 115–16.

32. In Loraux, *Invention of Athens*.

33. About the meaning of *kratos*, see Benveniste, *Vocabulaire des institutions indo-européennes*, vol. 2, pp. 74–77.

34. I summarize here the essential points of my *Children of Athena*.

35. Xenophon, *Hellenica* 2.4.20–22.

36. Plato, *Menexenus* 243–44a and 238a–39a. See the analysis of this text in Loraux, "*Oikeios polemos.*"

37. Similarly, Isocrates, *Panathenaicus* 48.120–25, opposes the origin myths of other cities, which are conspicuous for murder and crimes, to the Athenian one, characterized by peace reached through autochthony.

38. See Loraux, "*Oikeios polemos.*"

39. Aeschylus, *Eumenides* 858–66. In line 851, Athena describes all the other places where the Erinyes could go as *allophulon khthona* (a land of foreigners).

40. About the *isopsephos* ruling and Athena's "vote," see Loraux, "La Majorité, le tout et la moitié."

41. The contrast is even more striking in the French translation, which has the word "chest" (*poitrine*) instead of "viscera" (*entrailles*) — TRANS.

42. On the *Oresteia* in particular, see Loraux, "La Métaphore sans métaphore."

43. On *stasis* and sacrifice, see Detienne and Svenbro, "Feast of the Wolves," pp. 159–61. On *stasis* as killer of youths, see Aeschylus's *Eumenides* 956–57; *splankhnon neon* (859–60) evokes the *splankhna* of Thyestes's children (Aeschylus, *Agamemnon* 1221).

44. On the *oikeia kaka* (private ills) in Herodotus's description of Phrynichus's *Capture of Miletus*, and what it implies for Greek tragedy, see below, Chapter 6, as well as Vernant and Vidal-Naquet, "The Tragic Subject: Historicity and Transhistoricity," in *Myth and Tragedy in Ancient Greece*, pp. 237–48.

45. *Allēlophonous manias*: Aeschylus, *Agamemnon* 1575–78. In Arcadia, where the verb *erinuein* is equivalent to *thumōi khresthai*, to be furious (Pausanias 8.25.6), the Erinyes are designated by the noun for madness and called Maniai (Pausanias 8.34.1). I might also mention the Dorian word *emmanis* (for *emmenis*), which signifies the effectiveness of the divine curse as a sterilizing scourge (cf.

Watkins, "A propos de *Mênis*," pp. 200–201). Athena Polias does not use Dorian words, to be sure, but beyond metrics, which differentiates between long and short, is it really impossible to imagine at least an etymological link between the explicit *emmanes*, derived from *mania*, and the remote *emmanis*, derived from Menis, Wrath, which line 155 of the *Agamemnon* connects to *mnamon*, the Dorian form of *mnemon*?

46. We should compare lines 859–60 (*haimateras, aoinois* [without wine]) and lines 107 and 265 of the *Eumenides* for the description of the Erinyes (*aoinous, eruthron pelanon* [red blood]); concerning this last expression, see Vernant and Vidal-Naquet, "Hunting and Sacrifice in Aeschylus' *Oresteia*," in *Myth and Tragedy in Ancient Greece*.

47. Two articles devoted to images of these fights contain the principal textual references: Ph. Bruneau, "Le Motif des coqs affrontés dans l'imagerie antique," *Bulletin de correspondance Hellénique* 89 (1965), pp. 90–121, and H. Hoffmann, "Hahnenkampf in Athen," *Revue archéologique* (1974), pp. 195–220.

48. Aelian, *Historical Miscellany* 2.28, trans. N.G. Wilson (Cambridge, MA: Harvard University Press, 1997).

49. Compare Aelian's *Historical Miscellany* 2.28 with Aeschylus's *Persians* 402–405, where the list of motivations is the same, with the exception of glory and an added reference to women.

50. Including when they affirm that for both the winner and the loser the resulting ruin is the same; see Democritus frag. 249, who actually contradicts the opinion put forth in *Dissoi logoi* 8–10 that "[victory] is good for the winner, bad for the loser" (in *Ancilla to the Pre-Socratic Philosophers*).

51. See Loraux, "Solon au milieu de la lice" and "Corcyre 427, Paris 1871," pp. 107–12.

52. *Patraloias* is derived from *aloe*, the threshing floor, and according to Chantraine, *Dictionnaire étymologique*, s.v. *aloe*, it is an "expressive" word, or a euphemism. But however euphemistic it may be, the word is nonetheless fearsome, because it belongs to the "forbidden words," *aporrhēta onomata*; see Lysias, *Against Theomnestus* 1.6–8.

53. On the rooster tyrant (and Persian), see Aristophanes, *Birds* 483–85; on

the rooster parricide, see *Birds* 725–59 and 1341–70, trans. B.B. Rogers, *Aristophanes: The Peace. The Birds. The Frogs* (Cambridge, MA: Harvard University Press, 1961), as well as Aristophanes, *Clouds* 1424–30, trans. J. Henderson, *Aristophanes: Clouds. Wasps. Peace* (Cambridge, MA: Harvard University Press, 1998); on Aigisthos as a rooster, see Aeschylus, *Agamemnon* 1670, where the word *tharson* belongs to the same root as *thrasun* (Aeschylus, *Eumenides* 863); on incest, see Aeschylus, *Suppliant Maidens* 226. See also Vernant and Vidal-Naquet, "Hunting and Sacrifice."

54. See Loraux, "La guerre civile grecque."

55. Theognis 349.

56. For *oikeia bora*, see Aeschylus, *Agamemnon* 1220, with the observations by Vernant and Vidal-Naquet in "Hunting and Sacrifice," p. 150; for cannibalistic birds, see Aristophanes, *Birds* 1583–84; for Hesiod's definition of the status of man, see *Works and Days* 276–78; about the cannibalism of certain birds, see Aristotle, *History of Animals* 8.593b25.

57. The scholia to the *Eumenides* already offered this interpretation, observing that in line 861 "the bird is aggressive, and, although the other birds respect their kinship, it alone does not spare it," and glossing the house bird (866) thus: "The citizens who inhabit the city; it is a matter of war within the same lineage [*homophulos polemos*]." Note that the house bird is in the house (*enoikios*) while war is at the gates; about *thuraios*, see Benveniste, *Vocabulaire des institutions indo-européennes*, vol. 1, p. 313.

58. See below, Chapter 5.

59. They can undo the curse by the speech act carried out by the utterance of the verb *apennepō* (958), with which they "unsay" the curses they had uttered. Similarly, in Homer, *Iliad* 19.75, the Achaeans say not that Achilles put "an end to his wrath" but that he "denied" it, or even better, "unsaid" it, as was pointed out by Nagy, *Best of the Achaeans*. On this process in general, see Gernet, *Recherches*.

60. A few references: Alcaeus, frag. 143, Reinach-Puech; Theognis, v. 51; Solon, frag. 4 West, 19; Thucydides 3.81.5.

61. Commentators on the *Eumenides* have not failed to point out everything

at the end of the tragedy that implies a direct reference to Solon's fourth elegy (the so-called *Eunomia*).

62. Thus Edmunds, "Thucydides' Ethics as Reflected in the Description of *Stasis*," has convincingly demonstrated many allusions to the Hesiodic theme of the Iron race in Thucydides's explanation of *stasis* (3.82–83). On Hesiod the thinker of the city with regard to sacrifice, see Detienne, *Dionysos mis à mort*, p. 142, and Vernant in *Cuisine of Sacrifice*, p. 21.

63. See below, Chapter 7.

64. Aeschylus, *Eumenides* 830–31.

65. *Theogony* 226–27. Eris herself is the most powerful of the daughters of Night and is named at the end of the list, as is customary in Hesiodic poetry, where the last place is the place of honor (225). On this genealogy, where reproduction occurs through scissiparity, "through division and not through union," see Ramnoux, *La Nuit et les enfants de la Nuit dans la tradition grecque*, pp. 62–74.

66. The link between the two was already made by the Greeks. On Xenophanes, see the observations by Svenbro, *La Parole et le marbre*, pp. 103–104. On the story of Athena and Poseidon, see below, Chapter 8.

CHAPTER TWO: TO REPOLITICIZE THE CITY
This text was published, in a longer and somewhat different form, in a special issue of *L'Homme* 97–98 (1986), pp. 239–54, devoted to examining the current state of anthropology in France.

1. Lévi-Strauss, "Histoire et ethnologie," p. 1217.

2. See above, Chapter 1.

3. Lévi-Strauss, "Histoire et ethnologie," p. 1217.

4. However legitimate François Hartog's attempt to erase a division always emphasized by tradition, the split between the "Greece of shared knowledge" and its other does not seem close to being erased, inscribed as it is in the text.

5. François Hartog, "Histoire ancienne et histoire," *Annales ESC* 37 (1982), p. 692.

6. F.M. Cornford, *Thucydides Mythistoricus* (London, 1907). For a word of

warning about the gap between the Greeks' *muthōdēs* and "our" myth, see Marcel Detienne, *The Creation of Mythology*, trans. Margaret Cook (Chicago: University of Chicago Press, 1986).

7. See Catherine Darbo-Peschanski, "Les Barbares à l'épreuve du temps," *Mêtis* 4 (1989), pp. 233–50.

8. There is one notable exception: Vidal-Naquet, *Black Hunter*, pp. 47 and 253, who has read Cornford, suggests an anthropological interpretation of an episode from Thucydides in "Retour au chasseur noir," *Mélanges Pierre Lévêque* (Paris: Les Belles Lettres, 1989), vol. 2, p. 393.

9. I borrow this definition of *aiōn* from Benveniste, "Expression indo-européenne de l'éternité," *Bulletin de la Société de linguistique de Paris* 38 (1937), pp. 103–12.

10. The first list is taken from Lissarrague and Schnapp, "Imagerie des Grecs ou Grèce des imagiers," p. 283; the second one from the preface to Vidal-Naquet, *Black Hunter*, p. xxi, with the explicit difference that it is there ascribed to a *political* form of reason.

11. Putting this first part under the sign of the "city" is a way of not dissimulating my approach.

12. See Augé, *Théorie des pouvoirs et idéologie*, p. 216, as well as Augé, *Pouvoirs de vie, pouvoirs de mort*, pp. 100–102, on the "singular-plural."

13. On types, see Lissarrague and Schnapp, "Imagerie des Grecs ou Grèce des imagiers," p. 283. *La Cité des images* is the title of a work published in 1984 by the Institut d'archéologie et d'histoire ancienne de Lausanne and the Centre de recherches comparées sur les sociétés anciennes in Paris; for the English version, see *A City of Images: Iconography and Society in Ancient Greece*, trans. Deborah Lyons (Princeton, NJ: Princeton University Press, 1989).

14. Plato, *Phaedrus* 275d. Such a position is, of course, part of a general critique of *graphein* as a designation of writing, analyzed by Derrida in "Plato's Pharmacy," in *Dissemination*, trans. Barbara Johnson (Chicago: University of Chicago Press, 1981). *Zōographia* is painting as drawing (*graphē*) of living beings (*zōa*).

15. On the censorship of the political, see Lissarrague and Schnapp, "Image-

rie des Grecs ou Grèce des imagiers," pp. 282–84. In 1992, a workshop at the Conference on the Anthropology of Antiquity, held in Athens (proceedings forthcoming), was devoted to this question.

16. When Athenian painters, in illustrating one of Theseus's *erga*, take their inspiration from the famous sculpted group that represented the Tyrannoktones (the Tyrant Killers) on the *agora*, is it really appropriate to speak of a censorship of the political? In fact, the selection of images (those on vases, which are preferred over sculpted figures) is probably reduplicated and orchestrated by other image selections.

17. Lissarrague and Schnapp, "Imagerie des Grecs ou Grèce des imagiers," p. 282.

18. Jean-Pierre Vernant, preface to *City of Images*, p. 7.

19. This is Lévi-Strauss's expression, "Histoire et ethnologie," p. 1225, to which he adds the important specification that "it is no more the case that there are any completely 'cold' societies than it is that there are any completely 'flat' ones."

20. Plato, *Timaeus* 19b–c.

21. This is the title of a work by Pierre Clastres, *Society Against the State*, trans. Robert Hurley with Abe Stein (New York: Zone Books, 1987), who, however, does not equate the entirety of the political with the State.

22. See Loraux, "La Guerre civile grecque."

23. Gernet, *Les Grecs sans miracle*, p. 23, with the explanation on p. 17.

24. Despite what the title announces as a kind of manifesto, and despite the justifications offered by Vernant and Di Donato in the preface and postscript of *Les Grecs sans miracle*, Gernet does not appear in these texts to be an unambiguous opponent of the notion of humanism or even of the "Greek miracle."

25. On Gernet's method and works, see S.C. Humphreys, *Anthropology and the Greeks* (London: Routledge and Kegan Paul, 1978), pp. 76–106; Alberto Maffi, "Le *Recherches* di Louis Gernet nella storia del diritto greco," *Quaderni di storia* 13 (1981), pp. 3–54; Riccardo Di Donato, in Gernet, *Les Grecs sans miracle*, pp. 403–20, as well as in *Per una antropologia storica del mondo antico* (Florence: La Nuova Italia, 1990).

26. On Detienne and Vernant, eds., *Cuisine of Sacrifice Among the Greeks*, see Loraux, "La Cité comme cuisine et comme partage."

27. Here I roughly summarize Vernant, "The Spiritual Universe of the *Polis*," in *Origins of Greek Thought*, as well as Detienne, *Masters of Truth in Archaic Greece*, pp. 89–106.

28. Jean-Pierre Vernant, *Problèmes de la guerre en Grèce ancienne* (The Hague: Mouton, 1968), republished in Vernant, *Mythe et société en Grèce ancienne* (Paris: Maspero, 1974), with the title "La Guerre des cités," p. 40. Note that the assertion of the indissociable character of peace and conflict ("For the Greeks, it is impossible to dissociate the forms of conflict from those of union") pertains not to the classical city or the political universe but to religious thought and institutional practices relating to private revenge.

29. Homer, *Iliad* 18.497. *Neikos*: the scene is placed under the sign of the number two (two men, two camps: 498, 502), as it is when it comes to the city at war. On *neikos* in the *Iliad*, see Nagy, *Best of the Achaeans*, pp. 130 and 312.

30. Vernant, *Origins of Greek Thought*, p. 50.

31. See Loraux, "La majorité, le tout et la moitié."

32. A typical example of this point of view is found in the story of Maiandros in Herodotus 3.142–43; see also Marcel Detienne and Jesper Svenbro, "The Feast of the Wolves, or the Impossible City," in Detienne and Vernant (eds.), *Cuisine of Sacrifice Among the Greeks*, p. 151. The question of the tyrant urgently needs to be reexamined: it is not enough to repeat the Greek gesture of placing the tyrant outside the city, even if the Greeks wanted to believe in the tyrant's uncivic nature, for this is an ideological gesture of defense that obscures the question of power.

33. Like Phaeacia in the *Odyssey*, about which Vidal-Naquet, *Black Hunter*, p. 29, notes that it is "at once an ideal and an impossible society," adding that the Phaeacians "are ignorant of . . . political struggle."

34. Lévi-Strauss, "Histoire et ethnologie," p. 225.

35. See above, Chapter 1.

36. Augé, *Théorie des pouvoirs et idéologie*, p. 215.

37. Loraux, *Invention of Athens*, p. 331.

38. See Terray, "Un Anthropologue africaniste devant la cité grecque."

39. I borrow this expression from Thomas, "Se venger au forum," p. 65, who uses it in reference to vengeance, "which has never been studied except as that which is presupposed in the law that has superseded it." To postulate that conflict is always superseded, because it is always anterior, is a Greek discourse, beginning in the last book of the *Odyssey*; on this text, see Svenbro, "Vengeance et société en Grèce archaïque," with whose conclusions, however, I do not agree.

40. Detienne and Svenbro, "Feast of the Wolves," p. 162; see also Loraux, "La Guerre civile grecque."

41. Civic and not simply "civilized," a notion developed by Frontisi-Ducroux, "Artémis bucolique."

42. Lévi-Strauss, "Histoire et ethnologie," p. 1218.

43. See the observations made by Detienne and Svenbro in "Feast of the Wolves," p. 162.

44. *Ibid.*, p. 163.

45. See Loraux, "La Cité comme cuisine et comme partage."

46. See, for example, Aristophanes, *Acharnians* 971 (*eides, o pasa poli*), and Aristotle, *Politics* 4.1295b15–16 (*bouletai de ge he polis ex ison einai*).

47. To these examples, I will add the figure of the city-ideality, the prevalence of which is demonstrated in a discourse such as the Athenian funeral oration; see Loraux, *Invention of Athens*, pp. 263ff.

48. Detienne and Svenbro, "Feast of the Wolves," pp. 159 and 161.

49. M. Godelier, *L'Idéel et le matériel* (Paris: Fayard, 1984), pp. 284–85: "A Society is not a Subject"; Olivier de Sardan, *Les Sociétés songhay-zarma, Niger-Mali*: "The simple use of the basic terms of our field (society, culture, ethnicity) makes it possible to present what actually are only imaginary constructions of scientific thought as 'real' entities: how many times is 'society' implicitly described as a subject (even if only grammatically, preceding an active verb), whose functions and structures would constitute its modes of existence?"

50. Augé, *Théorie des pouvoirs et idéologie*, p. 69.

51. See Pierre Clastres, *Chronicle of the Guayaki Indians* (New York: Zone Books, 1998), pp. 107–108; and Pierre Clastres, *Recherches d'anthropologie politique*

(Paris: Le Seuil, 1980), pp. 154–55, where "unconscious" is used — certainly not very prudently, but in a way that is infinitely thought provoking — to name what leads "savages" to reject a coercive power of which they do not even have a notion; cf. Nicole Loraux, "Notes sur l'un, le deux et le multiple," in Miguel Abensour (ed.), *L'Esprit des lois sauvages: Pierre Clastres, ou, une nouvelle anthropologie politique* (Paris: Le Seuil, 1987), pp. 155–71.

52. Lévi-Strauss, "Histoire et ethnologie," p. 1231.

CHAPTER THREE: THE SOUL OF THE CITY

This essay is a modified and expanded version of a talk given at the Association française de psychoanalyse and published in *L'Ecrit du temps* 14–15 (1987).

1. See Certeau, *Writing of History*, on Freud's *Moses and Monotheism*.

2. See Loraux, *Invention of Athens* and *Children of Athena*, as well as above, Chapter 1.

3. Certeau, *Mystic Fable*, p. 9.

4. *Ibid.* p. 9.

5. While I tried to lean on the Freud of *Moses and Monotheism* to help me advance along an uncertain path — and this Freud, to be sure, is problematic for some psychoanalysts — I also understood that my interlocutors would have much preferred to see me confine myself to a discourse on myth, as a good Hellenist owes it to him- or herself to do.

6. The Greek *sumphorai* speaks of misfortunes in the form of events; *kaka* (which is implied by *mnesi-kaken*) denotes only sufferings.

7. See Loraux, *Invention of Athens*, pp. 198–201.

8. On *loimos*, or natural disaster, see, for example, Pindar's *Paean* 9.13–20; on the similarities to external war, see Thucydides 3.82.1; on the idea of the city as wounded, see Solon, frag. 4.17 (West).

9. Theognis 39–40: the city gives birth (*kuei*) to the tyrant (whence the *stasis*, 51–52); *ibid.* 1081–82: the city gives birth to the leader of *stasis*. On the sickness, see, for example, Plato, *Laws* 5.744d; but I should also mention the entire corpus of *stasis* from Alcaeus on. The idea of *stasis* as congenital to the city is implied in Plato, *Republic* 8.545c–d.

10. Freud, "Negation," pp. 235–39.

11. Plato, *Menexenus* 244a; Lysias, *Funeral Oration* 62. On *philotēs* (friendship) as the complete "negation of hate," see Glotz, *La Cité grecque*, p. 141.

12. See Loraux, *Mothers in Mourning*.

13. Cf. Watkins, "A propos de *Mênis.*"

14. Plutarch, *Obsolescence of Oracles* 418b–c. On *alastos*, see below, Chapter 6.

15. Homer, *Iliad* 19.67: *pauō kholon*, which the Achaeans immediately interpret correctly as a *menin apeipein*, a speech act that "unsays" wrath. See above, Chapter 1.

16. *Ibid.* 19.65.

17. I agree here with Nagy, "On Strife and the Human Condition," and "More on Strife and the Human Condition," in *Best of the Achaeans.*

18. I attempt this construction below, Chapter 4.

19. "Constructions in Analysis," *Standard Edition of the Complete Psychological Works of Sigmund Freud* (London: Hogarth Press, 1964), vol. 23, p. 258.

20. As in Freud, "Instincts and Their Vicissitudes," trans. James Strachey, in *Standard Edition of the Complete Psychological Works of Sigmund Freud* (London: Hogarth Press, 1957), vol. 14, pp. 109–40. On the "love of killing" in war, see Loraux, "*L'Iliade* moins les héros."

21. All the intellectual "heroism" of a Freud is necessary to introduce doubt as he explains in *Moses and Monotheism*; see also the observations by Marie Moscovici in her preface to *L'Homme Moïse et la religion monothéiste*, trans. C. Heim (Paris: Gallimard, 1986), p. 39, and Loraux, "*L'Homme Moïse* et l'audace d'être historien."

22. Poor in history but otherwise rather weighty. Because *ephialtēs* means nightmare in the sense of a demon and because a well-attested ancient etymology links it to *ephallomai*, to jump on someone (Chantraine, *Dictionnaire étymologique*, s.v.), this is a fateful name for someone who "led the attack against the Areopagus"; Ephialtes is also the name of a giant and of the traitor of [at] Thermopylae.

23. And also, as we have seen, from anthropologists; see above, Chapter 2.

24. Benveniste, *Vocabulaire des institutions indo-européennes*, vol. 2, p. 75.

25. *Sylloge Inscriptorium Graecarum [SIG]* 58. On the political use of *egkratēs*, see Plato, *Republic* 6.499d.4 and 501e3; on *kratos* and the empire, see *SIG* 54.1 and 147.60, as well as Aristotle, *Politics* 3.1284a40 (*egkratōs eskhe ten arkhēn*: the city obtained power [the empire] in the mode of domination).

26. Aristotle, *Politics* 4.1296a27–32 (commentary in Loraux, "Corcyre 427, Paris 1871," pp. 90–91). On victory in an assembly, see, for example, Thucydides 3.49.1; cf. Loraux, "La majorité, le tout et la moitié."

27. Because the Thirty have been invested with powers by an assembly — although the assembly voted under threat of violence — they are always designated as holding *arkhē* despite their "tyranny." See, for example, Xenophon, *Hellenica* 2.3.19 and 2.4.40 (Thrasybulus, leader of the democrats, speaks exclusively of *arkhē* in a context where *kratos* would be more appropriate).

28. For Theramenes's speech, see Xenophon, *Hellenica* 2.3.42.

29. See Loraux, *Invention of Athens*, pp. 172–220, with bibliography. Whatever the actual conditions of production of the word *dēmokratia*, the essential point is that the democrats behaved *as if* the name had been imposed on them by their adversaries.

30. Much more "democratic," for polemical reasons, than that of the democrats; cf. Loraux, "La Démocratie à l'épreuve de l'étranger (Athènes, Paris)."

31. One example is that of Aphrodite, institutionally Pandemos in Athens insofar as she presides over civic Love, which gathers the people into one whole. Although (should we be surprised?) it is the (antidemocratic) rereading of this epiclesis by Plato — who transforms the Pandemian Aphrodite into the earthly Aphrodite (*Symposium* 180d–182a) — that wins the day, to the point of completely obscuring the first meaning, in which *dēmos* included the totality of the people.

32. On *kratos* within the city, see Plato, *Statesman* 291e7 and *Laws* 4.713a and 714c; on *kratos* in the body, see Plato, *Republic* 4.444d; on *kratos* in the soul, see *ibid.* (to mention only a few examples).

33. Plato, *Menexenus* 238d3, 4, 8. Also note the expression *kratos dēmou* in

Plato, *Laws* 6.757d3. For *kratein* in Pericles's *epitaphios*, see Thucydides 2.39.2 and 40.3.

34. Piccirilli, "L'assassinio di Efialte," p. 12 (in French in the original), commenting on Aristotle's *Athenian Constitution* 25.1 and *adorodoketos*.

35. On the meaning that, according to Aristotelian logic, should be given to the claim that he took away "its extra powers" (Aristotle, *Athenian Constitution* 25.2), see Nicole and Patrice Loraux, "L'*Athenaion politeia* avec et sans Athéniens," *Rue Descartes* 1–2 (1991), pp. 57–79.

36. Aristotle, *Athenian Constitution* 35.2.

37. I confess I was not convinced by L. Marr's argument in "Ephialtes the Moderate," *Greece and Rome* 40 (1993), pp. 11–19, for a moderate Ephialtes, who wanted only to strip the Areopagus of its powers rather than destroy it, as extreme democrats wanted.

38. Herodotus 6.121.

39. See Anaximenes of Lampsacos, *Fragmente der griechischen Historiken* [*FGH*] 72 frag. 13, as well as, for example, Harpocration, s.v. *ho katothen nomos*.

40. Against the purely materialistic interpretation of this move by E. Will in *Revue de philologie* 42 (1986) pp. 134–35, see Ronald Stroud's observations in *The Axones and Kyrbeis of Drakon and Solon* (Berkeley: University of California Press, 1979), pp. 12–13. The gesture is parallel to that of Cleisthenes making Erechtheus go down to the *agora* (Bérard, "L'Héroïsation et la formation de la cité," p. 51), with the difference that Ephialtes brings the historical — rather than the mythical — past within everyone's reach.

41. As Piccirilli observes in *Efialte*, p. 78.

42. Lévêque and Vidal-Naquet, *Clisthène l'Athénien*, p. 122 and, more generally, pp. 117–22.

43. See Aristotle, *Athenian Constitution* 25; Diodorus Siculus 11.77.2–6; as well as Antiphon, *On the Murder of Herodes* 68, and Plutarch, *Pericles* 9–10.

44. Diodorus 11.77.2–6: *tēs nuktos anairetheis*. This wording is very close to that of Aristotle, *Athenian Constitution* 25.4 (*aneirethe ... dolophonetheis*) and that of Plutarch, *Pericles* 10.8 (*kruphaios aneilon*). It also recalls the "gray," or

euphemistic, diction of seditious murders in Thucydides (for example, 8.66: *krupha anelosan*; cf. Loraux, "Thucydide et la sédition dans les mots" and should not be the basis of preposterous hypotheses like that of D. Stockton in "The Death of Ephialtes," *Classical Quarterly* 32 (1982), pp. 227–28, according to which Ephialtes was struck down by a heart attack or a cerebral hemorrhage, and found dead in his bed one fine morning.

45. Is this Athens or Chicago? Pericles or Scarface? See especially Piccirilli, "L'assassinio di Efialte" and *Efialte*.

46. Cleisthenes is a *de facto* insurgent in the reform narratives of Herodotus and Aristotle; see Loraux, "Clistene e le nuovi caratteri della lotta politica."

47. Loraux, *Invention of Athens*, pp. 186–89.

48. Plutarch, *Pericles* 10.8; cf. 9.5.

49. A similar symmetry can be found in Aristotle's use of the compound forms of the same verb *hairein* (see Chantraine, *Dictionnaire étymologique*, pp. 146–47) to describe, on the one hand, Ephialtes's deed against the Areopagites (*aneilen*, 25.2; *hairethentas*, 25.3) and the powers of the Areopagus (*perieileto*, 25.2) and, on the other hand, his murder (*aneirethe*, 25.4).

50. Freud, *Moses and Monotheism*, p. 43.

51. *Ibid.*

52. Freud's audacity can serve as an inspiration; see *ibid.*, p. 100.

53. *Ibid.*, p. 132, 70, 99, 100.

54. On page 132 of *ibid.* ("it is not easy for us to carry over the concepts"), it would be better to translate *übertragen* as "to transfer"; see also page 126, where Freud uses *eintragen* when he claims that "it was not easy, to be sure, to introduce the idea of the unconscious into group psychology."

55. *Ibid.*, p. 72.

56. He treats it as a quasi identity; see Freud, *Thoughts for the Times on War and Death*, in *The Standard Edition of the Complete Psychological Works of Sigmund Freud*, vol. 14 (London: Hogarth Press, 1957), pp. 273–300, the "people-individuals of Europe."

57. Moscovici, "Un Meurtre construit par les produits de son oubli," p. 128.

58. Freud, *Moses and Monotheism*, p. 101.

59. I do not think we should have recourse to the notion of the politico-religious, which in this case would provide a purely verbal solution.

60. Freud, *Moses and Monotheism*, p. 100.

61. For *polis kai idiotēs*, see especially Thucydides 3.82.2 (examination of *stasis*), as well as 2.60.2–4, 2.65.7, 3.10.1, 4.61.2, 4.114.3.

62. Besides the countless occurrences of the oppositional *idiai/koinēi*, we also find the tragic version in Aeschylus's *Eumenides* 523–24 (*he polis brotos th' homoios*); among the orators, we note, for example, Demosthenes's *On the Crown* 95 (*andr' idiai kai polin koinēi*) and Aeschines's *Embassy* 164; finally, it falls to a historian like Polybius to utter the law according to which "public crimes . . . differ from private ones only in the extent and quantity of their results" (4.29.4, trans. W.R. Patton, *Polybius*, vol. 2 [Cambridge, MA: Harvard University Press, 1954.])

63. On fear, see Thucydides 1.23.6; on anger, see Thucydides 3.82.2 and 85.

64. "Deux modèles linguistiques de la cité," in Benveniste *Problèmes de linguistique générale*, vol. 2, pp. 272–80. The opposition of *polis* to *civitas* shows that the Greek model is in no way necessary, because it is not universal.

65. See Loraux, *Invention of Athens*, pp. 263–68.

66. Loraux, "Corcyre 427, Paris 1871, La guerre civile grecque entre deux temps," pp. 91–92.

67. Isocrates, *Panathenaicus* 138; Isocrates, *Areopagiticus* 14.

68. Plato, *Laws* 689a–b.

69. Plato, *Republic* 4.442.d4; see also *polis kai anēr* at *Republic* 4.442e, 4.444a, 9.577c, and so on.

70. An analogous phenomenon can be seen in Freud, *Moses and Monotheism*, p. 119, when, after reconstructing the evolution of Jewish religion toward greater spirituality, he writes: "The essential part of this course of events *is repeated* in the *abbreviated development* of the human individual" (my emphasis), as if the collective were the model of the individual.

71. Plato, *Republic* 8.544d–e.

72. See especially Homer, *Odyssey* 19.162–63.

73. Plato, *Republic* 4.435e–36a.

74. *Ibid.* 5.462c–d.

75. See V. Goldschmidt, *Le Paradigme dans la dialectique platonicienne* (Paris: PUF, 1947). The city, however, is always at the same time a paradigm in the sense of an ideal model; see Plato, *Republic* 8.545b–c, where the use of the verb *apoblepō* suggests this second sense.

76. Plato, *Republic* 8.545.b, where I gloss the word *enargesteron*.

77. *Ibid.* 4.434d–35a.

78. An interweaving in the form of *harmonia* between a "male" and a "female" piece, just as in a frame; on this notion, see below, Chapter 4.

79. Laurence Kahn, *Hermès passe* (Paris: Maspero, 1978), pp. 52–55.

80. Plato, *Republic* 4.445c and 8.544e.

81. See especially *ibid.* 4.442b, as well as 440b and 440e (where anger, in the *stasis* of the soul, takes arms on the side of the party of reason, as in Solon's law on civil war [see Aristotle, *Athenian Constitution* 8.5]), 444b, and 8.560d (*stasis*); 4.442c–d (harmony).

82. See especially Plato, *Republic* 9.591e–92a and 10.605b.

83. See Loraux, *Invention of Athens*, pp. 183–84.

84. Freud, *Moses and Monotheism*, p. 76.

85. Note, for example, the use of the plural in the French translation ("these transferences" in Freud, *L'Homme Moïse et la religion monothéiste*, p. 185) to avoid confusion with transference (*le transfert*) as a concept. It is nevertheless a fact that the text speaks, in the singular, of *this* transference (*ce transfert*).

86. "We might well lend the word '*Entstellung* [distortion]' the double meaning to which it has a claim but of which to-day it makes no use," Freud, *Moses and Monotheism*, p. 43.

87. Rey, "Freud et l'écriture de l'histoire," on Freud's *Moses and Monotheism*.

PART TWO: UNDER THE SIGN OF ERIS AND SOME OF HER CHILDREN

1. Hesiod, *Theogony* 226–32 and Hesiod, *Works and Days*, 11–13.

2. The essential work on this topic is Ramnoux, *La Nuit et les enfants de la Nuit dans la tradition grecque*.

3. See Loraux, "Sur un non-sens grec."

4. On this double register, see Detienne, *Masters of Truth in Archaic Greece*.

5. Hesiod, *Works and Days* 13.

CHAPTER FOUR: THE BOND OF DIVISION

This essay is based on a paper given at the Collège international de philosophie during a conference on community and published in 1987 in the *4ᵉ Cahier* of the Collège. The quotation is from van Effenterre, *La Cité grecque des origines à la défaite de Marathon*, p. 25.

1. Aeschylus, *Eumenides* 983–85.

2. *Ibid.*, 976–77 and 983–85.

3. Plato, *Republic* 5.462b.

4. On the bond as a frame, see Plato, *Laws* 7.793c7; on the bond of the *polis*, see Plato, *Republic* 7.519e–20a and *Laws* 12.945c–e; on the bond as a fabric, see Plato, *Statesman* 305e and *Laws* 5.734e–35a; for *sumplokē*, see *Statesman* 309e10; for *sundein* as opposed to *diaspan*, see *Republic* 5.462b–c and *Laws* 9.857a7; on *diaphora* and *stasis*, see *Statesman* 306b–307d.

5. See above, Chapter 3.

6. On *diatemno*, see Empedocles frag. 20, Diels-Kranz, 19–21 (see Aeschines 3.207, where the object of *diatemnō* is *politeia*, the constitution). To the Platonic examples of *diaspaō* already cited we can add Empedocles frag. 63 DK (Bollack, 641), where, despite what Bollack says in his commentary (pp. 552–53), it is indeed a question of division in two.

7. In Euripides, *sunaptō* (to tie) can have as its object an alliance by marriage (*Suppliant Women* 134), an exchange (*Phoenician Women* 569), negotiations (*Phoenician Women* 702), or a fight, *makhē* (*Suppliant Women* 144).

8. I borrow "at peace with itself" from Lyotard, *Le Différend*, pp. 199–200.

9. For *lusan d'agorēn*, see Homer, *Iliad* 1.305; for *luein ta sugkeimena*, see Lysias, *Against Andocides* 41; for *kataluein ten dēmokratian*, see Andocides, *On the Mysteries* 96; for *luē* (*lua*), see Alcaeus, frag. 36 Campbell and 70, 10–11 (*luē* that gnaws at the heart, and *emphulos makha*, the fight within the lineage); also see Pindar, *Nemean* 9.14, where *luē* is a commentary on the "horrible *stasis*."

10. Dividing is the primary meaning of *dia-*, according to Chantraine, *Dictionnaire étymologique*, s.v.

11. On the metaphor, see weaving, see Plato, *Statesman* 281a (*dialutikē*) and 282b (art of separating); see also Herodotus 4.76 (*diaplekon kai dialuon*). These occurrences of *luō* and *dialuō* are not taken into account in John Scheid and Jesper Svenbro's book devoted to weaving, *Le Métier de Zeus* (Paris: La Découverte, 1994).

12. For the use of *dialuō* in reference to an army disbanding, see Thucydides 2.23.3, 68.9, 78.2, 102; 3.1.2, 26.4; 5.83.2, and so on; in times of civil war, even secret societies can be disbanded (*ibid.* 8.81.3). For the use of *dialuō* in reference to a community breaking apart, see Plato, *Republic* 5.462b, as well as 1.342d, and Plato, *Laws* 1.632b. When used intransitively, *dialuein* can also mean "to break one's promise" (Aristotle, *Politics* 3.1276b14–15); on the breaking of a truce, see Tod, *Selection of Greek Historical Inscriptions*, 145, line 13, Argos in 361 B.C.

13. Euripides, *Phoenician Women* 435; Aristophanes, *Lysistrata* 569; Isaeus 2.40; Aristotle, *Politics* 5.1303b28 and 5.1308b30–31.

14. For the use of *dialuō* and *dialūsis* in reference to reconciliation after a dispute, see Lysias 4.1; Demosthenes, *Against Midias* 119 and 122; Aristotle, *Rhetoric* 1.1373a9; Polybius 4.17.6 and 9; see also P.M. Meyer, *Griechische Papyrusurkunde der Hamburger Stadtbibliothek* 1.13 (Berlin, 1911), no. 25, line 5 (mid-third century). For their use in reference to reconciliation after a civil war, see Thucydides 3.83.2; Xenophon, *Hellenica* 2.4.35 (Athens in 403 B.C.); Aristotle, *Athenian Constitution* 38.3 (Athens in 403 B.C.); Diodorus 15.89.1–90 (cf. Tod, *Selection of Greek Historical Inscriptions*, 145, line 5) and 201 (Mytilene in 324 B.C.), 2.46–47; Nenci, *Materiali e contributi*, p. 3 (Nakone, line 12); Pouilloux, ed., *Choix d'inscriptions grecques*, p. 21 (Samos around 280 B.C.), line 9, 2.14–15, 16, and 3 (Samos in 243 B.C.).

15. To borrow Freud's expression "antithetical meanings in primal words," which he himself borrowed from the linguist Karl Abel.

16. Nenci, *Materiali e contributi*, p. 3, line 12. On this inscription, see below, Chapter 9.

17. Chantraine, *Dictionnaire étymologique*, s.v. *luō*, lists *dialusis* and *sullusis* under the category "arrangement, settlement."

18. This is expressed by the adjective *emphulos*, internal, even inborn, to the group closed upon itself. See Loraux, *"Oikeios polemos."*

19. See Vernant, *Origins of Greek Thought*, pp. 47–48; Lévêque and Vidal-Naquet, *Clisthène l'Athénien*, pp. 18–24; Detienne, *Masters of Truth in Archaic Greece*, pp. 96–99; see also above, Chapter 2.

20. Alcaeus, frag. 208, trans. D.A. Campbell, in *Greek Lyric* (Cambridge, MA: Harvard University Press, 1982), vol. 1.

21. Homer, *Iliad* 9.440–43.

22. An assembly in which men stand is extremely rare (see *ibid.* 18.245–47). See also Silvia Montiglio, *Silence in the Land of Logos* (Princeton, NJ: Princeton University Press, 2000).

23. For trials in the *agora*, see Homer, *Iliad* 16.384–88. The epithet *kudianeira*, traditionally associated with fighting (*ibid.* 7.213, 8.448, 14.155), characterizes the assembly in *ibid.* 1.490–91. On *kudos*, see Benveniste, *Vocabulaire des institutions indo-européennes*, vol. 2, pp. 57–69.

24. The oath of the Amphictyons is in Aeschines, *Against Ctesiphon* 111.

25. Similarly, the Sanskrit word for village, *grama*, originally referred to troop. See Malamoud, *Cuire le monde*, p. 95.

26. Wars of words: *antibiois epeessin* (Homer, *Iliad* 1.304–305); see also the use of *antibion* in fighting (*ibid.* 3.20, 7.51, and so on), as well as the observations of G. Dunkel, *Journal of Indo-European Studies* 7 (1979), pp. 249–72. On the use of *agōn* to designate the assembly as a site of contest or conflict, see J.D. Ellsworth in *Classical Philology* 69 (1974), pp. 258–64, *Glotta* 54 (1976), pp. 228–35, and *Emerita* 49 (1981), pp. 97–104.

27. Homer, *Iliad* 18.497: *laoi d'ein agorēi esan athrooi*.

28. *Ibid.* 18.502.

29. On the quarrel as "archetypal," see Nagy, *Best of the Achaeans*, p. 109.

30. On *agōn*, see Gernet, *Recherches*, p. 90. For a general interpretation of the nature of conflict and its stakes, see Benveniste, *Vocabulaire des institutions indo-européennes*, vol. 2, pp. 241–42.

31. See above, Chapter 3, on Ephialtes.

32. Thucydides 3.49. See also Loraux, "La Majorité, le tout et la moitié."

33. On the institution of co-jurors and its relationship to the practice of counting votes, see Gernet, *Recherches*, pp. 90–91.

34. Democritus, frag. 249, in *Ancilla to the Pre-Socratic Philosophers*.

35. Loraux, "La Majorité, le tout et la moitié," and Loraux, "Sur la transparence démocratique."

36. Loraux, "Solon au milieu de la lice."

37. Aristotle, *Athenian Constitution* 8.5.

38. According to Chantraine, *Dictionnaire étymologique*, the anomalous formation of the word *stasiōtēs* can be explained with reference to the model of *patriōtēs*. In the language of Solon, however, the implicit model of *stasiōtēs* is probably to be found in *stratiōtēs*, the name of the soldier.

39. "We strike with atimia those we do not 'kill,'" Gernet, *Recherches*, pp. 110–11.

40. Aristotle, *Athenian Constitution* 39.6.

41. See, for example, Thucydides 3.82; Plato, *Republic* 8.545d2–3 and 6; and Aristotle, *Politics* 5.4.1304a36.

42. Plato, *Republic* 4.436c–39b.

43. Plato, *Sophist* 256b7.

44. Chantraine, *Dictionnaire étymologique*, under *histēmi*; Finley, "Démagogues athéniens," p. 94.

45. Plato, *Laws* 5.744d4.

46. The prehistory of this metaphor can be found in Homeric similes; see *Iliad* 16.765–71. Nagy, *Best of the Achaeans*, pp. 333–34, lists everything that connects Ares to winds.

47. Aeschylus, *Eumenides* 862–63. See above, Chapter 1.

48. If we link it to *sedere*; for another etymology, see Botteri, "*Stásis*: Le Mot grec, la chose romaine."

49. In inscriptions, *stasis* often refers to the action of erecting a statue. Erect Ares evokes Eris, who stands "erect" to the sky during the fighting (Homer, *Iliad* 4.443).

50. In using this phrase, borrowed from Breton's *L'Amour fou*, I agree with the analysis of the double meaning of *stasis* given by Desanti, "La Violence."

51. See, however, Loraux, "Corcyre 427, Paris 187," pp. 99–107.

52. Thucydides 3.82. See Loraux, "Thucydides et la sédition dans les mots."

53. *Stasis* is placed in a less dramatic register when it is used by historians who write about Rome in Greek. See Botteri, "*Stásis*: Le Mot grec, la chose romaine."

54. Benveniste, "Deux modèles linguistiques de la cité," in *Problèmes de linguistique générale*, vol. 2, p. 277.

55. "The abstract notion of a project conceived as objective realization," Benveniste, *Noms d'agent et noms d'action en indo-européen*, p. 80.

56. Heraclitus, DK, frag. 125, in *Ancilla to the Pre-Socratic Philosophers*. I accept the traditional reading, with the correction [*mē*] *kinoumenos*, and take into consideration the work done by Jean Bollack and Heinz Wismann, *Héraclite; ou, La Séparation* (Paris: Editions de Minuit, 1972), pp. 340–41, especially since I am not convinced by the manuscript reading.

57. Plutarch, *Moralia* 511b, with commentary by Battegazzore, *Maia*.

58. Battegazzore, "La funzione del gesto."

59. Aeschylus, *Agamemnon* 323–24, where we should note the terms *dikhostatount'* and *dikha*. Jean Dumortier, *Les Images dans la poésie d'Eschyle* (Paris: Société d'Edition Les Belles Lettres, 1935), p. 188, might be right to take this as an Aeschylean reworking of *Iliad* 4.450, although the originality of the tragedy is precisely in using the image of the impossible mixing.

60. See J. Taillardat, *Les Images d'Aristophane* (Paris: Société d'Edition Les Belles Lettres, 1965), nos. 597, 637 (Polemos), 698, 705, 707, 898, and esp. 701 (*ton dēmon diistanai*). In Homer, *Iliad* 21.240, *kukaō* describes the motion of the sea; see also *Homeric Hymn to Athena* 12.

61. Plato, *Phaedo* 101e9; Plato, *Cratylus* 439c5.

62. Homer, *Iliad* 4.439–53, trans. Richmond Lattimore, with modifications in the translation of *eris* and *neikos*.

63. On the reciprocity of war in its relationship to Ares, see Loraux, "Le corps vulnérable d'Ares." On *homoiios* (and its problematic relation to *homoios*), see Chantraine, *Dictionnaire étymologique*, s.v. ("what is equal for all, what spares no one"); Liddell and Scott's *Greek-English Lexicon* suggests "distressing" but

accepts "common to all, impartial"; Benveniste, *Vocabulaire des institutions indo-européennes*, vol. 2, p. 8, hesitantly suggests "cruel."

64. Homer, *Iliad* 18.309 (Hector), 19.275 (Achilles: *xunagōmen Arēa*); Heraclitus, frag. 80. Kahn's commentary, *Art and Thought of Heraclitus*, p. 205, exaggerates the difference between Heraclitus and Homer: war is already unifying in the *Iliad*.

65. Aeschylus, *Agamemnon* 437–38. Homer, *Iliad* 18.264: Achaeans and Trojans, standing in the middle of the plain, share equally in the fury of Ares (*en mesōi amphoteroi menos Arēos dateontai*); *en mesōi* describes the middle; *amphoteroi*, like *stasis*, designates the two parties that cannot be dissociated; *dateontai* is the verb of dividing and sharing.

66. Homer, *Iliad* 2.385–87 and 18.209; Homer, *Odyssey* 18.264 (with the commentary by Eustathius: *krinein*, that is *luein*, to unbind).

67. For Ares as deaf, see Homer, *Iliad* 13.295ff.; for Ares as blind, see Bacchylides 5.129–35; for Ares with his dice, see Aeschylus, *Seven Against Thebes* 414.

68. On the cut-up body of Patroclus (Homer, *Iliad* 18.236, 19.211, 19.319, 19.283, cf. 22.72), see Chantraine, *Dictionnaire étymologique*, s.v. *daïzō*.

69. Homer, *Iliad* 13.358–60, with commentary by Bollack, *Les Origines*, p. 57.

70. On *peirar* (Homer, *Iliad* 13.359, 7.402, 12.79, and Homer, *Odyssey* 22.33), see the observations of Detienne and Vernant, *Cunning Intelligence in Greek Culture and Society*, pp. 269–77. The use of the verb *ephaptō* (in the last three instances) evokes the idea of a knot, and the use of *tanuō* (13.359) links this passage to all those concerned with "straining the war": 11.336, 14.390, 17.389–401 (ox-hide simile).

71. Homer, *Iliad* 15.410–13 and 12.434.

72. See Theognis 543–44.

73. Homer, *Iliad* 15.707–15.

74. On *amphis*, separately, see Chantraine, *Dictionnaire étymologique*, under *amphi*. *Amphisbētein*, to dispute, and the Hesiodic *amphillogia*, debate, are also formed with *amphis-*.

75. Homer, *Iliad* 376–80 (Agamemnon), 16.219, 17.267. The classical version of this formula is *miai gnōmēi khrōmenoi* (Lysias, *Epitaphios* 17); *homothumadon* in Thrasybulus's speech in Xenophon, *Hellenica* 2.4.17.

76. Homer, *Iliad* 20.32–33.

77. Empedocles, frag. 19 DK (Bollack, 402), with the commentary of Bollack, *Les Origines*, pp. 309–10.

78. Homer, *Iliad* 15.508–10 (*autoskhediei mixai*), and so on, as well as Alcaeus, frag. 330 Campbell (*meixantes allalois areua*); *sumplokē*: Samos in 201–197 B.C. in Pouilloux, *Choix d'inscriptions grecques*, 14, line 30.

79. Homer, *Iliad* 23.710–13 (where the rafters are *ameibontes*, the exchanging); 11.214–16 (*histēmi* and joining: *artunō*, derived from the root *ar-*).

80. Benveniste, *Vocabulaire des institutions indo-européennes*, vol. 2, pp. 100–101.

81. Plato, *Phaedo* 92b1; Aristotle, *De anima* 407b–408a.

82. Solon, frag. 36 West, lines 16 and 19.

83. Bollack, *Introduction à la ancienne physique*, p. 154.

84. Empedocles, frag. 27 DK (Bollack 92), with Bollack's remarks in *Introduction à la ancienne physique*, pp. 134–35.

85. Heraclitus, frag. 51 DK, with the remarks by Bollack and Wismann, *Héraclite; ou, La Séparation*, p. 180, about the "mistake that consists in isolating division and reunion"; see also Battegazzore, "La funzione del gesto," p. 18, n.31, about the technical and craft connotations of the word *harmonia*.

86. Heraclitus, frag. 10 DK, with translation ("the counter-thrust brings together") and observations by Kahn, *Art and Thought of Heraclitus*, p. 193.

87. Heraclitus, frag. 10 DK, where, against Bollack and Wismann, *Héraclite; ou, La Séparation*, pp. 82–83, I accept the reading *sunapsies*; see Heidegger, in Martin Heidegger and Eugen Fink, *Héraclite* (1973), pp. 185 and 188. See also Battegazzore, "*Haptesthai.*"

88. Bollack and Wismann, *Héraclite; ou, La Séparation*, p. 335, on *agkhibasiē*.

89. Heraclitus, frag. 54 DK; *kreittōn* is the expression of a *kratos*. See Kahn, *Art and Thought of Heraclitus*, pp. 202 and 210, about the primacy of the negative.

90. And also the ambivalence of Aristotle, who, against Plato, defines the city as being composed of *anomoioi* but also underlines the risk of disagreement posed in a colony by the existence of a population that is not *homophulos*.

91. C. Meier, "Clisthène et le problème politique de la *pólis* grecque," *Revue internationale des droits de l'Antiquité* 20 (1973), pp. 115–59, dwells on this word, pp. 123, 138, 158.

92. Solon, frag. 4 West, lines 33 and 40; Plutarch, *Roman Questions* 264a and 270b.

93. Theognis 17–18; see Nagy, *Best of the Achaeans*, pp. 299–300, as well as Nagy, "A Poet's Vision of His City," in Nagy and Figueira (eds.), *Theognis of Megara*, pp. 27–28.

94. On this etymology, see Sinos, *Achilles, Patroklos and the Meaning of Phílos*, pp. 33–34, who insists on Ares being a "god of an unwarlike society."

95. Aristotle, *Eudemian Ethics* 1235a25.

96. Homer, *Iliad* 1.6–7, glossed by Plato, *Republic* 8.545d8–e1, with the word *stasis*. Concerning the foundation of human order on *eris*, see Nagy, *Best of the Achaeans*, pp. 223–32 and 309–12.

97. For example, Plato, *Laws* 1.632b4 (which takes up *Republic* 1.343d5); note that the break can be positive when it cuts between soul and body (*Gorgias* 524b; *Laws* 8.828d4).

98. Plato plays on *diaphora/diaphthora* in *Sophist* 228a4–8. See Cambiano, "Pathologie et analogie politique."

99. Plato, *Symposium* 87a–b; see also Plato, *Republic* 4.436c–39b (similarly, the definition of injustice as *stasis* corresponds to the Heraclitean assimilation of justice to discord).

100. See Plato, *Menexenus* 244a7.

101. Aeschylus, *Eumenides* 332.

CHAPTER FIVE: OATH, SON OF DISCORD

This is a previously unpublished essay, based on a talk given in 1987 at the Center for Law and Culture of the University of Paris X-Nanterre.

1. Hesiod, *Theogony 231–32.*

2. Empedocles, frag. 115, 2.3–4, in *Ancilla to the Pre-Socratic Philosophers*, likens murder to the betrayal of an oath, because the latter obeys *neikos*.

3. Xenophon, *Memorabilia* 4.4.16.

4. On democracy, see, for example, Lycurgus's claim in *Against Leocrates* 79; for examples, see the Chersonesians' oath (*Sylloge Inscriptorum Graecorum* [*SIG*] 360), 2.5 ff. (*homonoeso... kai ou prodoso... alla diaphulaxō oude katalusō ta demōkratian...*) or the "constitutional" oath of the Dreriens (*SIG* 527), 2.54ff. (I shall not betray and shall not cause *stasis* nor stand by rebels); cf. *SIG* 526 (oath of the Itanians).

5. See above, Chapter 4.

6. Gernet, *Anthropology of Ancient Greece*, p. 172.

7. As Gernet claims, in Benveniste's footsteps, in "The Concept of Time in the Earliest Forms of Law," in *ibid.*, p. 223; see also "Law and Prelaw in Ancient Greece," in *ibid.*, pp. 172–73 and 191–92.

8. For a critique of Gernet's tendency to prefer prehistory to history and pre-law to law, see the introduction to *Du châtiment dans la cité*, p. 5.

9. The expression "vocal gesture" is also from Gernet, who does not exclude the possibility that the imprecation would have the same force as the original "sacred substance." The imprecation "manifests itself by a prohibition in the strong sense,... it outlaws," Gernet, "Le Droit pénal dans la Grèce ancienne," p. 12.

10. Hesiod, *Works and Days* 190 and 194.

11. Thucydides 3.83.2; see also 3.82.7. On Hesiod's influence on Thucydides, see Edmunds, "Thucydides' Ethics as Reflected in the Description of *Stásis*."

12. Ramnoux, *La Nuit et les enfants de la Nuit dans la tradition grecque*, p. 75; Dumézil, *L'Idéologie des trois fonctions dans les épopées des peuples indo-européens*.

13. For the use of Hesiodic diction, see the translators' note in Gregory Nagy, *Le Meilleur des Achéens: La Fabrique du héros dans la poésie grecque archaïque*, trans. Jeannie Carlier and Nicole Loraux (Paris: Le Seuil, 1994), p. 18.

14. Note the power of the enjambment that throws the verb *pēmainei* forward to the beginning of line 232.

15. In Homer, *Iliad* 3.299, the oath breaker is the *subject* of the verb *pēmaino*, and *horkia* is its object, as if it were a possession that men can harm. The Hesiodic shift is considerable because the oath becomes the subject and mortals the object.

16. Hesiod, *Works and Days* 804. On Hesiod, *Theogony* 792 (*Styx mega pēma theoisin*), West observes: "just as Horkos is *pēm' epiorkois*," which implies that all oath takers — god or mortal — are potential oath breakers.

17. Without mentioning Hesiod, Gernet, "Law and Prelaw," in *Anthropology of Ancient Greece*, makes a comment that illuminates our text: "Vengeance will come if need be; from now on there is commitment through consecration, for which punishment for perjury will, if necessary, be its automatic result."

18. Hesiod, *Works and Days* 219, with West's commentary on the simultaneity of *autika*.

19. Chantraine, quoting W. Luther, in Chantraine, *Dictionnaire étymologique*, s.v. *horkos*. This theory appeals to me, because it reduces *horkos* to the force of the imprecation.

20. Benveniste, *Vocabulaire des institutions indo-européennes*, vol. 2, p. 170. Chantraine and West both agree with this hypothesis, [ad] *Works and Days* 194.

21. On Clytemnestra and Penelope, see Homer, *Odyssey* 24.192–202, with the observations by Ioanna Papadopoulou-Belmehdi in *Le Chant de Pénélope* (Paris: Belin, 1994), pp. 73–76; On Autolykos, see Homer, *Odyssey* 19.395–96.

22. Torricelli, "*Hórkos* e la figura lessicale del giuramento," p. 135, n.131, takes a more moderate position: a guarantee that goes beyond its competency.

23. See Glotz, "Le Serment," p. 182 (a text that develops the article "Jusjurandum" published in 1899 in Daremberg and Saglio, *Dictionnaire des antiquités*); Benveniste, *Vocabulaire des institutions indo-européennes*, vol. 2, p. 175.

24. Gernet, *Recherches*, p. 114, on Empedocles frag. 115, which he compares with Aeschylus, *Libation Bearers* 295–96. See also Gernet, "Le Droit pénal dans la Grèce ancienne," p. 13.

25. Benveniste, *Problèmes de linguistique générale*, vol. 2, p. 256 ("La blasphémie et l'euphémie").

26. When the oath formula, after having mentioned the gods as guarantors,

contains an invitation to them to keep watch over the observance of the oath, they in fact are potential avengers, who are addressed by name and in the vocative. There is an example of this formula in *SIG* 360 (oath of the Chersonesians, early third century B.C.).

27. Isocrates, *Against Callimachus* 3.

28. Hesychius, glossing *horkoi* with *desmoi sphragidos*, with Chantraine's commentary, *Dictionnaire étymologique*, s.v.; Empedocles, frag. 115: *katesphregismenon*. On the etymological kinship between *horkos* and *herkos*, wall, see Glotz, *La Cité grecque*, p. 99.

29. Aeschines, *Against Ctesiphon* 233.

30. "This is not simply a manner of speaking: ... the essential point each time is the object itself and not the act of enunciation," Benveniste, *Vocabulaire des institutions indo-européennes*, vol. 2, pp. 168–69. The linguist, however, cannot completely deny the power of words, concerning which he speaks again in terms of "acts," p. 169.

31. See above, Chapter 1.

32. Aeschylus, *Eumenides* 417; this name is probably the right one (they use, in fact, the perfect *keklemetha*, 417; cf. Ruijgh, "L'Emploi onomastique de *keklēsthai*"), since they inhabit the underworld, and Athena's answer deems it authentic (*klēdonas t' epōnumous* 418). Note also that a funerary inscription from Neocesarea (Pouilloux, ed., *Choix d'inscriptions grecques*, 52 I 12) describes Ara as "the most ancient of daimons [*daimonon*]."

33. *Ibid.* 829–31.

34. *Ibid.* 812–18. *Leikhēn* (blight) was also the result of Apollo's wrath, able to unleash the Erinyes in the *Libation Bearers* 283–84.

35. This is what Vernant, *Origins of Greek Thought* and Detienne, *Masters of Truth in Archaic Greece*, call "magico-religious speech." Similarly, *humnos desmios*, "the binding song" of the Erinyes (Aeschylus, *Eumenides* 306), evokes the language of curse tablets.

36. On this logic, see Loraux, "Sur un non-sens grec."

37. The Erinyes' wishes for Athens reverse their curses word for word (*apennepō*, 958; Aeschylus, *Eumenides* 937–45, 956–67), whereas the Danaids'

wishes for Argos take the place of the imprecations they would have cast if the people had not welcomed them (Euripedes, *Suppliant Women* 998–1074).

38. Pouilloux, ed., *Choix d'inscriptions grecques*, 31 (law on the repression of anti-oligarchic plots): *mēde en tēi eparēi esto.*

39. *SEG* 23.320 (fourth century B.C.); Tod, *Selection of Greek Historical Inscriptions*, 127. See also the oath of the founders of Cyrene (Meiggs and Lewis, *Selection of Greek Historical Inscriptions*, 5, 2.46–51), whose imprecation, for once, begins with a wish of destruction for the oath breaker.

40. *SIG* 360.

41. Meiggs and Lewis, *Selection of Greek Historical Inscriptions,* 30 (around 470 B.C.): *apollusthai kai auton kai genos te kēnō genos.* See Parker, *Miasma*, p. 186, n.234 and 235.

42. Gernet, "Le Droit pénal dans la Grèce ancienne," pp. 11–12.

43. Homer, *Iliad* 3.297–301.

44. Andocides, *On the Mysteries* 1.98, in *Minor Attic Orators.* Whence the name *exōleia* given to this imprecation in civic oaths.

45. The first two quotations are from Glotz (1906), pp. 114 and 112; the third from Benveniste, *Vocabulaire des institutions indo-européennes*, vol. 2, p. 172.

46. Glotz, "Le Serment," p. 154; Benveniste, *Vocabulaire des institutions indo-européennes*, p. 164. For a critique of the theory of ordeal, see Gernet, *Anthropology of Ancient Greece*, p. 190.

47. *SIG* 527 (Dreros), 2.75ff: "and if I break my oath, may the gods by which I swore be full of wrath [*theous . . . emmanias*]." On the ritual and traditional character of the word *menis*, see Watkins, C., "À propos de *mênis*," pp. 201–202.

48. Torricelli, "*Horkos* e la figura lessicale del giuramento," pp. 129–34, links oath as a speech act with the elements risked, which have exchange value and underwrite the oath taker's identity.

49. See, for example, *SIG* 526.40ff. (imprecation of the oath of the Itanians).

50. Herodotus 6.86.

51. Hesiod, *Works and Days* 282–86

52. *Ibid.* 242–44.

53. Although the Athenian institution of ostracism, which punishes an individual for his overlarge *dunamis*, follows a similar logic.

54. On the imprecation as equivalent to the Roman *sacer esto*, by which the culprit is abandoned to the gods, see Gernet, "Le Droit pénal dans la Grèce anciene," p. 11; on the oath taker who is *enagēs*, at once cursed and "sacred," see Gernet, "Time in the Archaic Forms of Law, " in *Anthropology of Ancient Greece*.

55. Aeschines, *Against Ctesiphon* 110–11.

56. Similarly, female animals will not bear "natural offspring." Recall that the good king's city is recognizable in the sons resembling their fathers; see Hesiod, *Works and Days* 235. For other examples of monstrous births, see the oath of Dreros (*SIG* 527), illuminated by Marie Delcourt's study, *Stérilités mystérieuses et naissances maléfiques dans l'antiquité classique* (Paris: 1938; reprint, Paris: Les Belles Lettres, 1986), and which contains this formula, "If I do not respect the oath . . . may neither women nor beasts give birth *according to nature*."

57. See above, Chapter 4.

58. I am commenting here on Aeschylus, *Eumenides* 903–15: we pass from *nikē mē kakē* in line 903, in which we detect good politics, to prosperity in line 904 and following, up to line 909. The role played by Athena is described at 913–15.

59. The classical period reversed the Homeric order, in which the sacrifice, "a performance of the imprecation," is preceded by the oath; see Glotz, "Le Serment." But the classical sacrifice is a conditional imprecation; see Plescia, *Oath and Perjury in Ancient Greece*, p. 12.

60. Pausanias 5.24.10–11, as well as 3.20.9; see, for example, Glotz, "Le Serment," p. 114.

61. The oath of Cyrene makes explicit the equivalence between the wax *kolossoi*, doomed to melt, and the *genos* of the offender; see Gernet, *Anthropology of Ancient Greece*, pp. 170–71.

62. *Dia*, again and always. The oath sacrifice often assumes a division of the victim *into two*; see Plescia, *Oath and Perjury in Ancient Greece*, p. 10.

63. Is he standing on the victim (Glotz), which supposes that he puts his feet on top of it (Burkert, *Greek Religion*, p. 251)? A passage from Aeschines's

Against Timarchus suggests a touching with the hand, and the conflictual connotations attached to *stas* in the case of oath would suffice in themselves, with no need to add a superfluous dramatization (see Pausanias 3.20.9, 4.15.8, 4.24.9, as well as Demosthenes, *Against Aristocrates* 68).

64. Burkert, *Greek Religion*, p. 251.

65. Pausanias 4.15.8 and 4.24.9: *epi kaprou tomion*; on the sacrifices at the Areopagus, see Demosthenes, *Against Aristocrates* 68.

66. Dumézil (1947), pp. 147–51.

67. *Enualios* is not exactly the same as Ares either, but it is often his epiclesis; in Tymnos in Caria, for example, he is also honored by a triple sacrifice including a boar, a dog, and a goat (*SEG* 4, 171, 2.29–30).

68. Homer, *Iliad* 19.258–60, with the commentary of Torricelli, "*Hórkos* e la figura lessicale del giuramento," p. 132; Hesiod, *Works and Days* 803–804.

69. Aeschylus, *Eumenides* 382–83.

70. Rohde, *Psyche*.

71. See Glotz, "Le Serment," p. 101. Note that Ge can be replaced by Demeter, and Helios by Apollo.

72. For the oath at Dreros, see *SIG* 527. For the oath at Athens, see Tod, *Selection of Greek Historical Inscriptions*, p. 204.

73. For example, in the treaty of Smyrna and Magnesia (*Orientis Graeci Inscriptiones Selelectae* [*OGI*] 229, cf. also 266), where he is in the list of canonical gods whose names are paratactically juxtaposed, alongside additional gods, linked with each other by *kai*; cf. the treaty of the Aeolians and Boeotians (*SIG* 366) or of the Athenians and Spartans (*SIG* 434).

74. In this act of synoecism (about 360 B.C.), Ares is the common denominator between Zeus Ares, Athena Areia, and Inualios Ares. On this text, see P. Kretschmer, "Ares," *Glotta* 11 (1921), pp. 195–98, and Sinos, *Achilles, Patroklos, and the Meaning of Phílos*, p. 33.

75. See Plescia, *Oath and Perjury in Ancient Greece*, pp. 15ff.

76. Herodotus 1.153.

77. See Meiggs and Lewis, *Selection of Greek Historical Inscriptions*, 2 (constitution law of the Drerians, 650–500 B.C.), 5 (foundation of Cyrene, where the

designation of the act as *horkion tōn oikistērōn* coexists with the formula of political decision *edoxe tai ekklesiai*), and 13 (law of the Locrians, 525–520 B.C.).

78. This is what happens in the decree on the use of Athenian measures in the empire (see *ibid.*, 45, clause 12). See also Tod, *Selection of Greek Historical Inscriptions*, 141, 2.14–15 (decree of Keos/Histiaia, c. 364 B.C.).

79. See, for example, Meiggs and Lewis, *Selection of Greek Historical Inscriptions,* 52 (Athens and Chalkis), 63 (Athens and Rhegion), 64 (Athens and Leontinoi), all from the fifth century B.C.

80. For example, Tod, *Selection of Greek Historical Inscriptions*, 142 (relations between Athens and Ioulis, 362 B.C.), 1.17.

81. Thucydides 5.42.3.

82. Hesiod, *Theogony* 775–805.

83. Pindar, *Pythian* 4.168–69, in Pindar, *Victory Songs*, trans. Frank Nisetich (Baltimore, MD: Johns Hopkins University Press, 1980); *karteros horkos* should be translated not as "a mighty oath" but as "the oath that prevails." Similarly, the *diōmosia* of the Areopagus is *horkos megistos kai iskhurōtatos* in Antiphon 5.11.

84. Hesiod, *Theogony* 383–403, with West's commentary.

85. Plescia, *Oath and Perjury in Ancient Greece*, p. 6.

86. Thucydides 5, dedicated to the Peace of Nicias, a moment of armed peace when everything happens through the intermediary of oaths and sometimes even of rival oaths.

87. Glotz, "Le Serment," p. 100 (sentence added to the article "Jusjurandum" in Daremberg and Saglio, *Dictionnaire des Antiquités*).

88. Burkert, *Greek Religion*, p. 253.

89. Glotz, "Le Serment," pp. 148–49; Gernet, *Recherches*, p. 90 and n.108.

90. Glotz, "Le Serment," pp. 118–19.

91. In this case, the texts specify that the oath is sworn *allēlois*; see Xenophon, *Hellenica* 5.4.55 (at Thespiae), and Polybius 4.17.11. It also happens, however, that only the party left in the city swears to treat the exiles well; see Tod, *Selection of Greek Historical Inscriptions*, 202 (oath of Tegea, 324 B.C., with a

translation and commentary by Plassart in *Bulletin de correspondance hellénique* 38 [1914], which gives other examples of this practice).

92. See Aristotle, *Athenian Constitution* 39.6, which expresses this clause in the form of a prohibition — *tōn de parēleluthotōn mēdeni pros mēdena mnēsikakein exeinai* ("Otherwise no one was to recall the past misdeeds of anyone") — and also mentions oath without any other details (39.4 and 40.2). Cf. Xenophon, *Hellenica* 2.4.43.

93. Aristotle, *Politics* 5.7.1310a9–11, says that oligarchs explicitly swore oaths to destroy the *dēmos* in all the democratic cities. Cf. Glotz, "Le Serment," p. 117.

94. Andocides, *On the Mysteries* 97–98, in *Minor Attic Orators*, vol. 1.

95. See Torricelli, "*Horkos* e la figura lessicale del giuramento," p. 128 (on the Homeric formula *homosen te teleutesen te ton horkon*, which reminds us that the importance of the words used in the oath is indirectly revealed by the many instances of obligations evaded through verbal tricks).

96. Here I have adapted observations made in *ibid.*, pp. 134–35.

97. For example, see Meiggs and Lewis, *Selection of Greek Historical Inscriptions*, 40 (oath of the Athenian *boulē* toward Erythrea), 52 (relations between Athens and Chalkis, 446–445 B.C.): the *boulē* and the judges swear *ouk ekhsēlō...*

98. See, for example, *ibid.*, 52, line 19, and 32–33.

99. See *ibid.*, 63 (treaty of alliance between Athens and Rhegion, 433–432 B.C.), line 13 (*khsum makhoi esōmetha*), and 64 (treaty of alliance between Athens and Leontinoi, same date), lines 20–21 and 24–25. Similarly, in the treaty between Keos and Histiaia (around 364 B.C.), some clauses of the oath, quoted indirectly, include a third-person plural; see Tod, *Selection of Greek Historical Inscriptions*, 141.15–17).

100. Thus, in the treaty of alliance between Athens and the Bottiaeans (in Hermann Bengtson, *Die Staatsverträge des Alteroms*, vol. 2 [Munich: Beck, 1962–69] 187), the oath formula goes from the singular (lines 15–16) to the plural (line 17) and finally goes back to the singular (lines 20–21).

101. Aeschines, *On the Embassy* 87.

102. This is what the language of this oath postulates. Before assuming their functions, the judges swore an oath to listen impartially to the accuser and the

accused; see Demosthenes, *Against Timocrates* 149–51, with the observations of Glotz, "Le Serment," pp. 147–48.

103. On this formula with which the city's enemy, having made himself into an outlaw, is treated as if he were an enemy from the outside, see the observations of Gernet, *Platon: Lois IX*, pp. 85–86. Andocides, *On the Mysteries* 97, in *Minor Attic Orators*, vol. 1.

104. Some decrees even foresee *atimia* for anyone who refused to have his name inscribed on the stela; see Glotz, "Le Serment," p. 125, and Plescia, *Oath and Perjury in Ancient Greece*, p. 24. This is a reminder that the *idiōtēs* exists not through himself but through the city.

105. See Gernet, *Anthropology of Ancient Greece*, p. 214, n.340.

106. See above, Chapter 1.

107. The form is occasionally modified, as in Alipheira in Arcadia, where the citizens swear "to recall anger against no one (*mēdena mēdeni mnasikhōlē-sai*)"; see Te Riele, "Contributions épigraphiques à la connaissance du grec ancien," and Te Riele, "Le Grand Apaisement de Rogoziò."

108. *Ou mnēnasikakēsō tōn parēleluthotōn*; see Tod, *Selection of Greek Historical Inscriptions*, 142.1.17; cf. Aristotle, *Athenian Constitution* 39.6: *tōn parēlelutho-tōn mēdeni pros mēdena mnēsikakein exeinai.*

109. Tod, *Selection of Greek Historical Inscriptions*, 142, line 58ff.

CHAPTER SIX: OF AMNESTY AND ITS OPPOSITE

This essay is a modified version of a paper presented at the conference of Roy-aumont on the "Uses of Forgetting" in 1987 and published in *Usages de l'oubli* (Paris: Le Seuil, 1988).

1. This absence can be designated as repudiation, in a Lacanian mode, but I prefer to borrow the notion of retrenchment from Françoise Davoine and Jean-Max Gaudillière.

2. On the theme of *diaeresis* and scar, see Loraux, "Pour quel consensus?" pp. 18–19.

3. Plato uses *amnēstia* in a very general sense (*Menexenus* 239e). The sense of forgetting the deeds of *stasis* or conflict is a later use; see, for example, *SIG*

633, 1.36 = Miletus, second century B.C. On Athens, see Plutarch, *Praecepta gerendae reipublicae* 17.8 (Didot 993), who speaks of a "decree of amnesty [*psēphisma amnēstias*]. "

4. See above, Chapter 1.

5. Herodotus 6.21. I have elaborated on this text in Loraux, *Mothers in Mourning*. The long article by David Rosenbloom, "Shouting Fire in a Crowded Theater: Phrynichos' *Capture of Miletos* and the Politics of Fear in Early Attic Tragedy," *Philologus* 137 (1993), pp. 159–90, adds nothing essential from the point of view that is of interest here.

6. I take *pathos*, suffering, from the form *pathousi* describing the Milesians (6.21). The Athenians identify with the Milesians — which is expressed with *oikeion* — and see their own *pathos* in what is, after all, a drama.

7. On Herodotus's account, see the remarks of Mazzarino (who translates *oikeia* by "own") in *Il pensiero storico classico*, vol. 1, pp. 107–108. On *oikeios*, see Loraux, "*Oikeios polemos*," as well as Loraux, "La Main d'Antigone."

8. I modify here the too-strong claims written in 1988 about Aeschylus's *Persians*. See "Ce que les *Perses* ont peut-être appris aux Athéniens," *Epokhè* 3 (1993), pp. 147–63.

9. This is Vernant's reading, "The Tragic Subject: Historicity and Transhistoricity," in Vernant and Vidal-Naquet, *Myth and Tragedy in Ancient Greece*.

10. Isocrates, *Panathenaicus* 121–23.

11. Plutarch, *Precepts of Statecraft* 814b–c. This text, devoted to what it is necessary to recall from the past in order to offer it to the imagination, explicitly retains as objects of memory only acts that lead to forgetting.

12. See above, Chapter 5.

13. See examples listed above, Chapter 5.

14. Plato, *Letter VII* 336e–37a; Luc Brisson's translation, *Platon: Lettres* (Paris: Flammarion, 1987).

15. Before I elaborate further below in Chapters 10 and 11, see, for example, Aristotle, *Athenian Constitution* 40.2; Isocrates, *Against Callimachus* 23 (and 2, where *dikazesthai para tous horkous* is the strict equivalent of *mnēsikakein*); Lysias, *Against Nicomachus* 9; and Andocides, *On the Mysteries* 104 in

Minor Attic Orators. The act of inadmissibility evoked in *Against Callimachus* 2 shuts the entire Athenian system off from memory, just like the current prejudicial question.

16. Aristotle, *Athenian Constitution* 38.4.

17. Andocides, *On the Mysteries* 81. Also, Achilles proposes to Agamemnon to forget the past (Homer, *Iliad* 19.65).

18. Lysias, as a democrat disappointed in his hopes for citizenship, claims on the contrary and without ambiguity that for the *dēmos* forgetfulness is a fault or an error; see Lysias, *Against Eratosthenes* 85, as well as *Against a Charge of Subverting the Dēmocracy* 2.

19. See, for example, Marcel Detienne, "L'Espace de la publicité; ses opérateurs intellectuels dans la cité," in Detienne, ed., *Les Savoirs de l'écriture en Grèce ancienne.*

20. Plato, *Theaetetus* 187b.

21. Euripides, *Hecuba* 590, trans. W. Arrowsmith (Chicago: University of Chicago Press, 1955–59).

22. Andocides, *On the Mysteries* 76.

23. Aristotle, *Athenian Constitution* 40.3.

24. For the association of these two gestures, see Andocides, *On the Mysteries* 79.

25. Only Isocrates, *Against Callimachus* 26, explicitly faces the erasure of the reconciliation, because his speech targets a democrat who despite everything had initiated proceedings.

26. See below, Chapter 9.

27. See Isocrates, *Against Callimachus* 2–3. On the *paragraphe*, see above, Chapter 5, and below, Chapter 10. *Aition*: the unfortunate democrat probably was the first (*ērxato*) to *mnēsikakein*, rather than someone who "began to," as Georges Mathieu translates (Collection des universités de France).

28. Aristotle, *Athenian Constitution* 40.2.

29. See above, Chapter 4.

30. Some other oligarchic bodies are to be added: see Aristotle, *Athenian Constitution* 39.6, and Andocides, *On the Mysteries* 90. On the use made of it

by citizens accused of antidemocratic intrigues, see Lysias, 25.5, 25.16, 25.18.

31. Aristotle, *Athenian Constitution* 40.2 and 40.3 (where the Athenians "use" their misfortunes, just as in Herodotus they forbid anyone to "use" Phrynichus's tragedy); Isocrates, *Against Callimachus*, 46.

32. Plutarch, *Table Talk* 9.6 (*Moralia* 741b); Plutarch, *On Brotherly Love* 18 (*Moralia* 489b–c). See above, Chapter 1, and below, Chapter 8.

33. See Mossé, "Comment s'élabore un mythe politique."

34. Plutarch, *Solon* 21.2.

35. See Rousso, "Vichy, le grand fossé," as well as *Le Syndrome de Vichy, 1944–198?* and *Le Syndrome de Vichy de 1944 à nous jours.*

36. Isaac, *Les Oligarques*, p. 191.

37. But see Michel Winock, "Les Affaires Dreyfus," *Vingtième siècle* 5 (1985), pp. 19–37, on the "contemporaneity" of the Dreyfus affair.

38. Jules Isaac, *Péguy*, vol. 1 of *Expériences de ma vie* (Paris: Calmann-Lévy, 1963), p. 282.

39. See Jean-Michel Rey, *Colère de Péguy* (Paris: Hachette, 1987).

40. See above, Chapter 4.

41. Homer, *Odyssey* 24.482–85.

42. *Ibid.* 24.531 and 24.543.

43. This is obviously not the place to discuss the authenticity of this ending, questioned since Antiquity by readers who want the poem to end at 23.296. Be that as it may, the ending of the *Odyssey* seems very plausible to me.

44. Alcaeus, frag. 70, trans. D.A. Campbell, in *Greek Lyric* (Cambridge, MA: Harvard University Press, 1982), vol. 1. This time, the gods cause the division, and the forgetting is human: the notion has come a long way.

45. Detienne, *Masters of Truth in Archaic Greece*, pp. 63–64.

46. Hesiod, *Theogony* 55.

47. *Ibid.*, 98–103.

48. Homer, *Odyssey* 4.222–26

49. See especially Homer, *Iliad* 9.632–33 (criticizing Achilles walled in by his refusal, Ajax claims that one must accept compensation even from the murderer of a brother or a son, which suggests that the desire for vengeance is never

as strong as it is in this case), as well as Homer, *Odyssey* 24.433–35 (Eupeithes's speech).

50. This is the title of Roselyne Dupont-Roc and Alain Le Boulluec's essay, "Le Charme du récit (*Odyssée* IV.218–289)," in *Ecriture et théorie poétiques: Lectures d'Homère, Eschyle, Platon, Aristote* (Paris: Presses de l'ENS, 1976).

51. Homer, *Iliad* 22.83.

52. The word "unforgetful," which I have coined from the adjective "forgetful," has much in common with the "inflexible thing" that Lyotard considers in "A l'insu." On *alastos/alastōr* and the uncertainty between "unforgettable" and "unforgetful," see Slatkin, "Wrath of Thetis," p. 19n.

53. Cf. Te Riele, "Le Grand Apaisement de Rogoziò," who dates the inscription to the last quarter of the third century B.C., as well as Te Riele, "Contributions épigraphiques à la connaissance du grec ancien," p. 343.

54. Lysias, *Against Eratosthenes* 96.

55. Sophocles, *Electra* 176–77.

56. *Ibid.* 222.

57. *Ibid.* 259–60.

58. *Ibid.* 140–42, 230, 1246–48. *Aluton* in Homer, *Iliad*: the fetters (13.37) and the bond of war (13.360). On *dialusis* as an untying of the strongest of bonds, see above, Chapter 4.

59. As regards Achilles, Slatkin, in "Wrath of Thetis" and *Power of Thetis*, pp. 85–105, suggests that the hero's *menis* is a displaced rereading of the "wrath" of his mother, Thetis.

On anti-(ante-) politics, see Loraux, *Mothers in Mourning*. The anti-political is probably a fiction; in fact, the verb *mēniō* in Herodotus designates a collective behavior. Cf. Gernet, *Recherches*, p. 148.

60. Among Lyotard's categories in *Le Différend*, p. 157, it comes under "identical repetition," a mode of sentence in which the mark is on the speaker and not, as in the "Jewish" sentence, on the addressee.

61. There are nineteen instances in Sophocles's *Electra* of the *aei* of Electra (as soon as Orestes takes action, this *aei* disappears without returning). On *aei* and institutional memory, see Lysias, *Against Andocides* 25, where it is the entity

Athens (Athenai), not the collectivity of Athenians (Athenaioi), that is the sub-ject all-memory (*aeimnēstoi*).

62. Cf. Watkins, "A propos de *mênis*," pp. 187–209. Recall that what Achilles puts an end to is his *kholos*.

63. Popular etymology links *menis* with *menō*, because it is a long-lasting wrath (Chantraine, *Dictionnaire étymologique*, s.v.).

64. Despite Chantraine's remarks, I am convinced by the etymology that makes *menis* a deformation of an original **mnanis* (Watkins, "A propos de *Mênis*," pp. 205–206).

65. See Pietro Pucci's remarks in *Odysseus Polutropos: Intertextual Readings in the "Odyssey" and the "Iliad"* (Ithaca, NY: Cornell University Press, 1987), p. 199.

66. Gernet, *Recherches*, pp. 324–25. Gernet glosses *alastein* as "to be irri-tated by a wrath that does not forget."

67. As Nagy writes, in the mode of "as if," in *Comparative Studies in Greek and Indic Meter*, p. 258.

68. Achilles's *menis* against Agamemnon arises out of the loss of his *time*, not of someone dear to him; yet not only does he behave precisely as if he had lost more than a son or a brother, which, though it would still require compensation (*Iliad* 9.632 ff.), largely exceeds all *time*, but it will not be long before he knows —because of this very *menis*—the *alaston penthos* of having lost his double. See B. Duroselle, "La Mesure de la mort," *Epokhè* (1995).

69. Homer, *Odyssey* 24.174.

70. *Ibid.* 4.108; Sophocles, *Oedipus at Colonus* 1672.

71. Homer, *Iliad* 22.261.

72. Plutarch, *Greek Questions* 25 (*Moralia* 297a).

73. *Alitérios* has a different etymology, but its closeness to *alastōr* makes it practically a doublet of this word (Chantraine, *Dictionnaire étymologique*, s.v. *aleites*). Xanthippus, who is described as such on an Athenian *ostrakon* (Meiggs and Lewis, *Selection of Greek Historical Inscriptions*, 21), is probably "cursed," in an allusion to the pollution of the Alcmeonids.

74. Bernard Abraham van Groningen, *In the Grip of the Past: Essay on an Aspect of Greek Thought* (Leiden: E.J. Brill, 1953).

75. Aeschylus, *Eumenides* 690–93 and 700–706.

76. The *stasis* is *alitēriōdēs* in Plato, *Republic* 5.470d6: on conflict as a "specter" haunting the city.

77. Plutarch, *Obsolescence of Oracles*, 418b–c.

78. For an attempt to construct a history of the word, see Chantraine, *Dictionnaire étymologique*, s.v. *alastōr*. On the idea of a "law of participation," see Gernet, *Recherches*, pp. 319–20.

79. Parker, *Miasma*, pp. 108–109, would like to make "the polluting act" the unifying principle, because he centers everything on pollution.

80. Sophocles, *Electra*, 481–485. See Simondon, *La Mémoire et l'oubli dans la pensée grecque*, pp. 218–19.

81. Aeschylus, *Choephoroi* 491–93, trans A.F. Garvie (New York: Oxford University Press, 1986).

82. Note that the weapon is no longer a tool but a subject credited with the killing of Agamemnon; thus in the Prytaneum, Athenian law judges objects that have "caused" the death of a man.

83. We may add to this list the evocation of Phineus's sons, who are blinded by a stepmother; the "circles of their eyes" are labeled *alastōr* in Sophocles, *Antigone* 974, in *Sophocles*, vol. 2.

84. Sophocles, *Electra* 1246–47.

85. Paul Mazon (CUF) retreats before the evidence and resorts to the passive voice. Simondon, *La Mémoire et l'oubli dans la pensée grecque*, chooses a "voluntarily equivocal" translation: "who cannot know forgetting." With Jebb, the illustrious English editor of Sophocles, we must understand "one sorrow which cannot forget."

86. Perhaps something of this undividedness can still be seen in the double accusative — of the person recalling and of the object recalled — governed by *anamimneskō* (the verb that designates Phrynichus's intervention in Herodotus).

87. Sophocles, *Electra* 223–24.

88. *Ibid.* 230–31.

89. *Ibid.*, 103–10. On the nightingale as slayer of her young, see Nicole

Loraux, "Le Deuil du rossignol," in the *Varia* of the *Nouvelle Revue de psych-analyse* 34 (1986), pp. 253–57.

90. Grammatical distortions in Sophocles do have a meaning: for examples in *Antigone*, see Loraux, "La main d'Antigone," pp. 165–96.

91. Sophocles, *Electra* 131–132.

92. Cf. Watkins, "A propos de *mênis*," p. 209, commenting on the formula *ou . . . lelēthē* (Solon, 13 West, 25).

93. On this form of the future perfect as indicating rightful designation, see Ruijgh, "L'Emploi onomastique de *keklēsthai*," p. 379.

94. Homer, *Iliad* 19.67, 19.35, 1974–75.

95. On "the Forgotten," see Jean-François Lyotard, *Heidegger and "the Jews,"* trans. Andreas Michel and Mark S. Roberts (Minneapolis: University of Minnesota Press, 1990).

96. In comedy, the prohibition is often expressed directly (Aristophanes, *Lysistrata* 590 and *Ploutos* 1146); but, spoken to a single addressee, it becomes burlesque.

97. For historians' narratives, see Xenophon, *Hellenica* 2.4.43; Aristotle, *Athenian Constitution* 39.6 (cites the text of the agreement); see also Andocides, *On the Mysteries* 77, 79, 81, as well as Thucydides, 4.74. For the citations of ora-tors, see Aeschines, *On the Embassy* 176.

98. On *rhēma*, see Aeschines, *Against Ctesiphon* 208; on the noncurrency of the citation, see Lyotard, *Le Différend*, p. 55.

99. Lyotard, *Le Différend*, p. 218.

100. See above, Chapter 5.

101. Nagy, *Comparative Studies in Greek and Indic Meter*, p. 258.

102. See the brief but suggestive remarks of Isocrates, *Against Callimachus* 3 and 23–25.

CHAPTER SEVEN: ON A DAY BANNED FROM THE ATHENIAN CALENDAR
A first version of this essay, as a paper given to the conference of the centennial of the Ecole pratique des hautes études, Fifth Section, was published in Philippe Gignoux, ed., *La Commémoration* (Louvain and Paris: Peeters, 1988)

1. On this notion, see Loraux, *Invention of Athens*, pp. 133–71. If the Athenian history of Athens has its place in the *epitaphioi*, it is important that Plato mentions the episode in the *Menexenus* right after the obligatory evocation of autochthony: *amphisbētēsantōn peri autōs theōn eris kai krisis* (237c8–d1).

2. The month of Boedromion, third of the religious year, corresponds roughly to our month of September.

3. It is true that in the great quarrel that rages over the Athenian calendar, literary sources, when they are extant, seem incomparably more dependable than mutilated inscriptions, whose reconstruction gives rise to all kinds of speculations. As Pritchett and van der Waerden, "Thucydidean Time-Reckoning and Euctemon's Seasonal Calendar," p. 21, write: "The evidence [Plutarch's texts] is fortunately literary and not epigraphical."

4. On the dedication of an altar to Lêthê, see above, Chapter 1. On the subtraction of the second of Boedromion, see Plutarch, *Table Talk* 9.6 (*Moralia* 741a).

5. Plutarch, *On Brotherly Love* 18 (*Moralia* 489b).

6. About brothers as Greek "parents" par excellence, and the conflict between brothers, see below, Chapter 8. The quotation is from *ibid.*

7. Mommsen, *Feste der Stadt Athen im Altertum*, pp. 132–33.

8. On *aei* and its relation to *aiōn*, see Benveniste, "Expression indo-européenne de l'éternité."

9. On the pediment of the Parthenon, see Pausanias 1.24.5 (the birth of Athena is on the east, and the *eris* between Poseidon and Athena for Attica is on the west). On *epitaphioi*, see Plato, *Menexenus* 237c.

10. The quarrel bears *witness* (*marturei* 237c8) and is simultaneously a eulogy of the city by the gods (*hen de theoi epenesan* 237d1).

11. Mikalson, *Sacred and Civil Calendar of the Athenian Year*, p. 47, where he cites Proclus, *In Timaeum* 53d. Mommsen, *Feste der Stadt Athen im Altertum*, p. 171, is more moderate and tries to compromise by placing the Niketeria on the third or fourth of Boedromion.

12. This is the cautious formula of Pritchett and van der Waerden, "Thucydidean Time-Reckoning and Euctemon's Seasonal Calendar," p. 22.

13. I will resist the temptation to date this act to the very end of the fifth century or the beginning of the fourth century by assimilating the divine *eris* to the recent *stasis*, because there are good reasons to be suspicious of an excessively coherent construction and also because the passage on *eris* in the *Menexenus* presupposes that official rhetoric actually included it as a requisite point in the eulogy of Athens.

14. Pritchett, *Ancient Athenian Calendars on Stone*, p. 343, dates it to the Hellenistic period. Archinus's suppression of the days remaining for inscribing exile candidates in 403–402 B.C. (Aristotle, *Athenian Constitution* 40.1) seems to me to require a different explanation, insofar as it corresponds to an immediate policy and not to a comprehensive strategy of official memory.

15. Aristophanes, *Frogs* 1287 (*Sphigga, dusamerian prutanin kuna*). About this text, see also Ana Iriarte, "L'Ogresse contre Thèbes," *Mêtis* 2 (1987), pp. 91–108, particularly 98.

16. Plutarch, *Table Talk* 9.6.

17. Lucian, *Pseudologistés* 13, with the observations of Mikalson, "*Heméra apophras*," p. 20.

18. At least during the republican period, for the empire would make important changes to the calendar. See A. Fraschetti, "Temps de la cité, temps du prince," preface to *Ovide, les Fastes* (Paris: Les Belles Lettres, 1990), pp. vii–xv.

19. According to Varro, *De lingua Latina*, this would be the only holiday put on the calendar "because of men" and not "because of gods." See *ibid.*, p. vii. Is it in order to reduce this anomaly that the ill-fated day was supposed to commemorate not the defeat itself but the sacrifices offered by the military tribune before battle (Aulus Gellius, *Attic Nights* 5.17)? On the Allia as a symbolic defeat, see Cicero, *Letters to Atticus* 9.5.2. According to Aulus Gellius, *Attic Nights*, the battle of Cannae was also at the origin of an "ill-fated day."

20. Plutarch, *Camillus* 19.2–3 and 12; Plutarch, *Roman Questions* 269e–f.

21. According to Aulus Gellius, *Attic Nights*, 4.9, who considers that the "vulgar ignoramus" mistakenly confuses an ill-fated day and a *religiosus* day.

22. On *dies fasti* and *nefasti*, see Michels, *Calendar of the Roman Republic*, pp.

48–52 and 61–67. There are also, of course, days unsuitable for legal business in Greek cities; for example, in Thasos at the end of the fourth century B.C. (see *SEG* 17 [1960], 415). But the forbidden day is assigned to some trials.

23. If we add *dies ater* (black day) to *dies nefasti* and *religiosi*; cf. Michels, *Calendar of Roman the Republic*, pp. 65–66.

24. See Mikalson, "*Heméra apophrás*," p. 20, on Lucian, and p. 22, on Plutarch.

25. See, for example, the text quoted by Mommsen, *Feste der Stadt Athen im Altertum*, p. 83.

26. Plutarch, *Camillus* 19.6.

27. Mikalson, "*Heméra apophrás*," p. 21, gives references.

28. Lucian, *Pseudologistés* 11–12 (*epikhōrion onoma; oikeian kai autokhthona*) and 14 (on the permanence of the meaning of the word *apophras*).

29. See Mikalson, "*Heméra apophrás*," pp. 19–20, on the definition from Lucian, *Pseudologistés* 12. Claiming that there were neither trials nor religious ceremonies on these days (on which the Areopagus passes judgment on murder cases and the Plynteria is celebrated), Lucian in fact defines a *dies nefastus* or a *dies ater*. The moderns (who often confuse the *hēmerai apophrades* with the *hēmerai aphetai*, on which the *boule* did not meet) are just as confused as Lucian; see, for example, Chantraine, *Dictionnaire étymologique*, s.v.

30. Plutarch, *Alcibiades* 34.2, taking up with reference to the Plynteria an idea expressed by Xenophon, *Hellenica* 1.4.12.

31. Mikalson, "*Heméra apophrás*," p. 26.

32. A passage in Plato's *Laws* 7.800d8 opposes the terms *kathara* and *apophrades*. Lexicographers often propose the equivalent *miarai hēmerai*. On the impurity of these days, see especially Parker, *Miasma*, pp. 158–59; for "taboo" days, see Pritchett, *Religion*, pp. 221–22, who takes up an expression of Farnell's.

33. See Mikalson, *Sacred and Civil Calendar of the Athenian Year*, p. 160, and Mikalson, "*Heméra apophrás*," pp. 23–24.

34. *Anepitēdeion*, says Xenophon, *Hellenica* 1.4.12, of the coincidence of Alcibiades's return to Athens with the ceremony. For other connotations of this euphemism, see Loraux, "Thucydide et la sédition dans les mots," pp. 121–22.

35. See Deubner, *Attische Feste*, p. 22 (quotation from Pollux 8.141), and Burkert, *Greek Religion*, p. 79.

36. Hesychius, s.v. *Plunteria*; cf. Parker, *Miasma*, p. 28.

37. See *Etymologicum magnum* 131.13, s.v. *apophradas*. The end of the month is *apophras* not in itself but because of the trials that take place then; cf. Mikalson, "*Heméra apophrás*," pp. 24–26.

38. Cf. Pollux 8.117, with the observations by Pritchett, *Religion*, p. 224, on the open-air trials which Lucian says were held at night.

39. Plutarch, *Roman Questions* 297a; see above, Chapter 6. Hesiod uses the verb *aleasthai* or *aleuasthai* to describe days to be avoided or mistrusted.

40. Scholia to Aeschines, *Against Timarchus* 188.

41. Hesiod, *Works and Days* 802–804.

42. This is Mommsen's theory, *Feste der Stadt Athen im Altertum*, p. 88. Mikalson's study, *Sacred and Civil Calendar of the Athenian Year*, however, shows the existence of at least two meetings of the *ekklēsia* and of one *boulē* on the fifth of a month, as well as of an official decree bearing such a date.

43. About this festival, see S. Georgoudi, "Commémoration et célébration des morts dans les cités grecques: Les Rites annuels," in Philippe Gignoux, ed., *La Commémoration* (Louvain and Paris: Peeters, 1988), pp. 73–89.

44. Hesychius, s.v. *apophrades*; see also the scholia to Plato, *Laws* 7.800d.

45. Among the first on this list are the last two days of the Anthesteria (on Hesychius's belief, s.v. *miarai hēmerai*). See, for example, Deubner, *Attische Feste*, p. 111.

46. The chthonic color of the number two is attested from Plato (*Laws* 4.717a–b) on to John the Lydian (*De mensibus* 2.2), who in fact mentions the second of Boedromion as proof of the "unpure [*ou katharos*]" character of the number two.

47. Mikalson, *Sacred and Civil Calendar of the Athenian Year*, p. 15, based on Plutarch, *Roman Questions* 270a–b.

48. Lysias, *Against Kinesias* frag. 2.

49. Its name evokes the mythical help (*boethēia*) given by Ion to the Athenians in the (victorious) fight against the Thracian Eumolpos. Divine events and

memories of the Persian Wars are associated with Boedromian: the third, like each month's, is the birthday of Athena (and thus could have included the Nike-teria), but it is also reminiscent of the victories of Platea and Mycale; the sixth is devoted to the celebration of the memory of Marathon, and around the twentieth, that of Salamis (Plutarch, *Camillus* 19.5–6). Finally, from the end of the fifth century on, the Athenians celebrate freedom on the twelfth of Boedromion, in memory of the return of Phyle.

50. It was harmful only for the city's women; see Loraux, *Children of Athena,* pp. 113ff.

51. Aeschylus, *Eumenides* 903; cf. Democritus, frag. 249. The *stasis emphulos* is an evil (*kakon*) because it means ruin for both winners and losers. Similarly, the "Cadmean" victory of Oedipus's sons is the "worst [*kakistēn*]," in Plutarch, *On Brotherly Love* 488a.

52. Plato, *Republic* 2.378b–c, and Plato, *Critias* 109b (*ou kat' erin*). But before Plato, Pindar, *Olympian* 9.40–41, already condemned all notions of war between the Immortals.

53. We can link *muthon . . . plasantes* with *muthous plasthentas* (Plato, *Republic* 2.377b), as well as *diaphorai . . . pros oikeious kai sugeneis* with *ekhthras . . . pros suggeneis te kai oikeious* (ibid. 2.378c).

54. Recall Xenophon, *Hellenica* 1.4.12: *anepitēdeion* describes the return of Alcibiades to Athens on the day of the Plynteria.

55. Plato, *Republic* 2.378b–c.

56. *Ibid.* 2.378c.

57. See Lysias, *Against Theomnestos.*

58. Pollux 8.141, s.v. *pariskhoinisai.* The close position of *paraphraxai* and *apophrasi* is certainly not an accident.

59. Eustathius, *ad Od.* 5.294 (p. 1538, 19): *hōs me hoia te ousa phrazesthai;* see also *ad Od.* 19.572. See Chantraine, *Dictionnaire étymologique,* p. 351: "accursed, that one must not say."

60. Estienne's *Thesaurus,* after quoting Eustathius, links it with the Latin *nefas* (*quasi a non fando*). But the utterance does not have the same value in both cases: on one side, the prohibition has to do with the very quality of the day "that

should not be mentioned," and on the other, the prohibition against pronouncing words that initiate a legal action (Michels, *Calendar of the Roman Republic*, p. 48) serves to name the day metonymically.

61. Is it by chance that Plutarch uses *aporrhēta* and *apophradēs* in the space of a few lines when he comments on the Plynteria in *Alcibiades* 34.1–2?

62. I owe a great deal to the study of the verb *phrazō* by Iriarte, *Las redes del enigma*. See also Battegazzore, "La funzione del gesto," pp. 12–13.

63. Hesiod, *Works and Days* 765–67, with West's interpretation, *ad loc.* Mazon (CUF) uses different punctuation in the line but reaches a similar translation: *pephradmen*, to make known.

64. In later periods, a*pophrazomai* is used to mean to forbid; see John the Lydian, *De mensibus* 3.10.

65. I apply to these days what Gernet, *Recherches*, p. 238, writes about the expression *onomata aporrhēta*, which "does not really mean the words that are forbidden to be uttered by law ... but, strictly, the abominable words, words that are an attack in themselves" — words that are effective in themselves.

66. See Cicero, *Against Verres* 2.52 (speaking of lunar months), as well as Diodorus 1.50.2 (who uses the verb *huphairein* just as Aristotle, *Athenian Constitution* 40, does about purely political maneuvers).

67. On these two calendars, see Pritchett and van der Waerden, "Thucydidean Time-Reckoning and Euctemon's Seasonal Calendar," pp. 19–20.

68. Plutarch, *Table Talk* 9.6.

69. On this distinction, which goes back to Solon, see Benjamin Dean Meritt, "The Hollow Month at Athens," *Mnemosyne* 30 (1977), pp. 217–42.

70. J.A. Walsh, "The Omitted Date in the Athenian Hollow Month at Athens," *Zeitschrift für Papyrologie und Epigraphik* 41 (1981), pp. 107–24 and p. 107, n.2.

71. *Ibid.*, p. 115.

72. *Ibid.*, p. 119, explains the word *exairesis* in this way.

73. Cf. Benjamin Dean Meritt, *The Athenian Year* (Berkeley: University of California Press, 1961), pp. 206–207, n.11.

74. Pritchett, *Ancient Athenian Calendars on Stone*, pp. 342–45, notes that "a

people who could strike out, say, 'September 2' certainly had a very different attitude toward the calendar from ours." Thus we can deduce an exceptional norm from the exception.

75. I have used this expression about myth in the city in Loraux, "Le Mythe: Cités grecques."

76. Herodotus 7.162; Aristotle, *Rhetoric* 1.1365a33. See Nicole Loraux, "*Hèbè* et *andreia*: Deux versions de la mort du combattant athénien," *Ancient Society* 6 (1975), pp. 1–31.

77. On tragedy, see Plato, *Republic* 3.394b5 (as well as 3.387d1, 3.387d4, and 3.387e9, and *Theaetetus* 143c5). On letters in words, see Plato, *Cratylus* 414d7 (there are seven other occurrences). On Aristarchus, see Plutarch, *How to Listen to Poetry* 8 (*Moralia* 26f.), about *Iliad* 9.456–61.

78. Cf. West, *Hesiod: Works and Days*, ad 822. The Hesiodic calendar actually compiles a list of *propitious* days; if they are bad for one thing, they are good for another. The only exceptions to this rule are the fifth days (line 802).

79. Hesiod, *Works and Days* 780 and 798.

80. The Hesiodic system *aleasthai/exaleasthai* can be compared with the opposition that Plutarch makes, in a different register, between the *apophras* day, of which one is wary (see the use of the verb *paraphulattein* in *Camillus* 19.9), and the second of Boedromion, object of *exairein*.

81. B. Moreux, "Sens non marqué et sens marqué: *Epi* et *ek* en prose attique," *Bulletin de la Société de linguistique de Paris* 76 (1979), pp. 267–79.

82. In a significant scene in *Table Talk*, the peripatetic Menephylos, who, as a good Aristotelian, praises the gentleness of Poseidon and the power of Lêthê, simply *has forgotten* to cite this day to back up his theory, which his interlocutor brings to his attention (*ekeino se lelēthen, hoti*...).

83. On extraction and the recurrence of the surgical metaphor concerning forgetting and memory, see Loraux, "Pour quel consensus?" pp. 18–21.

84. Similarly, "the content of a repressed image or idea can make its way into consciousness, on condition that it is *negated*" (Freud, "Negation," p. 235.)

85. At least we can rely on the support of a few texts, as rare as they are precious because they are authorized (Freud) or because they somehow show

solidarity. In this category, aside from the works of Gregory Nagy or Charles Malamoud, I must mention the article by Laura Slatkin on insults in the *Iliad*, "Les Amis mortels," *L'Ecrit du temps* 19 (1988), pp. 119–32.

PART THREE: POLITICS OF RECONCILIATION

1. I adapt here, with important modifications, an analysis outlined in Loraux, "Pour quel consensus?" pp. 11–12.

2. Sophocles, *Antigone* 166.

3. This is, among others, the translation of Mazon (CUF).

4. See above, Chapters 1 and 7, on this notion.

5. *Antigone* 144. My translation attempts to make clear the etymological affinity between *stugeros* and Styx.

6. Unless the chorus, without knowing it, anticipates Antigone's logic by treating Polyneices in the same way as Eteocles.

7. Sophocles, *Antigone* 146: *dikrateis logkhas*.

8. This is a way of being defeated by oneself; see Loraux, "La Main d'Antigone." On the sons of Oedipus as twins, see Alaux, *Le Liège et le filet*, pp. 73–111.

9. That tragedy knows no realized reconciliation is evident in Jocasta's failure to reconcile the brothers in Euripides's *Phoenician Women*; in tragedy, reconciliation occurs only in death, which is what actually happens with Oedipus's sons. On the civic formula of amnesty, see above, Chapter 6.

10. See Polybius 4.17–21 on the *stasis* of Kynaitha; cf. Loraux, "La Guerre civile grecque."

11. See Xenophon, *Hellenica* 2.4.43: *eti kai nun . . . tois horkois emmenei ho dēmos* (end of the narrative); cf. Aristotle, *Athenian Constitution* 40.3.

12. A rational mind, for example, is found in Critias. On oligarchic perjuries after a reconciliation, see Thucydides 4.74.2–3; remember that the democrats in Kynaitha are slaughtered by the former exiles.

13. On the Athenian democrats' attitude, see below, Chapter 11.

14. Ozouf, "La Révolution française et l'idée de fraternité," p. 181.

CHAPTER EIGHT: POLITICS OF BROTHERS

A shorter version of this essay was presented at a conference in Rouen on sociability and kinship, and was published in the proceedings of the conference,
Françoise Thélamon, ed., *Aux sources de la puissance: Sociabilité et parenté*
(Rouen, 1989), pp. 21–36. I discovered the quote from Saint-Just, taken from the
report to the Convention on the twenty-sixth Germinal year 2, while reading
Sophie Wahnich's thesis on the question of the foreigner in the French Revolution (University of Paris I, December 1994).

1. See below, Chapter 9.

2. See Asheri, "Osservazioni storiche sul decreto di Nakone," pp. 1033–53,
as well as Asheri, "Formes et procédures de réconciliations dans les cités grecques," and Loraux, "*Oikeios polemos.*"

3. Asheri, "Osservazioni storiche sul decreto di Nakone," p. 1044, and Asheri, "Formes et procédures de réconciliations dans les cités grecques," pp. 144–45.
Phrateres, members of a phratry, are "brothers" in a purely classificatory sense.

4. Glotz, *La Solidarité de la famille*, p. 903.

5. This would doubtless be a contradiction with regard to political practices
but not when it is a question of artificial kinship, indicated by *hairetos* as opposed
to *ek genous*. See Loraux, "*Oikeios polemos*," pp. 31–32.

6. See Loraux, "Le Mythe: Cités grecques."

7. Plato, *Republic* 3.414d–15a: *adelphōn kai gegenōn*, as in *Menexenus* 239a,
where autochthonous citizens are "the children all of one mother." Although it
etymologically means "from the same womb," *adelphos* for a Greek perhaps also
meant "brother of father and mother"; see Perpillou, "Frères de sang ou frères
de culte?" pp. 210–12. In the context of autochthony, however, the word — is this
an etymological trick by Plato? — refers to the maternal line only. Children of
one mother are considered more intimately connected, as is shown by the
Athenian prohibition on marriage between brother and sister from different
fathers but from the same mother. For analogous representations in an African
society where children from one mother are united by affection and children
from one father by rivalry, see Olivier de Sardan, *Les Sociétés songhay-zarma,
Niger-Mali*, p. 41 and 63–64.

8. See Sissa, "La Famille dans la cité grecque."

9. Xenophon, *Hellenica* 2.4.20–22.

10. Plutarch, *On Brotherly Love* 149d.

11. See Loraux, "*Oikeios polemos*," pp. 31–32.

12. Plutarch, *On Curiosity* 518a.

13. See Nicole Loraux, "*Poluneikes eponumos*: Le Nom des fils d'Oedipe entre épopée et tragédie," in Claude Calame (ed.), *Métamorphoses du mythe en Grèce antique* (Geneva: Labor et Fides, 1988), pp. 151–66.

14. I am not taking into account here the "private" phenomenon, well attested in legal speeches, of quarrels between brothers about sharing inheritance, which in fact is also the *eris* of Oedipus's sons. See Strauss, p. 68, where I find the only occurrence of the question.

15. Lysias, *Against Eratosthenes* 92.

16. Plato, *Laws* 9.869c–d.

17. Gernet, *Platon: Laws, livre IX*, p. 140, is more interested in this question than in the specific case of the murder of a brother (which a misprint transformed into "father").

18. Ozouf, "La Révolution française et l'idée de fraternité," p. 177.

19. Hesiod, *Works and Days* 182–84.

20. Note that the reciprocity between hosts and companions is expressed with the repetition of *xenos* and *hetairos* but that when it comes to brothers, a single mention of *kasignētos* is sufficient (*oude kasignētos philos essetai*). It is as if the reciprocity suggested by *philos* were never as obvious as in the case of the brother.

21. Herodotus 6.52.

22. There is a similar expression in Herodotus 3.61 (murder of Smerdis by his brother Cambyses) and 3.145, where the context, however, more clearly suggests an adversative force.

23. For quarrels, see Herodotus 1.92, 1.173, 3.139–40, 3.145, 5.104 (kings, barbarians, and tyrants), 6.52 (Spartan kings). For murders, see *ibid*. 1.35, 2.107–108, 3.30, 3.39, 3.61, 3.64, 3.65, 4.76, 4.160, 9.107–13. Quarrels and murders practically disappear when the Greeks come to the forefront of the scene

during the Persian Wars. For barbarians, kings, and tyrants, see *ibid.* 2.100, 3.119, 4.5, 5.25, 5.99, 7.7, 7.39, 7.156; for Greeks, see *ibid.* 7.227, 9.33–35.

24. Perpillou, "Frères de sang ou frères de culte?" pp. 207–208 and 210.

25. Aristotle, *Nicomachean Ethics* 8.1155b32ff.; Aristotle, *Eudemian Ethics* 1234b–35a.

26. See Loraux, "La Main d'Antigone," as well as Loraux, "Corcyre 427, Paris 1871."

27. See Alaux, *Le Liège et le filet*, pp. 73–111, on Oedipus's sons, as well as Jean Alaux, "Fratricide et lien fraternel: Quelques repères grecs," in *Quaderni di storia* 46 (1997), pp. 107–32.

28. In the Aristotelian formulation of this ideal, in *Nicomachean Ethics* 8.1160a5–6 (*deinoteron ... mē boēthēsai adelphōi ē othneiōi*), "not to help" is as severe an offense as "to strike" when the father is the object. Because "to strike" is often a euphemism for "to kill" — thus in *patraloias*, the "forbidden" name of patricide — we can measure the strength of the prohibition that weighs over the abandonment of a brother.

29. Demosthenes, *On the Embassy* 238; Plato, *Republic* 2.362d and 4.427d.

30. For example, Homer, *Iliad* 5.474; 2.409 and 8.317; 19.293 and 6.421; 14.483–85 and 16.320.

31. Herodotus 3.32.

32. Hesiod, *Works and Days* 371–72.

33. *Ibid.* 707–708.

34. Commenting on the second passage quoted from Hesiod, Plutarch diverts its sense according to his own prejudices: because he puts the brother above everything, he credits Hesiod with mistrust of the friend and not of the brother.

35. Aeschylus, *Seven Against Thebes* 681–82.

36. Aristotle, *Nicomachean Ethics* 9.1167a21–34.

37. Aristotle, *Politics* 5.1305b2–18.

38. Benveniste, *Vocabulaire des institutions indo-européennes*, vol. 1, pp. 210–11; Plato, *Republic* 5.457d, 5.461d, 5.471d.

39. On the singular form of *phrater*, see Perpillou, "Frères de sang ou frères de culte?"; but also see the doubts expressed by Lévêque, "Observations sur la communication de Marcel Piérart," pp. 189–90, on the word *aphretor*, which is obviously institutional (Homer, *Iliad* 9.63). On the plural form, see Benveniste, *Vocabulaire des institutions indo-européennes*, vol. 1, p. 221; cf. Chantraine, *Dictionnaire étymologique*, s.v.

40. *Ibid.*, vol. 1, p. 213, as well as Szemerényi, "Studies in the Kinship Terminology of the Indo-European Languages," pp. 22–23.

41. Roussel, *Tribu et cité*, p. 142.

42. Lévêque, "Observations sur la communication de Marcel Piérart," p. 190.

43. Homer, *Iliad* 9.63–64: *aphrētōr, athemistos, anestios*, with the commentary by Glotz, *La Solidarité de la famille*, p. 991.

44. See the scholia to Homer, *Iliad* 2.362–63, which speak of *suggeneia* and link it to *phulē*; Stephanus of Byzantium, s.v. *patra*, as well as Aristotle, *Politics* 2.1262a12.

45. Benveniste, *Vocabulaire des institutions indo-européennes*, vol. 1, p. 258, shows the asymmetry between *phratria* and *curia* (from *co-uiria*, the *uiri* as a whole) and challenges the legitimacy of the equivalence accepted without discussion by Fustel de Coulanges in *La Cité antique*, pp. 133–43 and 149.

46. Chantraine, *Dictionnaire étymologique*, s.v. See also Henri Jeanmaire, *Couroi et courètes* (1939; reprint, New York: Arno Press, 1975), p. 136.

47. Homer, *Iliad* 2.366; see Roussel, *Tribu et cité*, p. 117.

48. Aristotle, *Politics* 2.1264a8, 3.1280b37, 5.1309a12, 6.1319b23–24.

49. Roussel, *Tribu et cité*, p. 142.

50. Lejeune (1960).

51. See Benveniste, *Vocabulaire des institutions indo-européennes*, vol. 1, p. 221, and Lévêque, "Observations sur la communication de Marcel Piérart," p. 190, about Hesychius's gloss, *kasioi*.

52. Szemerényi, "Studies in the Kinship Terminology of the Indo-European Languages," p. 23.

53. Pierre Chantraine, "Note sur l'emploi homérique de *kasígnetos*," *Bulletin*

de la Société de linguistique de Paris (1960), pp. 27–31, correctly insists on the legitimate character of *kasignētoi*, adding that the word "regains in juridical importance" what it loses in precision (for the same root *gnē-*, see *gnēsios*).

54. Relative, that is, cousins: see Homer, *Iliad* 15.545 (with scholia), 15.456, 15.674 (with scholia), and especially Homer, *Odyssey* 16.115ff. (related through males in the case of two collateral lines that have only sons). On descending from brothers, see Herodotus 1.171; on natural allies, see Homer, *Odyssey* 16.97–98 (repeated at 115–16). On the role of collateral relatives, see Glotz, *La Solidarité de la famille*, p. 78.

55. The Scythians, to be sure, are the most Greek of the barbarians; see Hartog, *Mirror of Herodotus*. Yet if the notion of city is unknown to them, it is also unknown *a fortiori* to the Agathyrses.

56. Herodotus 4.104.

57. See above, Chapter 2, n.46, for the Aristotelian formulation "the city wants to be."

58. I summarize here a long passage from Aristotle, *Nicomachean Ethics* 8.1161b11–62a15. About the "sphere of use" of the words *etas, hetairos*, "excluding that of family structures," see Henri van Effenterre, "Ambiguïté du vocabulaire de la sociabilité dans la cité grecque archaïque," in F. Thélamon (ed.), *Sociabilité, pouvoirs et société: Actes du colloque de Rouen 1983* (Université de Rouen: 1987), p. 47.

59. Even if we slip first cousins and other *suggeneis* as reinforcements in between the brother and the companion (Aristotle, *Nicomachean Ethics* 8.1161b11–62a15).

60. To Hesychius's gloss, I add the following: *kasēs helikiōtēs*; see Calame, *Morphologie, fonction religieuse et sociale*, pp. 377–79.

61. *Hetairoi* are *de facto* contemporaries. On brothers and the question of age, see Aristotle, *Nicomachean Ethics* 8.1161a3–6.

62. See *ibid.* 8.1159b25ff., where brothers and companions are the only figures that can be superimposed on those of citizens, and 9.1164a29–33, where *parrhēsia* (democratic freedom of speech) is ascribed to the relations between companions and brothers, parents, *phuletes*, and citizens.

63. See Homer, *Odyssey* 21.216; Homer, *Iliad* 4.441, with Glotz's observations in *La Solidarité de la famille*, pp. 85–89.

64. The host and suppliant are compared to brothers in Homer, *Odyssey* 8.546 (*anti kasignetou*); see also 8.585–86.

65. *Ibid.* 8 and Theognis 97–99. See Aristotle, *Nicomachean Ethics* 8.1159b35–60a2 (from the family to *hetairoi* and citizens); see also 8.1161b25–26 (from brothers to *hetairoi* and citizens). There is the same movement in Aristotle, *Eudemian Ethics* 9.1242.

66. Plato, *Republic* 3.414d–15a and *Menexenus* 239a. This brotherhood certainly does oppose the city to the outside, but in the context of the Greek city it is not the "xenophobic brotherhood" (Ozouf, "La Révolution française et l'idée de fraternité," p. 174) later invented by Jacobinism; see Nicole Loraux, "Les Bénéfices de l'autochtonie," *Le Genre humain* 3–4 (1982), pp. 238–53.

67. Plato, *Laws* 1.627c and 9.888b5; see also 9.869c–d.

68. Plato, *Menexenus* 238d–39a; Aristotle, *Nicomachean Ethics* 8.1160a28–30.

69. Aristotle, *Eudemian Ethics* 9.1241d26ff.

70. Lysias, *Against Eratosthenes* 92.

71. Homer, *Iliad* 9.632–33 and 24.46–47; Homer, *Odyssey* 4.225, as well as 24.434. See also Aeschylus, *Agamemnon* 327 (*andron kasignēton*).

72. See Meiggs and Lewis, *Selection of Greek Historical Inscriptions*, 5 (foundation of Cyrene), 2.38–39, which can be compared with Herodotus 4.153; see also Meiggs and Lewis, *Selection of Greek Historical Inscriptions*, 20 (law of the Eastern Locrians concerning the colonization of Naupactus), 1.7.

73. Thus Adrastus, in Herodotus 1.45, involuntarily kills the son of Croesus and is described as *phoneus tou kathērantos*, destroyer of his purifier — Croesus himself, who had purified him when he welcomed him in his house: to kill the son is the same as killing the father.

74. Thucydides 3.81.5. See Loraux, "*Oikeios polemos*," pp. 20–21, for a comparison with Aristotle's silence on this type of murder in tragedy (*Poetics* 1453b19–22) and for an evaluation of the murders, respectively, of son and brother.

75. See Jal, *La Guerre civile à Rome*, pp. 269–70 and 414–15; we should especially note Velleius Paterculus 2.67 and Appian, *Civil Wars* 4.12–14 (Sulla's proscription). As for singular cases (Appian 4.17–30), François Hinard's prosopography in *Les Proscriptions de la Rome républicaine* (Rome: Ecole Française de Rome; Paris: Diffusion de Boccard, 1985), where it is essentially the responsibility of sons and brothers, scarcely strays from the literary sources.

76. Lucan, *Pharsalia* 2.148–51, trans. J.D. Duff, *Lucan* (Cambridge, MA: Harvard University Press, 1957). See Jal, *La Guerre civile à Rome*, pp. 406–11.

77. See Jal, *La Guerre civile à Rome*, pp. 406–11, about the *antiques fratrum discordiae*, even though Jal insists on Augustus's efforts to eliminate the theme of fratricide from the legend of Romulus (p. 408); see also pp. 401–405 on Greek influence and its limits.

78. These are seven murders of brothers for eight murders of fathers in book 7 of the *Pharsalia*. For intensity, see especially Velleius Paterculus 2.67.2, who characterizes the degree of loyalty of each member of the *familia: filiorum nullam.*

79. Lucan, *Pharsalia* 1.1.

80. Thomas, "*Parricidium* I: Le Père, la famille et la cité," p. 714. See also Mazzarino, *Il pensiero storico classico*, vol. 3, p. 73, on Vipitanus Messala, who associated the civil war of 69 with parricide, telling the tragic story of a son who kills his father in combat.

81. Without taking sides on the etymological question (murder of the same or murder of the brother?), I am interested in the representation of this act.

82. See Thomas, "Se venger au forum," pp. 77–78.

83. See Thomas, "Paura dei padri e violenza dei figli," pp. 120, 122–23, 135, as well as P. Botteri, "Figlio pubbici e padri privati," M.-A. Bonnefond, "Senato e conflitti de generazione nella Roma repubblicana," and J.-M. David, "Sfida o vendetta, minaccia o ricatto," in Ezio Pellizer and Nevio Zorzetti (eds.), *La Paura dei padri nella società antica e medievale* (Rome and Bari: Laterza, 1983). On the *patria potestas* at the center of this representation of the war of sons against fathers, see Thomas, "*Parricidium* I: Le Père, la famille et la cité," p. 690, and Thomas "Se venger au forum," passim.

84. Jal, *La Guerre civile à Rome*, pp. 469–70; Thomas, "*Parricidium* I: Le Père, la famille et la cité," pp. 653 and 690–95.

85. Fustel de Coulanges's completely "Roman" choice, projected onto Greece, leaves no room for *brothers*, except in inheritance division, and in the index of *La Cité antique*, the entry "father" is very well supplied, whereas the entry "brother" does not exist.

86. Maffi, in Pellizer and Zorzetti (eds.), *La Paura dei padri*, pp. 9–11. See also Strauss, *Fathers and Sons in Athens*, pp. 130–78, especially 153–66 (Aristophanes) for a more nuanced discussion of the "reality" of the tension between fathers and sons.

87. If time of war, in which fathers bury their sons, is the reverse of the normal order, in which sons bury their fathers, *stasis* goes beyond the absolute limit of horror when a father kills a son.

88. Cf. Jal, *La Guerre civile à Rome*, pp. 295–96 ("fraternization"). Occurrences of "fratricide," even when the word used is actually *parricidalis* (as in Petronius's *Satyricon* 80.1), are numerous; see Thomas, "*Parricidium* I: Le Père, la famille et la cité," p. 682.

89. Jal, *La Guerre civile à Rome*, pp. 19–21 and 36.

90. *Ibid.*, p. 394.

91. See Polybius 6.52–54, with the observations by Loraux, *Invention of Athens*, p. 20.

92. See Thomas, "Se venger au forum," p. 66.

93. See Botteri, "*Stasis*: Le Mot grec, la chose romaine," pp. 88–89 and 99–100.

94. See Loraux, "*Oikeios polemos*," about the Greek particulars.

95. Sissa, "La Famille dans la cité grecque," p. 183.

96. Isaeus, *Succession of Chiron* 35. See also Plato, *Laws* 4.718a7, for the distinction *ekgonoi/suggeneis*.

97. Aeschylus, *Eumenides* 985.

98. In Aeschylus, *Seven Against Thebes* 883, the mortal rivalry between the brothers is indissociably familial and political, and they are reconciled only "by the help of steel" (see also 941: *pikros lutēr neikeōn*); cf. Alaux, *Le Liège et le filet*, pp. 73ff.

CHAPTER NINE: A RECONCILIATION IN SICILY

A first version of this essay was presented at the Institut de droit romain.

1. On the geography (close to Entella, southeast of Segesta, halfway between Palermo and Selinonte), see van Effenterre, *La Cité grecque des origines à la défaite de Marathon*, and on the circumstances of the decree (probably from 345 B.C.), see Dubois, "Actualités dialectologiques. III."

2. The inscription was first published in 1980 by Giuseppe Nenci in *Annali della Scuola Normale Superiore* and later was systematically published in Nenci, ed., *Materiali e contributi*, by Asheri, and commented on in articles by S. Alessandri and I. Savalli, in Savalli, "Alcune osservazioni sulla terza iscrizione da Entella," pp. 1055–67; Asheri entered the discussion again later in "Formes et procédures de réconciliation dans les cités grecques," as did P. Gauthier, L. Dubois, H. and M. van Effenterre in *Annali della Scuola Normale Superiore* (1985). I have also commented on the question of brothers in Loraux, "*Oikeios polemos.*"

3. See Asheri, "Osservazioni storiche sul decreto di Nakone," p. 1038.

4. See above, Chapter 7.

5. I translate *homonoia* in this way to avoid the Roman tones of "concord."

6. On *diallaktēres*, see above, Chapter 4.

7. Like most scholars commenting on this text, I interpret *klaros* as the "lot" of each person. This is contrary to the opinion of Dubois, "Actualités dialectologiques. III," who understands *klaros* to mean plot of land, interpreting the decree as a division of land after a *stasis*.

8. This is a Doric form of the word *hieromnēmones*. On *mnēmones*, see above, Chapter 1.

9. Asheri, "Osservazioni storiche sul decreto di Nakone," p. 1035; Thucydides 8.54.4 (preparation for the overthrow by the oligarchs) bears witness that *arkhai* (public offices) could be the object of *stasis*, as well as Aristotle, *Athenian Constitution* 12.2 (after Solon). The bond of *agōn* with *stasis* is in fact clear in Thucydides 6.38.2 (*staseis kai agōnas*).

10. Asheri, "Osservazioni storiche sul decreto di Nakone," p. 1034, and Asheri, "Formes et procédures de réconciliation dans les cités grecques," p. 139.

11. Savalli, "Alcune osservazioni sulla terza iscrizione da Entella," pp. 1058–59 and 1060 ("a deep civic discord").

12. Van Effenterre, "L'Acte de fraternisation de Nakônè."

13. Much like *stasis*, as a matter of fact, as Moses Finley notes in *Politics in the Ancient World* (Cambridge, UK: Cambridge University Press, 1983), p. 105, when he describes it as a "portmanteau-word."

14. See Loraux, "La Majorité, le tout et la moitié," and Loraux, "La Démocratie à l'épreuve de l'étranger (Athènes, Paris)."

15. Savalli, "Alcune osservazioni sulla terza iscrizione da Entella," p. 1060.

16. For example, at Elis, where the state of *diaphora* precedes seditious acts themselves (Xenophon 7.4.15), or at Kynaitha (Polybius 4.17.10).

17. As Plato's analysis of this word implies; see *Republic* 5.470b and 5.471a–b (where the word's sense includes *polemos* and *stasis*), as well as *Laws* 862c (where it is opposed to *philia*). See also Cambiano, "Pathologie et analogie politique," p. 444 and n.15, on a passage of the *Euthyphro*.

18. See the examples listed by Savalli, "Alcune osservazioni sulla terza iscrizione da Entella," p. 1060, who contrasts them with the use of *stasis* by historians, without being aware that the formulation of a decree does not follow the same rules as historiographical narratives.

19. See, for example, the decree of Knossos for Hermias of Kos (end of third century B.C., *SIG* 528.2.4–7: the *stasis* of Gortyn).

20. Plato, *Menexenus* 243d; Xenophon 3.1.1.

21. See, for example, Pouilloux, ed., *Choix d'inscriptions grecques*, n.21, 2.5, 8–9, 11 and 16.

22. Xenophon, *Hellenica* 2.4.22 and 2.4.43 (two instances). See also *OGI* 229, 2.64–65: *politeusomai astasiastos*.

23. This practice, frequent in Hellenistic cities, evokes the *katartistēres* of the Archaic period; see above, Chapter 4.

24. Does *es ton loipon khronon* (line 5) mean, as has been suggested, "as long as old adversaries who have become friends will live?" I do not believe so, because even though the institution of brothers will end with the death of the

participants, the lasting agreement proclaimed at the beginning of the decree belongs to a very different plane of generality.

25. Aristotle, *Politics* 4.1296a10.

26. Fictitious and not "practical," as van Effenterre, "L'Acte de fraternisation de Nakônè," proposes, just after correctly observing that "there is no reason for the two opposing parties to have numbered exactly thirty men each."

27. Plato, *Republic* 5.471b.

28. Aristotle, *Athenian Constitution* 39.6.

29. See above, Chapter 4, as well as Loraux, "Corcyre 427, Paris 1871."

30. Rather than "all those of the citizens for whom the disagreement happened," a translation that is made unlikely by the word order.

31. At any rate, this was the Athenian city's plan for the men of Phyle, whom it was necessary to distinguish from the crowd of "those of the Piraeus" (cf. Aeschines, *Against Ctesiphon* 187: *boulē, skepsamenē hosoi epi Phulēi epoliorkhetesan...*), as well as the orphan sons of genuine citizens (decree of Theozotides, in *Hesperia* 40 [1971], line 4: *hosoi Athenaion apethanon...*).

32. See the observations by van Effenterre, "L'Acte de fraternisation de Nakônè," on the global nature of the drawing of lots.

33. See Loraux, "La Main d'Antigone," pp. 179–82, and Loraux, "Corcyre 427, Paris 1871." For one of many examples, see Polybius 4.22.4: *estasiazon pros sphas*.

34. Isocrates, *Against Callimachus* 30: *pisteis* [...] *tas pros hēmas autous gegenēmenas* [...] *lusomen* (but in 46, we find *pisteis allēlois edomen*).

35. See Dubois, "Actualités dialectologiques. III," pp. 102–103, on lines 19, 26, and 27.

36. By virtue of the grammatical rule that the repetition of a personal pronoun can substitute for the use of a reflexive pronoun; see Loraux, "La Main d'Antigone," for examples.

37. In Thucydides, they are interchangeable even in their language; see Loraux, "Thucydide et la sédition dans les mots." The perfect resemblance postulated by some Latin texts seems more external, see Jal, *La Guerre civile à Rome*, pp. 322–26.

38. See, for example, Plato, *Republic* 5.470d, with the observations of Asheri, "Formes et procédures de réconciliation dans les cités grecques," p. 140, n.5.

39. On the use of *hekateroi* to describe the relationship between opposites within an antithetical pair, see Cambiano, "Pathologie et analogie politique," p. 443.

40. See Plato, *Menexenus* 238d3–4, for the opposition of *hairetoi* and *ek genous*.

41. Calame, *Morphologie, fonction religieuse et sociale*, pp. 377–79, has shown how the Spartan *kasioi* and *kasies* do not depend on the same "fathers."

42. The Athenians instituted a cult of *dēmokratia*, but in the fourth century B.C. *dēmokratia* became a more and more empty word, synonymous with *homonoia*.

43. John Scheid, *Romulus et ses frères: Le Collège des frères arvales, modèle public dans la Rome des empereurs* (Rome and Paris: Ecole française de Rome, 1990).

44. Ozouf, M., "La Révolution française et l'idée de fraternité," pp. 167–68.

45. On the very controversial question of the phratry in the Cleisthenian reform, see Oswyn Murray, in Oswyn Murray and Simon Price (eds.), *The Greek City: From Homer to Alexander* (New York: Oxford University Press, 1990).

46. I owe this hypothesis to a suggestion by John Scheid.

47. Our lack of knowledge about the structures of the Nakonian city allows only for hypotheses.

48. See above, Chapter 8, on the connotations of *adelphos*.

49. See Savalli, "Alcune osservazioni sulla terza iscrizione da Entella," who gives references.

50. This would make more sense in the case of an arbitral-type structure.

51. Insofar as the three "neutrals" would function as arbitrators.

52. Plato, *Republic* 5.464d.

53. We have seen (above, Chapter 8) that the same applied to brothers.

54. The use of the plural, suggesting the concreteness of the brotherhoods, indicates that this has nothing to do with juridical procedures; yet we should not translate the word vaguely as "association," as does Dubois, "Actualités dialectologiques. III," p. 102, who seems to have difficulties with the fraternal theme.

55. Asheri, "Formes et procédures de réconciliation dans les cités grecques," pp. 1040–41. Carlo Alfonso Nallino has a similar approach in *Intorno al divieto romano imperiale dell' affratellamento e ad alcuni paralleli arabi* (Palermo, 1933), a study brought to my attention by Salvatore D'Onofrio.

56. The idea of a Carthaginian model is problematic if we must, with Dubois, "Actualités dialectologiques. III," link this reconciliation with the troubles caused in Sicily by the Carthaginian Hanno's expedition (345 B.C.).

57. See above, Chapter 8.

58. Perceptively observed by van Effenterre, "L'Acte de fraternisation de Nakônè."

59. Asheri, "Osservazioni storiche sul decreto di Nakone," pp. 1034–35.

60. See Loraux, "*Oikeios polemos.*" Since writing that essay, I have been led by Yan Thomas's arguments to reexamine the question.

61. Gernet, *Recherches*, pp. 88–93, about, it is true, blood trials.

62. Savalli, "Alcune osservazioni sulla terza iscrizione da Entella," p. 1062.

63. "Apparently a general assembly with jurisdictional power," in Asheri, "Formes et procédures de réconciliation dans les cités grecques," p. 139, a very common institution in Sicily and Magna Graecia; see Savalli, "Alcune osservazioni sulla terza iscrizione da Entella," and also Asheri, "Osservazioni storiche sul decreto di Nakone," p. 1040. In Athens, *hēliaia* is the generic name of the civic court.

64. The word *prographo* gives to the drawing up of the list the character of a real accusation, as M. Humbert brought to my attention. See also Savalli, "Alcune osservazioni sulla terza iscrizione da Entella," who observes that this verb literally translates the Latin *proscribere* in the Greek historians of Rome.

65. In terms of the numbers of Indo-European harmonics, we may think, for example, of the *Mahabharata*, which opposes two groups of five brothers. See Lévêque and Vidal-Naquet, *Clisthène l'Athénien*, pp. 92–96, on the number five in a study of the Cleisthenian ten.

66. Two is the number of division (and of the feminine), three that of completeness (and of the masculine); but we could also count two adversaries plus three *arbitrators*.

67. Asheri, "Osservazioni storiche sul decreto di Nakone," p. 1038, who interprets "in all justice and friendship" (lines 20–21) as the reference to a judgment through a majority vote. See also Asheri, "Formes et procédures de réconciliation dans les cités grecques," p. 141: "with friendly help or the majority vote of the three."

68. See Aristotle, *Athenian Constitution* 64.3: *kata pente*.

69. Asheri, "Osservazioni storiche sul decreto di Nakone," p. 1038.

70. Cf. Aristotle, *Athenian Constitution* 53, with the observations by Gernet, *Droit et société dans la Grèce ancienne*; see below, Chapter 10. Aristotle mentions public arbitrators in the list of officials whose functions are assigned by drawing lots.

71. See, for example, Tod, *Selection of Greek Historical Inscriptions*, 201, and especially Pouilloux, ed., *Choix d'inscriptions grecques*, 21, 2.13–15, 22–23 (opposition between *edikasan* and *dielusan, dialuō* being effectively used in the sense of "to settle a lawsuit").

72. Aristotle, *Athenian Constitution* 53.2, makes this the first stage of arbitration, which may or may not be followed by a legal stage.

73. This argument owes much to Yan Thomas's suggestions.

74. Van Effenterre, "L'Acte de fraternisation de Nakone," offers a similar idea.

75. Plato, *Menexenus* 243e5–6: *hos hasmenos kai oikeios allelois sunemeixan*.

76. The Sicilian version of *hoi aei en arkhēi ontes*, this expression means "on the feet," and hence "who follow each other." This is the clear formulation of a continuity in the form of a chain.

CHAPTER TEN: OF JUSTICE AS DIVISION

This essay is an expanded version of a paper presented at a conference on the subject of the trial (Association de philosophie du droit, Cour de cassation) in November 1993 and published in *Archives de philosophie du droit* (1994).

1. Heraclitus, frag. 80, in *Ancilla to the Pre-Socratic Philosophers*.

2. See [Xenophon], *Athenian Constitution* 1.16–18.

3. Aristophanes, *Wasps* 800–804, trans. B.B. Rogers, *Aristophanes* (Cambridge, MA: Harvard University Press, 1982).

4. Aristotle, *Athenian Constitution* 9.1.

5. See the enlightening observations on this point by Paoli, *Studi sul processo attico*, p. 71.

6. Aristotle, *Politics* 3.1275a22–23 and 3.1275b5ff; see also 3.1275b17ff.

7. *Ibid.* 6.1317b26ff., Athenian judges were chosen very democratically by drawing lots. Even the venerable court of the Areopagus, despite its aristocratic past, was indirectly recruited on the same basis; it was composed of archons, at least from 487 B.C. on, when "the nine archons were appointed by lot on a tribal basis, from a short list of five hundred elected by the members of the demes," Aristotle, *Athenian Constitution* 22.5.

8. Plato, *Laws* 6.767e–68b.

9. Plato, *Republic* 5.464d.

10. Plato, *Laws* 3.679d.

11. Aristotle, *Politics* 5.1306a31ff.

12. Thucydides 3.70.3 (Corcyra); see also 8.54.4.

13. Xenophon, *Memorabilia* 4.4.8. See also the observation by Paoli, *Studi sul processo attico*, p. 70.

14. For a complete study, see, for example, MacDowell, *Law in Classical Athens*.

15. On the generalization of the scheme of private justice in Athens, see the remarks by Gernet, "*Les Lois* et le droit postif," p. 135.

Cases not brought before popular tribunals were trials for homicide, which were judged by the Areopagus or other special law courts (the Ephetai at the Delphinion, the Prytaneion, and so on), and some trials concerning security of state, judged by the *Ekklēsia*.

16. On these functions, see Paoli, *Studi sul processo attico*, p. 82, who notes that the magistrate's sphere of action is further limited by the law (pp. 57 and 60).

17. On the expression *telos ekhei hē dikē* (the trial has reached its end), see Gernet, *Droit et société dans la Grèce ancienne*, pp. 69 and 81, and Gernet, "*Les Lois* et le droit positif," p. 134.

18. Gernet, *Droit et société dans la Grèce ancienne*, p. 63; Gernet, "*Les Lois* et le droit positif," p. 140.

19. Gernet, *Droit et société dans la Grèce ancienne*, p. 65, my emphasis.

20. To allude to one of Aristotle's very rare puns, in the *Nicomachean Ethics* 5.1132a31–32, between *dikē* and *dikha*.

21. See above, Chapter 4, as well as Loraux, "Reflections of the Greek City on Unity and Division," pp. 39–43. For an example of *diaphoron*, see Thucydides 2.37.1.

22. Chantraine, *Dictionnaire étymologique*, s.v. *dia*, gives to the prefix the original sense of "dividing, whence the notion of distinction, difference, rivalry"; on *dia-* and division, see above, Chapter 4, as well as Loraux, "Reflections of the Greek City on Unity and Division." According to Gernet, *Droit et société dans la Grèce ancienne*, pp. 99–100, "the prefix . . . presupposes two parties put on the same level and between which it is necessary to decide." This putting on the same level is completely fulfilled in the *diadikasia*, in which there are no accusers or defendants but only two or more equal adversaries.

23. For *diairein*, see Aeschylus, *Eumenides* 472 and 488, and Plato, *Statesman* 305b. For *diagignōskein*, see *Eumenides* 709 (with Gernet's comment [1917a] pp. 88–89). For *diakrisis*, see Plato, *Laws* 6.768a3 (although at a1, the word *krisis* is used).

24. See Hesiod, *Theogony* 535 and 882 (conflict dividing gods and men or Titans). See also Aeschylus, *Eumenides* 677: *pōs agōn krithēsetai*. Cf. Gernet, *Recherches*, p. 90 and n.106.

25. See especially Benveniste, *Vocabulaire des institutions indo-européennes*, vol. 2, pp. 109–10: "Carrying out justice is not an intellectual process requiring meditation or discussion."

26. Especially by Paoli, *Studi sul processo attico*, p. 67, as well as Gernet, *Recherches*, p. 450, and Gernet, *Droit et société dans la Grèce ancienne*, p. 110.

27. Paoli, *Studi sul processo attico*, p. 67.

28. "The fundamental notion is that of *dikaion* [the just], directly known by conscience," as Gernet notes, *Droit et société dans la Grèce ancienne*, p. 67.

29. Gernet, *Recherches*, pp. 86 and 91–92, and Gernet, *Droit et société dans la Grèce ancienne*, pp. 66–76.

30. Aristotle, *Politics* 3.1282a34–38.

31. Gernet, *Droit et société dans la Grèce ancienne*, p. 69.

32. Sometimes they appeared twice, in certain cases of homicide and in many private trials, which made it possible for the plaintiff, who was first to speak, to answer his adversary in his second speech. See MacDowell, *Law in Classical Athens*, pp. 119 and 249.

33. *Ibid.*, pp. 251–52, stresses the difference on this point with modern trials.

34. Xenophon, *Hellenica* 1.7.4–34.

35. MacDowell, *Law in Classical Athens*, pp. 187–88.

36. Gernet, *Droit et société dans la Grèce ancienne*, p. 70; see also p. 79 on the question of assessing punishment.

37. Paoli, *Studi sul processo attico*, p. 68.

38. On the honor of getting meals at the Prytaneum, see Pauline Schmitt Pantel, "Les Repas au Prytanée et à la Tholos dans l'Athènes classique: *Sitésis, misthos* et *trophè*," in *Annali dell'Istituto orientale di Napoli* (1980), pp. 55–68.

39. I owe this insight on the importance of this fundamental rule of legal thought to Yan Thomas.

40. Aristotle, *Politics* 2.1268b9–11.

41. The expression used by Aristotle, *ouk estin*, depends on "this does not exist" understood as "this is not possible" when the verb is accented.

42. Gernet, "*Les Lois* et le droit positif," p. 143, on the passage from Aristotle.

43. Aristotle repeats this verb twice (1268b7 and 10), as if its utterance in itself communicated an obvious absurdity.

44. The presuppostions of this wager on the majority are elaborated by Terray, "Un Anthropologue africaniste devant la cité grecque," pp. 21–24.

45. Plato, *Laws* 6.766d5ff., with the comments by Gernet, "*Les Lois* et le droit positif," pp. 140–41; 9.876b.

46. Aristophanes, *Wasps* 587, trans. J. Henderson, *Aristophanes* (Cambridge, MA: Harvard University Press, 1998), vol. 2, a claim that Bdelycleon himself recognizes as just. Much could be said about this privilege, which is outrageous in a system where providing an account is the rule and which, insofar as it can

verge on irresponsibility, gives to Athenian judges the intoxicating feeling of power derided by comedy.

47. Plato, *Laws* 6.761e. At 6.767e, a suit to the benefit of the injured party is allowed against the author of an unjust sentence.

48. We saw, however, that Plato, *Laws* 6.767e–68b, recognized the necessity of a popular basis for justice in his city. In fact, the account in the *Laws* is still very much inspired by the Athenian model, whose influence Gernet, "Les Lois et le droit positif," passim, stresses.

49. Plato, *Laws* 9.855e.

50. This preference is evident before and even during the trial, until the moment when the judges decide; see Gernet, *Droit et société dans la Grèce ancienne*, p. 114. This strongly implies that private arbitration, far from being only an alternative to legal action, coexisted with it and could even fit within it.

51. Plato, *Laws* 6.767b.

52. Aristotle, *Politics* 4.1297a5–6. Doubtless, the extant speeches presuppose by their mere existence that the intervention of such a mediator was not enough and that it was necessary to have recourse to the service of judges as "dividers"; it remains that in most cases, arbitration would have preceded – as if to avoid – recourse to the justice of tribunals.

53. This is the title of a chapter in Gernet's study *Droit et société dans la Grèce ancienne*, pp. 103–119.

54. Aristotle, *Athenian Constitution* 53.2–3.

55. Gernet, *Droit et société dans la Grèce ancienne*, p. 115, as well as Gernet, "*Les Lois* et le droit positif," p. 141.

56. Note the formula *ekhei telos hē dikē*.

57. Gernet, *Droit et société dans la Grèce ancienne*, p. 104.

58. There is always this primacy of the ancient in Gernet . . .

59. Gernet, *Droit et société dans la Grèce ancienne*, p. 113, quoting Aristotle, *Rhetoric* 1.13.1374b (*to epieikes*). Plato, *Letters* 7.325b, praises the Athenian *dēmos* in 403 B.C. for its equity (*epieikeia*).

60. See above, Chapter 9, on Nakone.

61. For *dialusis*, see Aristotle, *Athenian Constitution* 38.3, 39.1, 40.1; on the

connotations of this word, see above, Chapter 4. For *diallattein* and *diallagē* in about 403 B.C., see Xenophon, *Hellenica* 2.4.38, and Isocrates, *Against Calli-machus* 25.

62. Gernet, *Droit et société dans la Grèce ancienne*, p. 117, n.3, and p. 114.

63. In Pericles's funeral oration in Thucydides 2.37.1, this is a mandatory prelude to the praise of democracy: "When it is a question of settling private disputes [*pros ta idia diaphora*], everyone is equal before the law."

64. This is also attested by the fact that jury men, as judges, swore a special oath of amnesty (Andocides, *On the Mysteries* 91), reduplicating and detailing the one they had sworn *koinēi* as citizens (*ibid.* 90).

65. See above, Chapter 9.

66. Anger is so fundamental to *stasis* that a reconciliation in the Arcadian city of Alipheira (third century B.C.; see Te Riele, "Contributions épigraphiques à la connaissance du grec ancien," p. 343) substitutes the verb *mnasikholan* (to forget the anger) for the traditional *mnēsikakein*.

67. This is a recurrent theme in Aristophanes's *Wasps*, in which a bias against the accused seems to be the norm (see 880–81, 893–94, 942–43); but it gains its significance in a speech such as Lysias's *Against Eratosthenes*, spoken in the midst of the democratic restoration and in front of a popular tribunal against one of the Thirty (*orgizomenoi*, 90; *orgisthēte*, 96).

68. Aristotle, *Athenian Constitution* 40.2. This is a procedure of *apagōgē* excluding all trial in front of a tribunal.

69. Remember that he was considered the plaintiff and would have to speak first in front of the tribunal; see Paoli, *Studi sul processo attico*, pp. 99 and 121–22. On *Against Callimachus*, see J.-H. Kühn, "Die Amnestie von 403 v. Chr. im Reflex der 18. Isokrates-Rede," *Wiener Studien* 80 (1967), pp. 31–73.

70. This is especially true in that if Athenian justice "is made ... to sanction the order that is introduced once society has found stability again" (Gernet, *Droit et société dans la Grèce ancienne*, p. 67), the introduction of a trial putting the reestablished order at risk — by reexamining the confiscation of goods under the Thirty — in itself contradicts this essential principle.

71. This is, in fact, the usual ground for trial after a *stasis*.

333

72. Xenophon, *Hellenica* 5.2.10, trans. C.L. Brownson, *Xenophon, Hellenica, Books I–V* (Cambridge, MA: Harvard University Press, 1957).

73. But what exactly were its terms? If the *dikēi diakrithēnai* of Xenophon is an actual quote and not a condensed version, it was a matter of civic law courts for the people of Phlius, but the vagueness of the formula allows for countless interpretations.

74. Xenophon, *Hellenica* 5.3.10 (CUF).

75. *Ibid.* The verb *diadikazesthai* implies recourse to civic jurisdictions composed of *dikastai*; the exiles themselves are asking that there be a decision (*krinesthai*).

76. I would translate the adjective *isos* as "equitable."

77. Thus at Nakone, where "foreigners" reconcile citizens with each other, see above, Chapter 9.

78. It is a peculiar *anakrisis* that, instead of beginning the trials of the "guilty," simply gives them a sentence of life or death.

79. Xenophon, *Hellenica* 5.3.25.

80. Usually denoted by *isos*: thus Agesilaus interprets the exiles' demand in his own way.

81. Xenophon gives this information at 5.3.16 before giving his account of the "scheme" imposed by Agesilaus.

CHAPTER ELEVEN: AND ATHENIAN DEMOCRACY FORGOT *KRATOS*
I presented a first version of this essay at the European psychoanalytic conference "Mémoire, oubli, responsabilité" in Paris, November 1990, and an expanded version at the conference "Die Notwendigkeiten des Vergessens," Einstein Forum at Potsdam, November 1993.

1. Bloch, *L'Etrange défaite*, p. 30. For other references to Marc Bloch on past/present and for a meditation on the position of the historian of the ancient world, see Loraux, "Eloge de l'anachronisme en histoire."

2. Andocides, *On the Mysteries* 90, in *Minor Attic Orators*, vol. 1. This rendering of account is an eminently democratic practice.

3. Aristotle only quotes it indirectly in *Athenian Constitution* 39.6. There is

a complete bibliography on this oath in Loening, *Reconciliation Agreement of 403/402 B.C. in Athens.*

4. Andocides, *On the Mysteries* 90. On the word "misfortunes," see Catherine Darbo-Peschanski, "Que faire? Par où commencer? Où s'arrêter," *L'Inactuel* 2 (1994), pp. 125–37.

5. Lysias, *Against Eratosthenes* 82 and 84.

6. Probably while he was giving his accounts.

7. Lysias, *Against Eratosthenes* 79. The *dikē* demanded by Lysias is transcendent and not limited to indicating the trial itself.

8. Lysias, *On the Scrutiny of Evandros* 16–17.

9. See, for example, Lysias, *On the Confiscation of the Property of the Brother of Nicias* 18–19.

10. Isocrates, *Against Callimachus* 38. Recall that one of the first democrats coming out of exile who tried to introduce a lawsuit was arrested and, as an example, put to death without a trial; see Aristotle, *Athenian Constitution* 40.2.

11. Lysias, *Defence Against a Charge of Subverting the Democracy* 33.

12. Aristotle, *Athenian Constitution* 40.3.

13. Not everyone agrees with this assessment; see the preface to the second French edition of Loraux, *L'Invention d'Athènes* (Paris: Payot, 1993), p. 17.

14. Aristotle, *Athenian Constitution* 41.1.

15. *Ibid.* 41.2. On the word *kurios* (which he translates as "sovereign") and the root **kleu-*, see Benveniste's remarks, *Vocabulaire des institutions indo-européennes*, vol. 2, p. 183, and vol. 1, p. 250.

16. Not all fourth-century writers share this perspective: in Xenophon's *Hellenica*, in which the democrats' troops are roughed up by the Spartans, Pausanias oversees the reconciliation; on the trustworthiness of this narrative, see Cloché, *La Restauration démocratique à Athènes*, pp. 78–79.

17. Isocrates, *Against Callimachus* 17; cf. Isocrates, *Areopagiticus* 67 (*kratesantes*). Lysias, *Against Eratosthenes* 92 and 79.

18. See Loening, *Reconciliation Agreement of 403/402 B.C. in Athens*, p. 147, for whom the equitable division of advantages and disadvantages in the reconciliation prohibits characterizing it as a victory for the exiled democrats.

19. See above, Chapter 3. I could also mention Aristotle, *Athenian Constitution* 35.4, on the Thirty who held the city *ekkratesteron*. On *kratos*, see Benveniste, *Vocabulaire des institutions indo-européennes*, vol. 1, pp. 71–83, who seeks to distinguish two roots to remove the negative connotations of the neutral meaning; but see also Nagy, *Best of the Achaeans*, p. 86, §31 n.4.

20. See Loraux, *Invention of Athens*, chap. 4.

21. Aristotle, *Politics* 3.3.1276a12–13: *politeias tōi kratein ousas*. The passage explicitly speaks of continuity through a change of regime.

22. There is some flattery in these claims that renew, to the benefit of the *dēmos,* the *topos* of Athenian generosity.

23. Plutarch, *Table Talk* 9.6 (*Moralia* 741). See above, Chapter 1.

24. Thucydides 3.82.7.

25. See above, Chapter 10, as well as Gernet, *Droit et société dans la Grèce ancienne*, p. 66.

26. The verb *spheterizō* is then used, because the rebels make political life into their own thing. See Loraux, "Corcyre 427, Paris 1871."

27. Thus, praising the *dēmos* for not wanting more rights than the others (Lysias, *Funeral Oration* 64), the official discourse of funeral oration takes up the praise of the people on behalf of the city.

28. Lysias, *Defence Against a Charge of Subverting the Democracy* 1. There is no doubt that the orator recognizes the cogency of such an anger, but it is interesting that he credits his client with this idea.

29. *Ibid.* 28. Think of Thrasybulus's exhortation in Xenophon, *Hellenica* 2.4.42.

30. Isocrates, *Against Callimachus* 25.

31. Aristotle, *Athenian Constitution* 40.2. "The sentence of Archinus could be translated as 'the democracy will be loyal to the amnesty or it will not exist,'" Cloché, *La Restauration démocratique à Athènes*, p. 151.

32. On the twelfth of Boedromion, see Mikalson, *Sacred and Civil Calendar of the Athenian Year*, p. 53.

33. These motley troops are described as *pantodapoi* in Xenophon, *Hellenica* 2.4.25, which is characteristic of democracy for Plato, *Republic* 8.557c1–2.

I might add that for Aristotle, *Politics* 5.1303b10–12, the Piraeus in itself is more "democratic" than the city.

34. The decree, published by A.E. Raubitschek in *Hesperia* 10 (1941), pp. 284–95, granting an olive crown to these worthy citizens is in fact owed to Archinus.

35. Aeschines speaks of the men of Phyle (*Against Ctesiphon* 181, 187, 195, 208), whereas Demosthenes evokes the "*dēmos* of the Piraeus" (*Against Leptines* 149; cf. *On the Embassy* 277, but in 280, Thrasybulus leads back "the people from Phyle"). *The Athenian Constitution* goes from "men from Phyle" (38.1–2) to "men from the Piraeus" (38.3–4) to end with the evocation of the "return from Phyle and the Piraeus."

36. Compare Lysias, *Against Eratosthenes* 53, 55–56, 59, 92, 95, 97 (cf. Lysias, *Funeral Oration* 61, 66) and Lysias, *Against Agoratus* 63 and 77.

37. On the capture of Phyle by Thrasybulus, see Lysias, *Against Eratosthenes* 52; Xenophon, *Hellenica* 2.4.2; Aristotle, *Athenian Constitution* 37.1. Yet in Demosthenes's *Against Timocrates,* Archinus captures Phyle; and whereas the leaders of the people during the return to Athens are Anytos and Thrasybulus in Xenophon, *Hellenica* 2.3.44, they are "Archinus and Thrasybulus" in Aeschines, *On the Embassy* 176.

38. Aristophanes, *The Plutus* 1146, trans. B.B. Rogers, *Aristophanes* (New York: G.P. Putnam's Sons, 1931), vol. 3. Here we can see clearly on what the real weight of amnesty rests.

39. Lysias, *Against Eratosthenes* 78 (now we call on Theramenes); Aristotle, *Athenian Constitution* 36.1 (Critias fears that Theramenes may become the leader of the people); Diodorus 14.3.6 and 14.4.1.

40. Isocrates, *Against Callimachus* 32.

41. For *Epieikeia,* see Plato, *Letter* 7.325b. Gernet, *Droit et société dans la Grèce ancienne,* p. 67 n.3, translates *epieikeia* as "equity" in a passage from Aristotle's *Rhetoric* in which equity is linked with an arbitral judgment of conciliation. But we should recall that *epieikeia* is typical of "decent people" in Xenophon's *Athenian Constitution*; in Isocrates's *Areopagiticus,* the Athenian *dēmos* is credited with *epieikia* for having paid the Thirty's debt, going much further than prescribed by conventions.

42. Lysias, *Against the Subversion of the Ancestral Constitution of Athens* 5.

43. See Paula Botteri and Mouza Raskolnikoff, "Diodore, Caius Gracchus et la démocratie," in Claude Nicolet (ed.), *Dēmokratia et aristokratia: A propos de Caius Gracchus: Mots grecs et réalités romaines* (Paris: Université de Paris I, 1983), pp. 59–101.

44. Isocrates, *Panegyricus* 39: Athens was the first to establish laws and a constitution (*politeian katestesato*); this should be compared with the very similar passage in Lysias, *Epitaphios* 18, which credits the Athenians with having established a democracy (*dēmokratian katestesanto*). See also *Panegyricus* 106 (Athenians establish among others the same constitution as in Athens).

45. Isocrates, *Panathenaicus* 118.

46. Isocrates, *Areopagiticus* 70, *Isocrates*, vol. 2.

47. Isocrates, *Panathenaicus* 151 and 197, in *Isocrates*, vol. 2; cf. 164.

48. *Ibid.* 148.

49. See again *ibid.* 130–31 (two ways to distort democracy: make it an aristocracy, or use the empty name *politeia koinē*, common government).

50. In book 3 of the *Politics*, Aristotle, focusing on the question of the city's eternity across its different governments, expresses his skepticism toward such a notion (3.1276b1–6); yet after having closely linked the city's identity with the permanence of its constitution, he keeps *hē polis* as the subject of the clause "when the city changes its constitution."

51. In Aristotle's *Athenian Constitution*, the city "is pleased" at first with the rule of the Thirty (*ekhairon hē polis*, 35.3), but at the beginning of the next paragraph it is "declining" (36.1).

52. See above, Chapter 6.

53. This is how Isocrates, in his speech *On the Peace* 51, makes a parallel between the Athenians' zeal for the constitution and their zeal for the safety of the entire city; similarly, Plato, *Republic* 8.563b5, uses *polis* where we might expect *politeia*.

54. Aristotle, *Athenian Constitution* 40.3 and 39.6.

55. Recall that the Thirty, as magistrates chosen by an assembly, are usually

called *arkhē* — just as we speak of the French State with reference to Vichy — and not *kratos*.

Xenophon's formulation in *Hellenica* 2.3.1 is unambiguous: *edoxe tōi dēmōi triakonta andras helesthai*; the Thirty had to put in writing the laws of the ancestors by virtue of which they ruled. When all is said and done, the takeover was formally "legal." This is what we call the "Weimar syndrome"; see Gothot, "Le Passé et l'avenir."

56. *Idiai* concerns the renunciation made by private individuals of lawsuits seeking to reclaim their violated rights whereas *koinēi* concerns the reimbursement of the debt. Thus the second point is more important than the first.

57. Aristotle, *Athenian Constitution* 40.3.

58. See above, Chapter 6.

59. On this theme, see the preface to the second French edition of Loraux, *L'Invention d'Athènes*, p. 17.

60. *Phasi ton dēmon helesthai sunegkein auton*: this *auton* of initiative is the exact opposite of Lysias's *autos ouk etolmese metaskhein*. "To take its place" would have meant "to appropriate [*spheterizein*] public affairs strongly enough not to leave any bit of authority to the losers," which means, as a passage in Plato, *Laws* 4.715a–b, attests, to develop in one's adversary the memory of the wrongs inflicted in the past.

61. Demosthenes, *Against Leptines* 11–12, trans. J.H. Vince, *Demosthenes: Olynthiacs, Philippics; Minor Public Speeches; Speech Against Leptines* (London and New York: William Heinemann and G.P. Putnam's Sons, 1930).

62. Aristotle, *Athenian Constitution* 38.4.

63. As Cloché insistently does in *La Restauration démocratique à Athènes*, pp. 343, 350, 404, 407, 410.

64. Xenophon, *Hellenica* 2.4.20–22.

65. *Ibid.* 2.4.13–17.

66. *Ibid.* 4.40–42.

67. Isocrates, *Areopagiticus* 20: *politeian . . . onomati tōi koinotatōi kaì praotatōi prosagoreuomenēn*.

68. See, for example, Demosthenes, *Against Androtion*, 52 and *Against Timocrates*, 163–4.

69. Lysias, *Against the Subversion of the Ancestral Constitution of Athens* 1.

70. *Ibid.* 2.

71. Aristotle, *Athenian Constitution* 41.1 and 41.2.

72. This is the theme *proteron men/nun de*, the framework of the narrative on the constitution; see, for example, Aristotle, *Athenian Constitution* 54.1.3, 48.3 (*pote/nun*), 51.3, 53.1 (*proteron men ... meta de tēn epi tōn triakonta oligarkhian*), 54.3, 55.1 (*ex arkhēs / nun de*), 55.4, 56.3, 56.4, 61.1, 62.

73. I rely on Diodorus's distinction at 14.3.3 between *tēn palaian katastasin*, the oligarchs' demand, and *tēn tōn paterōn politeian*, the democrats' slogan. This is reminiscent of the strategy adopted by the French Republic toward the "Vichy interlude."

74. Xenophon, *Hellenica* 2.4.42.

75. Chantraine, *Dictionnaire étymologique*, s.v.

76. Loraux, *Invention of Athens*.

77. This is attested by Xenophon's play on words in the following sentence in *Hellenica* 2.4.43, where, once they have divided up the duties (*arkhas*), the Athenians *epoliteuonto*.

78. See, for example, Demosthenes, *On the Embassy* 227 and 280; Aeschines, *On the Embassy* 78 and 147, and Aeschines, *Against Ctesiphon* 187 (decree of Archinus at the Metroon), 188, 190.

79. Isocrates, *Concerning the Team of Horses*, 26, and Isocrates, *Areopagiticus* 16.

80. In Isocrates, *Areopagiticus* 16, the sentence "we should be willing to restore that earlier democracy which was instituted by Solon ... and which was reestablished by Cleisthenes, who drove out the tyrants and brought the people back into power [*palin ex arkhēs katestesen*]" is doubly a retrospective projection, because the idea of a democracy of Solon is a "myth" of the fourth century B.C.; see Mossé, "Comment s'élabore un mythe politique."

81. See Lévêque and Vidal-Naquet, *Clisthène l'Athénien*, pp. 117–22.

82. For a detailed analysis of this operation, see Loraux, "Clistene e le nuovi caratteri della lotta politica."

83. This is how in 412 B.C., the reference to Cleisthenes functioned in

Cleitophon's amendment inviting the *probouloi* to examine "the traditional laws which Cleisthenes had enacted when he set up the democracy"; see Aristotle, *Athenian Constitution* 29.3.

84. See above, Chapters 10 (judges) and 5 (oath).

85. See above, Chapter 7.

86. I am alluding here to the central statement in the dream of the dead father, which Freud examines in *The Interpretation of Dreams*.

87. Lysias, *Against Eratosthenes* 87, 92, 94, 96; Lysias, *Against Agoratus* 43–44 and 48. See also Lysias, *Against the Subversion of the Ancestral Constitution of Athens* 2.

88. Lysias, *Against Eratosthenes* 90: show what is your judgment (*gnōmēn*) of the events. This is almost an invitation to vote on the past.

89. *Ibid.* 91.

90. According to Gernet's commentary on this speech (CUF), it seems the matter was not directly linked with the "misfortunes" of the city; yet they are recent enough to be evoked as the decisive argument.

91. Lysias, *On the Confiscation of the Property of the Brother of Nicias: Peroration* 18–19.

92. On *ainos*, see Nagy, *Best of the Achaeans*, pp. 235–41, and Nagy and Figueira, eds., *Theognis of Megara*, p. 24 ("a mode of poetic discourse that is unmistakably understandable only to its intended audience"); see also Gregory Nagy, *Pindar's Homer* (Baltimore, MD: Johns Hopkins University Press, 1990), pp. 314–38.

93. See Lysias, *Against the Subversion of the Ancestral Constitution of Athens* 10 (appeal to justice for those who were wronged).

94. See fragments from Lysias, *Against Hypotherses*, in which, after recalling that the democrats came back *hōs adikoumenoi*, the orator claims that they will be deprived of their property as if they were guilty (*hōs adikountes*), whereas justice would have required them to yield to anger (*dikaios an [orgizoisthē]*), 5.

95. Xenophon, *Hellenica* 2.4.20.

96. *Ibid.* 2.4.13: *ouden adikountas.*

97. *Ibid.* 2.4.40.

98. *Ibid.* 2.4.41–42.

99. I am alluding here to events current in the Berlin news in November 1993. On the monument, see Reinhart Koselleck, "Allemagne, le mémorial de l'oubli," *Libération*, Jan. 17, 1994.

100. On the question of mourning as it is formulated in Germany, see Alexandre Mitscherlich and Margarete Mitscherlich, *Le Deuil impossible* (Paris: Payot, 1972); see also Loraux, "Pour quel consensus?"

101. Lacan, *L'Ethique de la psychanalyse*, p. 272.

Bibliography

Classical works

Aeschines, *The Speeches of Aeschines*, trans. Charles Darwin Adams (New York: G.P. Putnams's Sons, 1919).

Aeschylus, *Agamemnon*, trans. David Grene and Richmond Lattimore, in *The Complete Greek Tragedies* (Chicago: University of Chicago Press, 1997), vol. 1.

————, *Eumenides*, trans. Richmond Lattimore (Chicago: University of Chicago Press, 1953).

————, *The Seven Against Thebes*, trans. Herbert Weir Smyth, in *Aeschylus* (Cambridge, MA: Harvard University Press, 1973), vol. 1.

————, *Suppliant Maidens*, trans. S.G. Benardete (Chicago: University of Chicago Press, 1953).

Ancilla to the Pre-Socratic Philsophers, trans. Kathleen Freeman (1948; reprint, Cambridge, MA: Harvard University Press, 1983).

Aristotle, *The Athenian Constitution*, trans. P.J. Rhodes (London: Penguin, 1984).

————, *Basic Works of Aristotle*, ed. Richard McKeon (New York: Random House, 1941).

Gellius, Aulus, *The Attic Nights of Aulus Gellius*, trans. John Carew Rolfe (Cambridge, MA: Harvard University Press, 1954).

Herodotus, *The Persian Wars*, trans. George Rawlinson (New York: Modern Library, 1942).

Hesiod, *Works and Days, Theogony, The Shield of Herakles*, trans. Richmond Lattimore (Ann Arbor: University of Michigan Press, 1959).

Homer, *Iliad*, trans. Richmond Lattimore (Chicago: University of Chicago Press, 1951).

———, *Odyssey*, trans. Richmond Lattimore (New York: Harper & Row, 1965).

Isocrates, *Isocrates*, trans. George Norlin and Larue Van Hook, 3 vols. (Cambridge, MA: Harvard University Press, 1945).

Lysias, *Lysias*, trans. W.R.M. Lamb (New York: G.P. Putnam's Sons, 1930).

Minor Attic Orators, trans. K.J. Maidment (Cambridge, MA: Harvard University Press, 1941).

Plato, *The Collected Dialogues of Plato*, eds. Edith Hamilton and Huntington Cairns (Princeton, NJ: Princeton University Press, 1961).

Plutarch, *Obsolescence of Oracles*, trans. Frank Cole Babbitt, in *Plutarch's Moralia* (Cambridge, MA: Loeb Classical Library, 1969), vol. 5.

———, *On Brotherly Love*, trans. W.C. Helmbold, in *Plutarch's Moralia* (Cambridge, MA: Harvard University Press, 1939), vol. 6.

———, *Plutarch's Lives*, trans. Bernadotte Perrin (New York: G.P. Putnam's Sons, 1916).

———, *Table Talk*, trans. E. Minar, F.H. Sandbach, and W.C. Helmbold, in *Plutarch's Moralia* (Cambridge, MA: Harvard University Press, 1961), vol. 9.

Sophocles, *Antigone*, in *Sophocles*, trans. Hugh Lloyd-Jones (Cambridge, MA: Harvard University Press, 1994).

———, *Electra*, in *Sophocles*, trans. Hugh Lloyd-Jones (Cambridge, MA: Harvard University Press, 1994).

Theognis, in *Elegy and Iambus*, trans. J.M. Edmonds (Cambridge, MA: Harvard University Press, 1968), vol 1.

Thucydides, *History of the Peloponnesian War*, trans. Rex Warner (London: Penguin, 1972).

Xenophon, *Memorabilia and Oeconomicus*, trans. E.C. Marchant (Cambridge, MA: Harvard University Press, 1953).

———, *Xenophon*, trans. Carleton Lewis Brownson (Cambridge, MA: Harvard University Press, 1968).

Secondary works

Alaux, Jean, *Le Liège et le filet* (Paris: Belin, 1995).

Asheri, David, "Formes et procédures de réconciliation dans les cités grecques," *Symposion 1982* (Santander and Valence, 1985), pp. 135–45.

————, "Osservazioni storiche sul decreto di Nakone," in Giuseppe Nenci (ed.), *Materiali e contributi per lo studio degli otto decreti da Entella*, Annali della Scuola Normale Superiore, Pisa, 1982.

Augé, Marc, *Pouvoirs de vie, pouvoirs de mort* (Paris: Flammarion, 1977).

————, *Théorie des pouvoirs et idéologie* (Paris: Hermann, 1975).

Battegazzore, A.M., "La funzione del gesto e la concordia civica: Una nuova interpretazione del fr. 1 di Eraclito alla luce di un passo plutarcheo," *Sandalion* 1 (1978), pp. 7–44.

————, "*Háptesthai*: La nozione eraclitea di contatto-ardore," *Sandalion* 3 (1980), pp. 5–17.

————, *Maia* 29 (1977), pp. 3–16.

Benveniste, Emile, "Expression indo-européenne de l'éternité," *Bulletin de la Société de linguistique de Paris* 38 (1937), pp. 103–12.

————, *Noms d'agent et noms d'action en indo-européen*, 2nd ed. (Paris: Adrien Maisonneuve, 1975).

————, *Problèmes de linguistique générale* (Paris: Gallimard, 1974).

————, *Vocabulaire des institutions indo-européennes*, 2 vols. (Paris: Minuit, 1969).

Bérard, Claude, "L'Héroïsation et la formation de la cité: Un Conflit idéologique," in *Architecture et société: De l'archaïsme grec à la fin de la République romaine* (Rome and Paris, 1983), pp. 43–59.

Bloch, Marc, *L'Etrange Défaite* (1940; reprint, Paris: Gallimard, 1993).

Bollack, Jean, *Introduction à l'ancienne physique*, vol. 1 of *Empédocle* (Paris: Editions de Minuet, 1965).

————, *Les Origines: Commentaire, 1 et 2*, vol. 3 of *Empédocle* (Paris: Minuit, 1969).

Botteri, Paula, "*Stásis*: Le Mot grec, la chose romaine," *Mêtis* 4 (1989), pp. 87–100.

Burkert, Walter, *Greek Religion* (Cambridge, MA: Harvard University Press, 1985).

Calame, Claude, *Morphologie, fonction religieuse et sociale*, vol. 1 of *Les Chœurs de jeunes filles dans la Grèce archaïque* (Rome: Ateneo and Bizzari, 1977).

Cambiano, Giuseppe, "Pathologie et analogie politique," in *Actes du IVᵉ colloque hippocratique* (Lausanne), Geneva, 1983, pp. 441–58.

Certeau, Michel de, *The Mystic Fable*, trans. M.B. Smith (Chicago: University of Chicago Press, 1992).

———, *The Writing of History*, trans. Tom Conley (New York: Columbia University Press, 1988).

Chantraine, Pierre, *Dictionnaire étymologique de la langue grecque* (Paris: Klincksieck, 1968).

———, *La Formation des noms en grec ancien* (Paris: Klincksieck, 1933).

———, "Les Verbes grecs signifiant 'tuer,'" *Die Sprache* 1 (1949), pp. 143–49.

Cloché, Paul, *La Restauration démocratique à Athènes* (Paris: Ernest Leroux, 1915).

Desanti, Jean-Toussaint, "La Violence," *Monde-Dimanche*, Aug. 15, 1982.

Detienne, Marcel, *Dionysos mis à mort* (Paris: Gallimard, 1977).

———, *The Masters of Truth in Archaic Greece*, trans. Janet Lloyd (New York: Zone Books, 1996).

——— (ed.), *Les Savoirs de l'écriture en Grèce ancienne* (Presses Universitaires de Lille, 1988).

Detienne, Marcel, and Jean-Pierre Vernant, *Cunning Intelligence in Greek Culture and Society*, trans. Janet Lloyd (Atlantic Highlands, NJ: Humanities Press, 1978).

——— (eds.), *The Cuisine of Sacrifice Among the Greeks* (Chicago: University of Chicago Press, 1989).

Deubner, Ludwig, *Attische Feste* (Berlin: H. Keller, 1932).

Dubois, Laurent, "Actualités dialectologiques. III: Un Réfléchi en -*ta* dans l'ouest sicilien," *Revue de philologie* 60 (1986), pp. 102–105.

Du châtiment dans la cité: Supplices corporels et peine de mort dans le monde antique (Rome and Paris: Ecole française de Rome, 1984).

Dumézil, Georges, *L'Idéologie des trois fonctions dans les épopées des peuples indo-*

européens, vol. 1 of *Mythe et épopée* (Paris: Gallimard, 1968).

———, *Tarpeia* (Paris: Gallimard, 1947).

Edmunds, Lowell, "Thucydides' Ethics as Reflected in the Description of *Stásis*," *Harvard Studies in Classical Philology* 79 (1975), pp. 73–92.

Finley, Moses I., *Economy and Society in Ancient Greece* (London: Chatto & Windus, 1981).

———, *L'Invention de la politique*, trans. Jeannie Carlier (Paris: Flammarion, 1985).

Freud, Sigmund, *The Interpretation of Dreams*, in *The Standard Edition of the Complete Psychological Works of Sigmund Freud*, trans. James Strachey and Anna Freud (London: Hogarth Press, 1964).

———, *Moses and Monotheism*, in *The Standard Edition of the Complete Psychological Works of Sigmund Freud*, trans. James Strachey and Anna Freud (London: Hogarth Press, 1964), vol. 23.

———, "Negation," in *The Standard Edition of the Complete Psychological Works of Sigmund Freud*, trans. James Strachey and Anna Freud (London: Hogarth Press, 1964), vol. 19.

Frontisi-Ducroux, Françoise, "Artémis bucolique," *Revue de l'histoire des religions* (1980), pp. 29–56.

Fustel de Coulanges, Numa. *La Cité antique* (1864).

Gernet, Louis, *The Anthropology of Ancient Greece*, trans. John Hamilton and Blaise Nagy (Baltimore, MD: Johns Hopkins University Press, 1981).

———, *Droit et société dans la Grèce ancienne* (Paris: Sirey, 1955).

———, "Le Droit pénal dans la Grèce ancienne," in *Du châtiment dans la cité: Supplices corporels et peine de mort dans le monde antique*.

———, *Les Grecs sans miracle*, texts collected by Ricardo Di Donato, preface by Jean-Pierre Vernant, postscript by Ricardo Di Donato (Paris: Maspero-La Découverte, 1983).

———, "*Les Lois* et le droit positif," introduction to Plato, *Les Lois* (Paris: Les Belles Lettres, 1951), pp. v–ccvi.

———, *Platon: Lois, livre IX*, trans. and commentary by Louis Gernet (Paris: Ernest Leroux, 1917).

————, *Recherches sur le développement juridique et moral de la pensée grecque* (Paris: Ernest Leroux, 1917).

Glotz, Gustave, *La Cité grecque* (1928; reprint, Paris: A. Michel, 1968).

————, "Le Serment," in *Etudes sociales et juridiques* (Paris: Hachette, 1906).

————, *La Solidarité de la famille dans le droit criminel en Grèce* (1904; reprint, New York: Arno Press, 1973).

Gothot, Pierre, "Le Passé et l'avenir: Quelques remarques thérapeutiques à propos du syndrome de Weimar," *Le Genre humain* 27 (1993), pp. 61–76.

Hartog, François, *The Mirror of Herodotus: The Representation of the Other in the Writing of History* (Berkeley: University of California Press, 1989).

Iriarte, Ana, *Las redes del enigma: Voces femeninas en el pensamiento griego* (Madrid: Taurus, 1990).

Isaac, Jules (Junius), *Les Oligarques: Essai d'histoire partiale* (Paris: Minuit, 1946; rev. ed., Paris: Calmann-Lévy, 1989).

Jal, Paul, *La Guerre civile à Rome: Etude littéraire et morale* (Paris: PUF, 1963).

Kahn, Charles H., *The Art and Thought of Heraclitus* (Cambridge, UK: Cambridge University Press, 1979).

Lacan, Jacques, *L'Ethique de la psychanalyse*, book 7 of *Le Séminaire* (Paris: Le Seuil, 1986).

Lefort, Claude, and Marcel Gauchet, "Sur la démocratie: Le Politique et l'institution du social," *Textures* 2–3 (1971).

Lévêque, Pierre, "Observations sur la communication de Marcel Piérart: Sur l'évolution du **brother* indo-européen," *Revue des études anciennes* (1985), pp. 188–90.

————, and Pierre Vidal-Naquet, *Clisthène l'Athénien: Essai sur la représentation de l'espace et du temps dans la pensée politique grecque à la fin du VIᵉ siècle à la mort de Platon* (Paris and Besançon: Les Belles Lettres, 1964).

Lévi-Strauss, Claude, "Histoire et ethnologie," *Annales ESC* 38 (1983), pp. 1217–31.

Lissarrague, François, and Alain Schnapp, "Imagerie des Grecs ou Grèce des imagiers," *Le Temps de la réflexion* 2 (1981), pp. 275–97.

Loening, Th. C., *The Reconciliation Agreement of 403/402 B.C. in Athens: Its Con-*

tent and Application (Stuttgart: F. Steiner Verlag Wiesbaden, 1987).

Loraux, Nicole, "Back to the Greeks? Chronique d'une expédition lointaine en terre connue" (Paris: Le Cerf–Ecole des Hautes Etudes en Sciences Sociales, 1996), pp. 275–97.

———, *The Children of Athena: Athenian Ideas About Citizenship and the Division Between the Sexes*, trans. Caroline Levine (Princeton, NJ: Princeton University Press, 1993).

———, "La Cité comme cuisine et comme partage," *Annales ESC* (July–Aug. 1981), pp. 614–22.

———, "Clistene e le nuovi caratteri della lotta politica," *I Greci e noi* (Turin: Einaudi, 1997).

———, "Corcyre 427, Paris 1871: La Guerre civile grecque entre deux temps," *Les Temps modernes* (Dec. 1993), pp. 82–119, and (March 1994), pp. 188–90.

———, "Le Corps vulnérable d'Arès," *Le Temps de la réflexion* 7 (1986), pp. 335–54.

———, "La Démocratie à l'épreuve de l'étranger (Athènes, Paris)," in R.-P. Droit (ed.), *Les Grecs, les Romains et nous: L'Antiquité est-elle moderne?* (Paris: Le Monde Editions, 1991), pp. 164–88.

———, "Eloge de l'anachronisme en histoire," *Le Genre humain* 27 (1993), pp. 23–39.

———, *The Experiences of Tiresias: The Feminine and the Greek Man*, trans. Paula Wissing (Princeton, NJ: Princeton University Press, 1995).

———, "La Guerre civile grecque et la représentation anthropologique du monde à l'envers," *Revue de l'histoire des religions* 212 (1995), pp. 299–326.

———, "*L'Homme Moïse* et l'audace d'être historien," *Le Cheval de Troie* 3 (1991), pp. 83–98.

———, "*L'Iliade* moins les héros," *L'Inactuel* 1 (1994), pp. 29–48.

———, *The Invention of Athens: The Funeral Oration in the Classical City*, trans. Alan Sheridan (Cambridge, MA: Harvard University Press, 1986).

———, "La Main d'Antigone," *Mêtis* 1 (1986), pp. 165–96.

———, "La Majorité, le tout et la moitié: Sur l'arithmétique athénienne du vote," *Le Genre humain* 22 (1990), pp. 89–110.

349

————, "La Métaphore sans métaphore: A propos de l'*Orestie*," *Revue de philosophie* (1990), pp. 115–39.

————, *Mothers in Mourning*, trans. Corinne Pache (Ithaca, NY: Cornell University Press, 1998).

————, "Le Mythe: Cités grecques," in Y. Bonnefoy (ed.), *Dictionnaire des mythologies*, vol. 1 (Paris: Flammarion, 1981), pp. 203–209.

————, *Né de la terre: Mythe et politique à Athènes* (Paris: Le Seuil, 1996).

————, "*Oikeios polemos*: La guerra nella famiglia," *Studi storici* 28 (1987), pp. 5–35; published in French in *Klio* 5 (1997).

————, "Pour quel consensus?" introduction to *Politiques de l'oubli* (Paris: Le Seuil, 1988), pp. 9–23.

————, "Reflections of the Greek City on Unity and Division," in Molho, Raaflaub, and Emlen (eds.), *City States in Classical Antiquity and Medieval Italy*, pp. 33–51.

————, "Solon au milieu de la lice," in *Aux origines de l'hellénisme: La Crète et la Grèce: Hommage à Henri van Effenterre* (Paris: La Sorbonne, 1984), pp. 199–214.

————, "Sur la transparence démocratique," *Raison présente* 49 (1979), pp. 3–13.

————, "Sur un non-sens grec: Œdipe, Théognis, Freud," *L'Ecrit du temps* 19 (1988), pp. 19–36.

————, "Thucydide et la sédition dans les mots," *Quaderni di storia* (Jan.–June 1986), pp. 95–134.

Lyotard, Jean-François, "A l'insu," *Le Genre humain* 18 (1988).

————, *Le Différend* (Paris: Minuit, 1983).

MacDowell, Douglas M., *The Law in Classical Athens* (Ithaca, NY: Cornell University Press, 1986).

Malamoud, Charles, *Cuire le monde: Rite et pensée dans l'Inde ancienne* (Paris: La Découverte, 1989).

Mazzarino, Santo, *Il pensiero storico classico*, 3 vols., 2nd ed. (Rome and Bari: Laterza, 1983).

Meiggs, Russell, and David M. Lewis, *A Selection of Greek Historical Inscriptions* (Oxford: Clarendon Press, 1969).

Michels, Agnes Kirsopp, *The Calendar of the Roman Republic* (Princeton, NJ: Princeton University Press, 1967).

Mikalson, Jon D., *"Heméra apophrás,"* *American Journal of Philology* 96 (1975), pp. 19–27.

———, *The Sacred and Civil Calendar of the Athenian Year* (Princeton, NJ: Princeton University Press, 1975).

Molho, Anthony, Kurt A. Raaflaub, and Julia Emlen (eds.), *City States in Classical Antiquity and Medieval Italy* (Ann Arbor: University of Michigan Press, 1992).

Mommsen, August, *Feste der Stadt Athen im Altertum* (Leipzig: B.G. Teubner, 1898).

Moscovici, Marie, "Un Meurtre construit par les produits de son oubli," *L'Ecrit du temps* 10 (1985).

Mossé, Claude, "Comment s'élabore un mythe politique: Solon père fondateur de la démocratie athénienne," *Annales ESC* 34 (1979), pp. 425–37.

Nagy, Gregory, *The Best of the Achaeans: Concepts of the Hero in Archaic Greek Poetry* (Baltimore, MD: Johns Hopkins University Press, 1979).

———, *Comparative Studies in Greek and Indic Meter* (Cambridge, MA: Harvard University Press, 1974).

———, and Thomas J. Figueira (eds.), *Theognis of Megara* (Baltimore, MD: Johns Hopkins University Press, 1985).

Nenci, Giuseppe (ed.), *Materiali e contributi per lo studio degli otto decreti da Entella*, Annali della Scuola Normale Superiore, Pisa, 1982.

Olivier de Sardan, Jean-Pierre, *Les Sociétés songhay-zarma, Niger-Mali* (Paris: Karthala, 1984).

Ozouf, Mona, "Le Révolution française et l'idée de fraternité," in *L'Homme régénéré: Essais sur la Révolution française* (Paris: Gallimard, 1989), pp. 158–82.

Paoli, Ugo Enrico, *Studi sul processo attico* (Padua: A. Milani, 1933).

Parker, Robert, *Miasma: Pollution and Purification in Early Greek Religion* (Oxford: Clarendon Press, 1983).

Perpillou, Jean-Louis, "Frères de sang ou frères de culte?" *Studi micenei ed egeo-anatolici* 25 (1984), pp. 205–20.

Piccirilli, Luigi, "L'assassinio di Efialte," *Annali della Scuola Normale Superiore di Pisa* 17 (1987), pp. 9–17.

——, *Efialte* (Genoa: Il Melangolo, 1988).

Plescia, Joseph, *The Oath and Perjury in Ancient Greece* (Tallahassee: Florida State University Press, 1970).

Pouilloux, Jean (ed.), *Choix d'inscriptions grecques* (Paris: Les Belles Lettres, 1960).

Pritchett, W.K., *Ancient Athenian Calendars on Stone* (Berkeley: University of California Press, 1963).

——, *Religion*, vol. 3 of *The Greek State at War* (Berkeley: University of California Press, 1979).

——, and B.L. van der Waerden, "Thucydidean Time-Reckoning and Euctemon's Seasonal Calendar," *Bulletin de correspondance hellénique* 85 (1961), pp. 17–52.

Ramnoux, Clémence, *La Nuit et les enfants de la Nuit dans la tradition grecque* (Paris: Flammarion, 1959).

Rey, Jean-Michel, "Freud et l'écriture de l'histoire," *L'Ecrit du temps* 6 (1984).

Rohde, Erwin, *Psyche: The Cult of Souls and Belief in Immortality Among the Greeks* (London: Routledge and Kegan Paul, 1950).

Roussel, Denis, *Tribu et cité: Etude sur les groupes sociaux dans les cités grecques aux époques archaïque et classique* (Paris and Besançon: Les Belles Lettres, 1976).

Rousso, Henri, *Le Syndrome de Vichy, 1944–198?* (Paris: Le Seuil, 1987); 2nd ed., *Le Syndrome de Vichy de 1944 à nos jours* (Paris: Le Seuil, 1990).

——, "Vichy, le grand fossé," *Vingtième siècle* 5 (1985), pp. 55–79.

Ruijgh, C.J., "L'Emploi onomastique de *keklêsthai*," *Miscellanea tragica in honorem J.C. Kamerbeek* (Amsterdam: Apud A. Hakkert, 1976).

Savalli, Ivanna, "Alcune osservazioni sulla terza iscrizione da Entella," in Giuseppe Nenci (ed.), *Materiali e contributi per lo studio degli otto decreti da Entella*.

Simondon, Michèle, *La Mémoire et l'oubli dans la pensée grecque* (Paris: Les Belles Lettres, 1982).

Sinos, Dale, *Achilles, Patroklos, and the Meaning of Phílos* (Innsbruck: Institut für

Sprachwissenschaft der Universität Innsbruck, 1980).

Sissa, Giulia, "La Famille dans la cité grecque (V^e–IVe siècle av. J.-C.)," in A. Bur-guière, C. Klapisch, M. Segalen, and F. Zonabend (eds.), *Histoire de la famille* (Paris: A. Colin, 1986), pp. 162–93.

Slatkin, Laura, *The Power of Thetis: Allusion and Interpretation in the "Iliad"* (Berkeley: University of California Press, 1991).

————, "The Wrath of Thetis," *Transactions of the American Philological Association* 116 (1986).

Strauss, Barry S., *Fathers and Sons in Athens: Ideology and Society in the Era of the Peloponnesian War* (Princeton, NJ: Princeton University Press, 1993).

Svenbro, Jesper, *La Parole et le marbre: Aux origines de la poétique grecque* (Lund, 1976).

————, "Vengeance et société en Grèce archaïque," in Raymond Verdier and Jean-Pierre Poly (eds.), *La Vengeance: Vengeance, pouvoir et idéologie dans quelques civilisations de l'Antiquité* (Paris: Editions Cujas, 1984), pp. 47–63.

Szemerényi, Oswald, "Studies in the Kinship Terminology of the Indo-European Languages," *Acta Iranica* 16 (1978).

Te Riele, G.-J.-M.-J., "Contributions épigraphiques à la connaissance du grec ancien," *Mnemosyne* 21 (1968), pp. 337–46.

————, "Le Grand Apaisement de Rogoziò," *Acta of the Fifth Epigraphic Congress 1967* (Oxford: Blackwell, 1971), pp. 89–91.

Terray, Emmanuel, "Un Anthropologue africaniste devant la cité grecque," *Opus* 6–8 (1987–1989), pp. 13–25.

Thomas, Yan, "*Parricidium* I: Le Père, la famille et la cité," *Mélanges des écoles françaises de Rome et d'Athènes* 93 (1981), pp. 643–715.

————, "Paura dei padri e violenza dei figli," in Ezio Pellizer and Nevio Zorzetti (eds.), *La Paura dei padri nella società antica e medievale* (Rome and Bari: Laterza, 1983), pp. 115–40.

————, "Se venger au forum," in Raymond Verdier et Jean-Pierre Poly (eds.), *La Vengeance: Vengeance, pouvoir et idéologie dans quelques civilisations de l'Antiquité* (Paris: Editions Cujas, 1984), pp. 65–100.

————, "*Vitae necisque potestas*: Le Père, la cité et la mort," in *Du châtiment dans*

353

la cité: Supplices corporels et peine de mort dans le monde antique, pp. 499–548.

Tod, Marcus N., *A Selection of Greek Historical Inscriptions*, vol. 2 (Oxford: Clarendon Press, 1948).

Torricelli, Patrizia, "*Hórkos* e la figura lessicale del giuramento," *Atti della Academia nazionale dei Lincei* 36 (1981), pp. 125–39.

van Effenterre, Henri, "L'Acte de fraternisation de Nakônè," *Mélanges des écoles françaises de Rome et d'Athènes* (1988).

———, *La Cité grecque des origines à la défaite de Marathon* (Paris: Hachette, 1985).

Vernant, Jean-Pierre, *The Origins of Greek Thought* (Ithaca, NY: Cornell University Press, 1982).

———, and Pierre Vidal-Naquet, *Myth and Tragedy in Ancient Greece*, trans. Janet Lloyd (New York: Zone Books, 1988).

Vidal-Naquet, Pierre, *The Black Hunter: Forms of Thought and Forms of Society in the Greek World*, trans. Andrew Szegedy-Maszak (Baltimore, MD: Johns Hopkins University Press, 1986).

Watkins, Calvert, "A propos de *mênis*," *Bulletin de la Société de linguistique de Paris* 72 (1977).

West, Martin Litchfield, *Hesiod: Theogony* (Oxford: Clarendon Press, 1966).

———, *Hesiod: Works and Days* (Oxford: Clarendon Press, 1978).

Index

ACHILLES, 120.
adelphoi, 200–203, 206.
aei, 150, 164, 174.
Aelian, 136.
Aeschylus, 23, 24, 31–39, 41–42, 91, 112–13, 122, 129, 136–37, 148, 165, 179.
Agesilaus, 243, 244.
agōn, 100, 234–35.
agora, 98–100, 138.
aiōn, 47, 174.
alaston penthos, 90, 156, 157–58, 161.
alastōr, 161–63, 164.
Alcaeus, 39, 40, 98, 106, 107, 156–57.
Almaeon of Croton, 121.
Alētheia, 161.
Amnesty, 15–16, 29, 41–44, 128, 145–69, 173, 246–48.
anakrisis, 233.
Andocides, 246.
Anger, 66, 159–61, 241. *See also* *mēnis*.
Anthropology: and history, 16, 17–18, 19, 40, 45–62.
apophras, 174, 175–77, 182–84.
Appian, 205.
ara, 129–30.
Arbitration, 224–26, 238–41.

Archinus, 128, 152, 153, 341, 252–53.
Areopagus, meeting days of, 176.
Ares, 106, 112–13, 119–20, 136–37; *emphulios*, 35, 38–39.
Aristophanes, 27, 59, 110, 176, 229, 237, 254.
Aristotle, 20, 59, 72, 79, 102, 116, 149–53, 204–205, 206–208, 230, 232, 235, 236–37, 239, 248–55, 259–60.
Asheri, David, 215, 216, 218, 224, 225.
Athena, 156; quarrel with Poseidon, 172–75, 181–82.
Athens: amnesty in (402 B.C.), 146–55, 167–69, 226 ff.; as "the" city, 27 ff.; calendar of, 172–81, 184; trial procedures, 232–33, 236–38.
Aulus Gellius, 174.
Autochthony, myth of, 28, 30.
Autolycus, 127.

BELLUM CIVILE, 107–108.
Benveniste, Emile, 69, 79, 107, 129, 203.
Bloch, Marc, 245.
Boedromion, second day of, 172–90.

355

Bollack, Jean, 117.
Brotherhood, 197–206; in Nakone, 222–24.
Burckhardt, Jakob, 25.

CADMUS, 119.
Calendar, civic and lunar, 184–88.
Callixenos, 21–22.
Certeau, Michel de, 64.
City, representations of, 16–21, 48–50, 53, 55, 206–13; as subject, 59–62; and individual, 78–86. *See also* Athens.
Cleisthenes, 72–73, 206, 259–60.
Cleocritus, 9–10, 39, 198, 258, 263.
Conflict, in Greek political thought, 21 ff., 52–59, 70, 98, 112–16, 120–22. *See also* Eris and *stasis*.
Critias, 29.

DEMOCRITUS, 99.
dēmokratia, 27, 70, 249, 252, 254.
Demophantos, decree of, 131, 140, 142.
Demosthenes, 202, 257.
Detienne, Marcel, 52.
dialuō, 95–97.
dialusis, 96–97.
diaphora, 96, 101, 218–19, 234.
diastasis, 110.
dikē, 231–32.
Diodorus, 72, 73.
diomōsia, 135, 139.
Dionysus, theater of, 35.
Dumézil, Georges, 125–26, 134, 136.

EKSAIREIN, 184–87.
Empedocles, 94, 115–17, 127, 128.
Ephialtes, murder of, 20, 68, 71–75.
Erasure, 150–52, 181, 183–84. *See also* Ephialtes, murder of.
Erichthonius, 28.
Erinyes, 31–35, 38–42, 91, 93, 106, 122, 129, 135–37, 178–79.

Eris, 23, 90–92, 110, 112, 121–24, 135, 169, 181–82, 188–90.
Euripides, 146.
Eustathius, 180.

FAMILY, 31–39, 208–13, 224. *See also* Brotherhood.
Fertility, 133, 134–36.
Finley, Moses I., 24.
Forgetting, 42–44, 66, 155–61, 171, 172, 251, 257, 259, 261–64. *See also* Lêthê and Oblivion.
Freud, Sigmund, 65, 67, 74, 75–77, 82, 84–85, 145, 184, 257.
Funeral oration, 27–28.

GERNET, LOUIS, 51, 100, 164, 225, 233, 236.
Glotz, Gustave, 25, 139–40.

HARMONIA, 116–18, 119.
Harrison, Jane, 47.
Hartog, Francois, 46.
Hatzfeld, Jean, 238.
Heidegger, Martin, 117.
Heraclitus, 104, 108–10, 112; on *palintropos harmoniē*, 117–18.
Herodotus, 18, 46, 47, 88, 132, 137–38, 147, 159, 200–201, 202, 206.
Hesiod, 24, 37, 40, 43, 90, 123, 200, 228; on oaths, 123, 125–27, 132–33, 136, 138–39; on forbidden days, 177–79, 183, 185.
hetairos, 203.
Homer. *See* Iliad; Odyssey.
homonoia, 109, 256, 257, 262.
Horkos, 123–27, 187.

ICONOGRAPHERS, 49–50.
Ideology, use of, 41, 56–57.
Iliad, 98–99, 111–16, 120, 121, 131, 136, 158, 160, 169, 201, 204; Shield of Achilles, 16–17, 23–24, 53, 99–100.

Isaac, Jules, 154.
Isocrates, 44, 79–80, 128, 148, 153, 221, 241, 248–55, 258.
isonomia, 30.

KASIGNĒTOS, 205–206, 207.
kinēsis, 110.
kratos, 68–71, 85, 139, 249 ff.; opposed to *arkhē*, 23, 56–57, 69–70.
krinein, 234.
kukaō, 110.
kukeōn, 108–109.

LACAN, JACQUES, 264.
Lêthê, 15, 43, 153–54, 169, 173, 187.
Lévi-Strauss, Claude, 45, 56, 62.
Lucan, 209–10.
Lyotard, Jean-François, 167.
Lysias, 180, 199, 208–209, 242–49, 255, 258.

MĒNIS, 66, 132, 160–61.
meson, 50, 52, 53, 54–55, 98, 102, 154.
Mikalson, Jon, 177–79.
mnēsikakein, 149–50, 153, 161, 248.
Mourning, 158–63, 260.

NAKONE, RECONCILIATION OF, 197, 215–28.
Negation, 65–66, 163–67, 171, 189–90.
neikos, 23, 100, 112–14.
Nicias, nephews of, 262.
Non-forgetting, 159–69.

OATHS, 90–91, 123–43, 193–94, 233–34; of 403 B.C., 9, 15, 41–42, 146, 148, 149, 167–69, 242; of Amphictyons, 134–36.
Oblivion, 90–91.
Odyssey, 155–58.

PARRICIDE, 210–12.
Pausanias, 242.
Peguy, and Dreyfus affair, 155–55.
Pericles, 20, 72, 73, 74, 186, 197.
Perjury, 124 ff., 139.
Perpillou, Jean-Louis, 201.
pharmakon, of Helen, 157–58.
Phlius, 242–44.
phratēr, 204–205.
Phrynichus, 142, 148, 149.
Phyle, 252–53.
Pindar, 88.
Plato, 30, 48–50, 70–71, 78–84, 91, 104–106, 110, 120–21, 149, 175, 181–82, 198–202, 203–204, 208, 219, 223–24, 227, 231–32, 237–38, 239, 260.
Plutarch, 43, 66, 108–109, 148, 153–54, 162, 164, 199, 203, 250–51; on Pericles, 72, 74–75; on second of Boedromion, 172–78, 181, 182, 184–88.
Plynteria, festival of, 178.
polis, 16, 17, 30, 32, 255, 257. *See also* City.
politeia, 17, 212, 234, 249, 254.
political, the, and politics, 53, 124–29, 153–54, 174.
Pollux, 182.
Poseidon, 153.
Proclus, 175.
Psychoanalysis and history, 68, 76–78, 84–86.

RAMNOUX, CLEMENCE, 125.
Repression, 76–78, 145–46.
Rhinon, 150, 257.
Roosters, 35–37.

SACRIFICE, 17, 25, 53, 55, 57; and oaths, 135–36, 142, 218.
Samos, 114.
Scheid, John, 218.
Semnai, 137, 178. *See also* Erinyes.

Solon, 39–40, 102–103, 152, 231.
Sophocles, 112, 159–60, 164–67,
    191–93, 205.
sphagē, 25, 57.
splankhna, 33–34.
stasis, 10, 24–26, 30, 35, 37, 40,
    64–67, 98, 104–108, 189, 198–200,
    219–20.
sumplokē, 30, 94, 97, 116.
suggeneia, 212–13.

THEMISTOCLES, 36, 72.
Theognis, 39, 65, 207.
Theramenes, 253.
Thirty Tyrants, 15, 29, 152, 208–209,
    246, 255–59.
Thomas, Yan, 210.
Thrasybulus, 115, 153, 250, 253, 258,
    259–60, 263.
Thucydides, 18, 20, 24–25, 39–40,
    47, 78–79, 100, 107, 125, 138, 143,
    209, 242, 234, 251.
Tragedy, reading of, 32–37; in Athens,
    148.
Transference, 84–86.

VERNANT, JEAN-PIERRE, 53, 53, 54.
Vichy, 154.
Victory, 21–23, 35–36, 40, 54, 101.
Vote, 101–102.

WOMEN, PLACE OF, 17, 28.
Wrath. *See* Anger and *mēnis*.

XENOPHON, 9, 20, 29–30, 39, 69,
    198, 219, 232, 234, 242–44, 258.

ZEUS, 156.